PEOPLE AND FOLKS

GANGS, CRIME AND THE UNDERCLASS IN A RUSTBELT CITY

Second Edition

by John Hagedorn
with Perry Macon

LAKE VIEW Press
Chicago

Lake View Press
P.O. Box 578279, Chicago, IL 60657

Library of Congress Cataloging-in-Publication Data

Hagedorn, John, 1947–
    People and folks: gangs, crime, and the underclass in a rustbelt city / by
John M. Hagedorn, with Perry Macon. — 2nd ed.
        p.   cm.
    Includes bibliographical references and index.
    ISBN 0-941702-45-6 — ISBN 0-941702-46-4
    1. Gangs—Wisconsin—Milwaukee—Case studies.   2. Urban poor—
Wisconsin—Milwaukee—Case studies.   3. Milwaukee (Wis.)—Social
conditions.   I. Macon, Perry.   II. Title.
HV6439.U7M554   1998
364.1'06'60977595—dc21   97-25593
                                                                                 CIP

Q. Is there anything else you want to add—maybe something I didn't ask you that maybe I should?

A. Just tell these young people to stay out of the gangs. Its just a bad way to go. Cause there's always two enemies, really three: the other gang member, the police, and yourself.

Q. How yourself? What do you mean by yourself?

A. Because say like you in a gang, and you had a gang fight that night, and you cut somebody. He be in the hospital seriously bleeding, in intensive care, they don't know if he goin' to die or live. That can screw a brother up seriously. Have him walking around every time he see a knife, go into shock, you know. They might have all tried to jump on him and he didn't never pick up the knife to protect himself...I put a dude in the hospital for four months with a nightstick. I still have a hard time when I see the police slap up their nightstick. Because when I hit him, blood was squirting all over my shirt, and oooh, four months he was in the hospital.

Chuck, Vicelords

CONTENTS

TABLES & CHARTS

PREFACE TO THE SECOND EDITION

I wrote the first edition of *People and Folks* hoping that it might be "provocative" in the sense that it might "provoke" the reader to think in a new way about gangs. Conventional wisdom had it that the members of Milwaukee's youth gangs were merely young hoodlums. What I saw, however, were troubled youth growing up and acting out—often destructively—in a strange, new, post-industrial world. I argued that gangs were not just a "crime problem," but could only be understood in the context of economic restructuring. *People and Folks* was the first book to apply William Julius Wilson's work to the study of gangs.

I concluded in the first edition that deindustrialization was changing the rules for gang members, as for many others in poor communities. What would happen to the gang members we studied as the good jobs left? They didn't know and I didn't know as the first edition went to press. This new edition answers that question, and lets male and female gang members interpret their experience for the reader in their own words.

This edition adds a single rather long chapter that updates the reader on what happened to the people and folks as they became adults. The new Chapter Eight reports some of the data from a five-year follow-up study of gangs and drug dealing in Milwaukee funded by the National Institute on Drug Abuse.

But the new chapter does more than report numbers. I argue in this chapter that many of the new criminological studies on gangs—including the first edition of *People and Folks*—have three serious flaws: (1) They do not pay sufficient attention to female gangs or to the importance of gender for both males and females; (2) they underestimate the influence of mainstream culture on gang members and the underclass; and (3) they do not fully appreciate the extent and importance of the informal economy for gangs and poor communities.

As with earlier chapters, Chapter Eight uses the voices of gang members themselves to discuss these issues. Among the questions explored in these pages are how drug dealing has in many ways replaced industrial jobs in some poor communities, and how that change impacts gangs. I present some shocking statistics on the state of the formal and informal economy in Milwaukee. I also discuss how the lives of female gang members differ from the lives of male gang members.

You will note that the gang members in these pages do not worship some deviant code of the street, but have deeply internalized the good, the bad, and the ugliness of American culture. Mainstream American culture, I've learned, has had far more influence on gang members' outlook than the "social isolation" they face in segregated ghettoes. *My fundamental conclusion is that underclass gang members differ from you and me not in their "culture," but in the different opportunities they face and the kinds of choices available to them.*

This conclusion may run against the grain of some current criminological thinking. But the intention of *People and Folks* was to be provocative, and I don't think the second edition will disappoint anyone on that account. The perceptive reader may discover in my argument the beginnings of a new theoretical perspective on understanding gangs—one that incorporates anomie theory and feminism, along with some elements of social disorganization theory. I believe the post-industrial revolution may have consequences for the urban poor that are as sweeping as those brought about by the industrial revolution. I've concluded we may need new theory to account for these phenomena, but I have not attempted to do more than outline elements of a new approach here.

I have kept the term "underclass" in the title of the book. This word has become so controversial that even William Julius Wilson no longer uses it. Some see the word "underclass" as stigmatizing minority males or as a surrogate term for the "disreputable poor." Others use it in a strict statistical sense to describe a portion of the urban poor, while still others use it vaguely to describe the victims of deindustrialization. This array of definitions of the term certainly makes us ask, like Alice in Wonderland, "whether you can make words mean so many different things?"

I agree with Wilson when he urges us not get hung up with words. But I'm also like Humpty Dumpty, who retorted to Alice, "When I use a word, it means just what I choose it to mean—neither more nor less." What I mean by underclass are those people in poor communities who have been most affected by economic restructuring and are surviving by some combination of low wage jobs, welfare, and/or work in the informal economy. This work includes drug selling, which, I argue, is transforming the nature of the post-industrial gang. This "underclass" is a distinct new social formation, and it needs a descriptive term.

Just as the first edition of *People and Folks* was a joint effort with former Vicelord Perry Macon, this chapter was also collaborative. Jerome Wonders, Lavell Cox, Angelo Vega, Jorge Silva, Rita Lewis, Amelia Holloway, Dora Rodriguez, Frances Turlock, and Clint Holloway all accepted the awesome responsiblity to interview 174 of their homeboys and homegirls and to convince them that research can be useful for them. I hope it will be. I have the greatest respect for how these young men and women transcended their gang experiences by becoming an integral part of a five-year social science research study. It was their constant questioning of what I thought I had found that taught me the most about gangs.

I've also learned from other social scientists, first of all from Joan Moore. Joan drummed the inductive method into me and promoted skepticism, scholarship, and love of the truth. She also constantly reminded me that no two gangs are alike, and we need to be cautious when trying to generalize from my Milwaukee data. The reader of this book should always keep that in mind.

I have great admiration for my colleagues in gang research, from whom I've learned that most of what I thought was new, wasn't. Jim Short and Meda Chesney-Lind have had perhaps the most influence on my thinking, but not always leading me in the same direction. I've especially appreciated the friendly criticism and warm counsel of David Curry and Mac Klein. I have the greatest respect for their work—yes, even their "courthouse criminology." I admire their critical spirit and I'm honored to count them as friends. I've also been priviliged to have discussed gang research with Irv Spergel, Richard Cloward, Albert Cohen, and Lewis Yablonsky.

Bob Bursik, Dwight Conquergood, Scott Decker, Eloise Dunlap, Jeff Fagan, Andy Hamid, Ron Huff, Karen Joe, Cheryl Maxson, Jody Miller, Felix Padilla, Claire Sterk, Carl Taylor, Lalo Valdez, Diego Vigil, the late Dan Waldorf, and Marjorie Zatz have all contributed to my thinking about gangs. I want to specifically thank Meda Chesney-Lind , David Curry, Mary Devitt, Greg Giglio, Clint Holloway, Rita Lewis, Perry Macon, Joan Moore, Jim Short, Angelo Vega, and Jerome Wonders for reading and commenting on various drafts of the new chapter.

Paul Elitzik has been more than my best friend. He has been an insightful critic and the best editor I could ever have. His questions have always helped me not only to write better, but also to clarify my often fuzzy thinking. Bob Brown did his usual outstanding job on the graphics and photos. Steve Percy and the UWM Center for Urban Initiatives and Research have been supportive as have Dennis Rosenbaum and my colleagues at the University of Illinois-Chicago. The research was supported by grant # RO1 DA O7218 from the National Institute on Drug Abuse.

The most important influence on my work has been the critical, lively, and thoroughly feminist mind of my partner, Mary Devitt. Our relationship has given me the opportunity to learn from her work and thinking and to join her in challenging old paradigms, as well as in trying to change some of my characteristically male behaviors.

I hope my thinking has grown as much as my children, as Tracey and Katie are now young women and Marty is no longer a little kid. Since the first edition, Zach and Jess have arrived to Mary's and my home and added to our pleasure in life. I think they are happy to be here too.

The first edition of *People & Folks* broke some new ground and upset some who had grown comfortable in the old theories. The second edition may upset some others who have grown comfortable in a new set of ill-fitting theoretical clothes. However, please don't mistake the passion of my argument for hubris. Like all social science "truths," my conclusions must be seen as tentative, not universal, as dynamic, not static, and as firmly rooted in a specific time and place. This book should still be read mainly as a method of analysis, not a new dogma.

The first seven chapters remain an accurate and analytical description of the formation and organization of adolescent male gangs. The new Chapter Eight attempts to make understandable the life experiences of male and female adult gang members in post-industrial Milwaukee. I alone am responsible for it. My goal in writing a new chapter remains to provoke you, the reader, to dare to think in new ways about gangs.

Milwaukee
June 1997

PREFACE

This book has been written for two kinds of readers. On the one hand it is aimed at all those concerned with understanding the gang problem in our cities. Policy makers, community activists, police and correctional officials, teachers and social workers, among others, should find this book readable as well as a challenge to traditional and stereotyped views of gangs. While sociological theories about gangs are discussed, they are presented in a straightforward manner which explores their strengths and weaknesses in explaining modern gangs, particularly in smaller cities.

On the other hand, we are also making an argument within sociological theory. We have critiqued the sources of knowledge about today's gangs and suggested we may know less than we thought we knew. New empirical research, like our work in Milwaukee, is clearly needed. Previous theories have treated gangs as largely immigrant, adolescent, working class phenomena. This book looks at the minority gangs of the 1980s as including both juveniles and young adults, and as a fraction of a forming underclass. Gangs today no longer fade away as their ethnic group climbs the ladder of social mobility; rather, they are becoming institutionalized within our central cities. Theories about gangs need to be revised in the light of the major economic, political, and demographic changes of the past decades.

The academic reader will find it useful to refer to the footnotes for some of the more complicated discussion which might divert other readers from following the argument in the text. The footnotes also contain anecdotes and data that bring some of our contentions to life, but were too cumbersome to include within the text.

We hope this book will be provocative, in the simple sense that it provoke thought, discussion and research, and contributes to formulating a new approach to the gang problem.

ACKNOWLEDGEMENTS

I am deeply indebted to the Milwaukee Foundation, which funded our rather unorthodox Milwaukee Gang Research Project. It would have been easy for them to say "no," but they found a way to support our efforts. The National Institute on Drug Abuse issued our project a Confidentiality Certificate No. DA 86-03, which enabled us to protect the identity of our research subjects and protect ourselves, our tapes, and our transcripts from subpoena. The study on which this book was based was initiated by a 1985 "pilot ethnography" looking at gang members' perceptions of drug and alcohol abuse programs funded by the Wadari Foundation.

I also wish to thank Urban Research Center of the University of Wisconsin-Milwaukee, which sponsored all our research and allowed us full use of their facilities. A special word needs to be said about Kathy Lelinski and Shirley Brah, who transcribed many of the interviews and patiently helped us get our materials ready for publication. Further thanks go to the Cudahy, Hazen, and Stackner Foundations and the State of Wisconsin, which combined to fund a Wingspread conference on gangs in small cities highlighting our research and increasing our knowledge of gangs outside Milwaukee. The Johnson Foundation did a magnificent job in hosting the conference.

Joan Moore deserves more thanks than I can give. She helped shape the methodology, provided a comparative perspective, and was there when needed for guidance and advice. While it may seem trite to say that without Joan Moore this book could not have been written, it is true. We also acknowledge Robert Garcia, who gave his frank insights from the beginnings of our research.

Paul Elitzik and Peggy Wiedmann must be thanked for their initial suggestion to convert our research into a book and their encouragement throughout. Jeannetta Robinson and Career Youth Development also deserve thanks for their support.

My deepest thanks go to those from Milwaukee's gangs who agreed to be interviewed. They took a chance their story would be told accurately and honestly. I especially want to thank those interviewed who helped us locate other "top dogs" of major gangs, assured them we were "all right," and put their own reputations on the line on our behalf. I hope we have captured the openness of those we interviewed concerning how their gangs formed, their gang structure, the status of adults in their gangs, and other related subjects. It is the common hope of our respondents and the authors that this book might lead to changes in how gangs are viewed and what must be done.

I also want to recognize Nancy Diaz, who was the first outreach worker in our 1983 gang intervention program. She put her heart into that job, and helped later with our research. Her struggle against the destructiveness of gangs, accompanied by her sympathy for gang members as human beings, pointed us in the right direction.

Perry Macon is cited as a co-author of this book. That is the appropriate designation for someone who has participated in all stages of our early program experience with gangs and has done more than anyone else to divert black, Hispanic, and white youth away from Milwaukee gangs. He helped design and gather the research, criticized it, and helped distribute and discuss our findings on playgrounds all over Milwaukee. Finally he helped write up our findings in a way, we hope, that "speaks the truth." Perry is one of those remarkable individuals who could leave gang activity behind, but still give of himself in struggling with and helping those still involved.

Finally, I need to thank my wife Kathe and my children Tracey, Katie, and Marty, for putting up with the financial and psychological hardships of the past three years. I'm grateful they shared my conviction that this task needed to be done.

John M. Hagedorn

PEOPLE AND FOLKS

INTRODUCTION

GANGS AND THE UNDERCLASS: A COMPARATIVE PERSPECTIVE
Joan Moore

Youth gangs are now a fact of life in smaller cities (Needle and Stapleton 1982). Until recently they were found only in big cities—Chicago, Philadelphia, Los Angeles.

What is happening? Are gangs simply an infectious idea as gang members move from one city to another? Are big city drug-dealing gangs simply establishing branches in smaller cities?

Who is telling us about the gangs? Must newspaper and television reporters be the only sources of information? Are city policemen and special "gang squads" more dependable sources? If none of these are reliable because of their special interests, how can the professionals working with gangs in smaller and medium-sized cities learn about the nature and extent of the youth gang problem? John Hagedorn and Perry Macon offer an entirely new perspective on the youth gangs. It is certainly the most accurate and insightful picture of youth gangs in a smaller city yet to appear. Yet valuable as it is, some of the background and critical points about gangs need explanation.

Particularly, we must keep in mind that social science has very little to offer about gangs. Virtually all of our new information comes from law enforcement, newspapers and television. Recent research serves to sound warnings about the dangers in drawing conclusions about gangs based on information from these sources.

First, we must be very careful about the word "gang." It can mean a group of adolescents who hang out around a candy store, something like "West Side Story," or a highly organized Mafia family with elaborate banking connections and a tradition of clever, if shady business deals. Both images appear almost interchangeably. Most law enforcement people refer to an organized crime conspiracy, although Hagedorn and Macon find no traces of it in Milwaukee. It is what Perkins (1987) sees in Chicago, but it is folly to spend public money and waste law enforcement on somebody else's gang.

Second, youth gangs are very different—one time from another, one place from another, one group from another in the same city. The time element is particularly important, as we see in Los Angeles. Compounding the difficulty is the fact that virtually all sociological theory about youth gangs dates from the 1960s—practically a millenium back into history, as far as our large cities are concerned. This fact is a warning about assumptions.

Third, there are some similarities among the gangs—and quite possibly, these similarities may offer guidelines for positive action. These similarities are most striking when we look at their interaction with city institutions over the years.

Fourth, if you have gangs in your community, be wary of your information. Gang members are quite adept at telling social workers and policemen self-serving lies. Glib misinformation is, in fact, a survival tool for many gang members. It is easy for outside people (and that is practically everybody) to believe social workers and policemen because they have direct contact with gang members. Yet this direct contact is often managed by the gang members themselves, sometimes for survival, sometimes even for self-glorifying exaggeration, and police and gang workers also have some self-interest in the images they purvey.

Fifth and finally: if you have gangs in your community, find out about them directly and use our research results in two other communities for comparison and appraisal. My colleagues and I have been studying Los Angeles youth gangs for more than a decade. Even this unique background in systematic research teaches us caution—and to say that the study of gangs is only in its infancy.

What Do We Mean by "Gang?"

The term "gang" calls up a wide range of associations. On the one hand there is the romanticized "West-Side Story" adolescent band whose members are aggressive and rebellious—but appealing. At the other extreme there is the "gang" of organized crime—the Capone gang, or the Mafia families.

Both in this book and in our Los Angeles research we refer to something that differs from either of these images. To begin with, the gangs we study do start out a little bit like "West Side Story." They are a friendship group of adolescents who share common interests, with a more or less clearly defined territory, in which most of the members live. They are committed to defending one another, the territory, and the gang name in the status-setting fights that occur in school and on the streets. Their families tend to live conventional lives; although some may be troubled, this is by no means true for all of them. Police harass the gang, and some members go into juvenile facilities for longer or shorter periods of time.

As its members age, the clique begins to splinter. Some of the members get married and settle down, while others remain involved in a street life-style. The community is still poor and marginalized, and in very short order, another clique of the gang comes into being. The gang is developing an age-graded system. This means that there are several fairly clearly defined subgroupings within the gang that are separated by age and history. In the case of the Los Angeles Chicano gangs that we have been studying, members call these age graded subgroups "cliques" (*klikas*). In Los Angeles the clique is fairly self-contained. It does not associate much with younger or older cliques, but it is more or less available to them for help when needed. In any event, these are clearly *not* hierarchical organizations, as in the Mafia image, nor are they paramilitary organizations, as in the image of several police departments.[1]

It is important to note that these gangs are not simply youth phenomena. Some of the members do, in fact, drop their gang ties as they mature. Others assume normal, conventional lifestyles but retain the close friendships that were formed during the years of gang activity. (Some of the Los Angeles gangs stage annual reunions, for example.) Others, enmeshed in the street lifestyle and periodically spending time in jail or prison, continue the old gang ties. They need one another in the prisons and in their marginal life on the streets. In both Los Angeles and Milwaukee, circumstances combine to make it increasingly difficult for young men and women to outgrow their youthful ties.

It is also important to remember that these are overwhelmingly black and Hispanic youth. They are not the ethnic Europeans of the gangs of the 1920s, whose marginality lasted only one generation. Nor are they the working class youth of so many studies, but rather they are increasingly a fraction of the urban underclass. In short, when we talk about gangs we are talking about quasi-institutionalized structures within the poorer minority communities.

What Do We Mean By "Underclass?"

The term "underclass" has recently become a media favorite. Many social scientists avoid it because it is vague enough to refer to anything from Skid Row bums to welfare mothers (Auletta 1983). Others avoid it because it carries connotations of long-standing racist stereotypes (cf. Wilson 1985). In the 1960s the "culture of poverty" seemed to imply that black Americans were sexually lax, shiftless and dangerous (*Moynihan Report* 1965; Rainwater and Yancey 1967). Conservatives revive these connotations in their attacks on the welfare state. The most widely read of these, Charles Murray's *Losing Ground*, explicitly focused on black welfare dependency, teen pregnancy, and crime. Recently the plight of inner-city black poor has become much worse (Wilson 1987). This has caused some liberal and left-leaning social scientists and black advocacy organizations to talk about an "underclass problem" affecting a sizable stratum "who are unable to participate in the mainstream economy" (National Research Council 1982). This particular definition is carefully neutral. It might refer to physical or mental handicaps, or even to legal barriers to participation in American society, such as those faced by undocumented Mexican workers.[2] But such barriers affect only one generation, and the *children* of the handicapped or undocumented workers usually do not face the same barriers as their parents. This neutral definition, then, refers to a stratum of unrelated individuals who have something in common. But we are more interested in a class, which might reproduce its lifestyle.

One major social scientist, William J. Wilson, has argued forcefully, and in the face of much controversy, for the usefulness of the term "underclass" in discussing the structure of black ghettos of the 1980s. He accepts the criterion that the underclass are "outside the mainstream of the American occupational system," and adds some specifics.

When he talks of the underclass, he refers to "individuals who lack training and skills. . . individuals who are engaged in street criminal activity and other forms of aberrant behavior, and families who experience long-term spells of poverty and/or welfare dependency" (1985, 546). Wilson's analysis is particularly useful in Hagedorn's and Macon's study of Milwaukee, because he, and they, focus on the consequences of the deindustrialization of cities in the North and Middlewest. And he concentrates on the black community, with particular interest in the exodus of middle class and working class blacks from the ghettos.

Though deindustrialization affects the Hispanic poor in cities like Chicago and Milwaukee as much as it affects blacks, some of the other after-effects of the civil rights revolutions (e.g., the opening up of jobs and housing to middle class minority group members) may not have been so important for Hispanics as for blacks. And, certainly few of the cities of the West where "new" gangs are especially to be found (Needle and Stapleton 1983) have suffered from deindustrialization. Quite the contrary, these are boom towns. How, then, have the Hispanic—largely Mexican American—populations in such cities suffered from marginalization? Perhaps the most convincing argument is two-fold. First, the boom didn't really reach into the poorest ghettos and barrios of the Southwest (cf. Feagin 1984). A booming service economy left few lucrative spots for poorly educated minorities, and older manufacturing plants which *did* offer good jobs left the Southwest in the 1980s, just as they had left the Midwest. Second, the massive Mexican immigration of the 1980s had a negative impact on the job opportunities of the poorest and least prepared of the native-born Chicanos in those communities (cf. Muller and Espenshade 1985; McCarthy and Valdez 1986). Thus those Chicanos who were "left over" in the barrios, along with the immigrant Mexicans, are in fact in much the same position as are the "leftover" poor blacks of Chicago and Milwaukee when middle and working class blacks moved out of the ghetto.

In this book the word "underclass" refers to a category of people that is even smaller than Wilson's people. These are men and women permanently excluded from participation in mainstream occupations. They survive, somehow, by a combination of economic resources. At any time this may include (a) temporary or part-time jobs in the secondary labor market, (b) temporarily living off relatives or spouse equivalents, (c) the use of transfer payments, like AFDC or General

Assistance, (d) subsidized employment, like OJT, CETA, and JTPA, (e) petty hustling or street crime (cf. Moore et al. 1979). As our respondents tell us in Los Angeles, this is the "bone." "I got my bone today; where am I gonna get my next bone when this one's chewed up?" (Moore, Salcido, and Garcia 1979). We are also concerned with the process by which this lifestyle is reproduced, and especially with the possible interfaces of the gang and the underclass.

The Possible Relation Between Gangs and the Underclass

Youth gangs may disappear after one or two cliques—or they may evolve in any one of a number of different ways. In neither of the Chicano communities we studied in Los Angles nor in the Milwaukee communities of Hagedorn and Macon have the gangs in any way become involved in an organized criminal infra-structure. (It is important to make this point, because of the Mafia-like connotations of the word "gang" and because Chicago's "supergangs" are so clearly seen as criminal structures.)

We suggest, rather, that a fraction of each gang clique moves off into the underclass—surviving from month to month by a variety of short-range devices. Some of these men and women have children and our long-range studies in Los Angeles show that many become conventional in their lifestyles.[3] Often they are reared by conventional grandparents or divorced wives.) But some fraction is again recruited into the gang during adolescence. Thus the gang itself tends to play a role in reproducing a lifestyle.

Kids from conventional families and from underclass families are continuously recruited into the gang. The opportunities available in the community at the time probably determine what fraction "matures out" and what fraction remains. Thus the gang becomes an institutionalized feature of some poverty communities, and plays a role in the perpetuation of the underclass. How do the gangs become an institutional feature of poor communities? A look at the history in Los Angeles tells one part of the story, and a comparison drawn from Hagedorn and Macon's work in Milwaukee tells another part.

How Did The Chicano Gangs Emerge in Los Angeles?

By the early 1920s, the Mexican American population of Los Angeles was clearly on the bottom of the heap in terms of jobs, and was also the target of considerable discrimination. Understandably, few of the Mexican immigrants relinquished the protections of Mexican citizenship to become naturalized. And, in its turn, Los Angeles justified this reluctance by a massive "repatriation" of thousands of Mexicans when the Great Depression hit. Immigration picked up again in the late 1930s and during the war years as jobs opened up.

During the 1920s, the little Mexican immigrant neighborhoods (or barrios) began to see the emergence of adolescent groupings that one sociologist called "boy gangs" (Bogardus 1926). These were somewhat in the Mexican tradition of barrio male groups that appeared as far back as the 19th century (cf. Redfield 1941). Members of these barrios fought with boys from other barrios at dances and parties, but by adulthood they had left the gang. The gangs we studied in Los Angeles built on this traditional base, but did not get under way until the later 1930s and early 1940s, among the children of Mexican immigrants (Moore, et al. 1978). A number of factors coincided during this period to transform the original barrio crowd into the kind of gang we are discussing. First, a cluster of events called the gangs into being. Second, a cluster of events crystallized and reinforced a newly institutionalized structure.

Events calling the gangs into being. A stylistic fad swept the youth of Los Angeles barrios in the early 1940s, the zoot-suit fad, just as it swept other poor communities throughout the nation. In Chicano communities, as elsewhere, the clothing style involved wide-shouldered, long jackets, pleated baggy pants with long watch chains, double-soled shoes and wide flat hats. Some of the barrio gangs innovated by adding tattoos and also developed a special Spanish-English argot—*pachuco* talk, or *calo*. The clothing style was universal throughout the barrios, according to informants active at the time, but the tattooing and *calo* tended to be confined to gang members. Fights continued at parties and dances, but without extensive inter-gang warfare.

However, in 1942 a party fight ended in a killing in an East Los Angeles spot known as "Sleepy Lagoon," and there were two major responses. First, there was massive, sensationalist press publicity both about the case and more generally about the Chicano gangs. For the first time, gangs became part of the anti-Mexican stereotype in Los Angeles (Gonzalez 1981). At the same time, the police reacted strongly, arresting twenty-two gang members on charges of conspiracy to commit murder. This was the first conspiracy charge to be leveled by prosecutors in cases involving gangs. Twelve defendants were convicted of first or second degree murder. Police also began "sweep arrests" of gang members—as a preventive procedure.[4]

In less than a year, another incident focussed on the gangs. This was the zoot-suit riot, starting in a fight at a dance hall between Chicano young men—reputedly gang members—and Anglo sailors. The ensuing riots were largely initiated by servicemen who indiscriminately beat up on all Mexican youngsters, stripping them of zoot suits, cutting their duck-tailed haircuts. Gangs fought back, and, in the process, tended both to strengthen their identity as gangs and also as Mexican, since these were clearly racial incidents.

The coincidence of the zoot suit fad, the sensationalist publicity, and sensationalized treatment of the gangs both in the Sleepy Lagoon case and in the zoot suit riots helped to precipitate the new gangs and to distinguish them from other barrio youth groups both in style and in the enhanced risk of involvement with criminal justice system.

How the gangs got institutionalized. As the gangs became crystallized, kids from neighborhoods that did not have gangs or which had very small gangs tended to be easy targets in fights. In many neighborhoods, gangs started up anew or strengthened themselves by recruiting more good fighters. At the same time, whole cohorts of young men who had been involved in the barrio youth groups were drafted into the armed forces of World War II. When they disappeared from the barrios they took with them many of the traditions and conventional linkages of the traditional youth groups. The predecessor of one of the gangs we studied, for example, had been associated with the barrio church, and was called by its name—La Purissima.

By the end of World War II, the gangs of East Los Angeles had already developed an age-graded structure. The gangs of that era might be viewed as transitional. Although barrio warfare was becoming endemic, the gangs still had many conventional linkages. The gang we studied no longer related to the barrio church, but it was still involved in sporting competitions, winning trophies offered by the YMCA. But in the late 1940s, heroin was introduced into the gangs, and many members became hooked. Shortly afterwards, in 1950, gang members began to go to prison in rather large numbers for the first time. The gangs became even more marginalized. In prison, the gang loyalties of new prisoners were revived as they turned to their homeboys for support. Thus the street scene—the loyalties and animosities of gang men—tended to be replicated in California's prisons.

As these men were released into their neighborhoods, usually more or less involved with heroin use and largely unemployable in mainstream jobs, we begin to see the formation of an underclass. We do *not*, however, see the formation of a Capone-type gang. Gang members and their individual friends dealt in drugs, for example, but with very rare exceptions the gangs themselves did not become involved in crime. They generally lived in a survival-oriented world, alternating between temporary pick-up jobs, spells of unemployment insurance, living with mothers or girlfriends, and petty hustling—the underclass life.

In short, the Chicano gangs in Los Angeles started out as a youth fad, which took on different characteristics through media publicity and criminal justice overreaction. The gangs became institutionalized largely as a pattern of illicit drug use and marketing developed, which meant that they also functioned as support groups in prisons.

How Do Milwaukee Gangs Compare with Los Angeles Gangs?

Many of the processes we see in Los Angeles also appear as gangs formed in minority communities in Milwaukee in the 1980s. But there are major differences in context. As Hagedorn and Macon document, Milwaukee attracted a number of minority immigrants to its strong, unionized plants during and after World War II. In the 1950s, the children of this first large-scale minority immigration began to develop gangs. But, like the children of European immigrants earlier, and like Los Angeles' Chicano gangs of the 1920s, these gang members grew older and matured out of the gangs, and the early gangs themselves faded out.

Despite the availability of good jobs during one period in its history, Milwaukee has not been perceived as a "good" town for minorities. When local factories began to close, unemployment rates among the minority populations soared. Hagedorn and Macon detail these processes and their effects in the second chapter of this volume. It is clear that there were some very real differences between the way in which Los Angeles of the 1940s and Milwaukee of the 1980s functioned for their immigrant minority populations. There was much more overt discrimination in 1940's Los Angeles, and much more economic and institutional exclusion in Milwaukee in the 1980s. However, as in Los Angeles, Hagedorn and Macon delineate both a cluster of events that called the Milwaukee gangs into being and a cluster of events that crystallized and reinforced—and, perhaps, institutionalized—the "new" kind of age-graded gang structure.

Events calling the gangs into being in Milwaukee. In Milwaukee, as in Los Angeles, the emergence of some of the gangs was associated with a youth fad. Hagedorn and Macon tell us how breakdancing and drill teams swept the black communities. In some cases, the transition from dance groups to gangs came about as fights broke out after dance competitions. But there were also a number of traditional corner boy groups already in existence at the time. As fighting between groups became more common, the corner boys, like the dance groups, began to define themselves as gangs.

So far, this sounds much like Los Angeles—with a fad and fighting shifting traditional youth forms into the gang direction. But, in addition, Milwaukee is a satellite of Chicago, and four of the gangs started through Chicago roots, usually when an individual former gang member moved to Milwaukee. The diffusion from Chicago exerted a real cultural influence. Rather quickly, most of the Milwaukee gangs began responding to Chicago gang symbols. But they vigorously resent the notion that they are "branches" of Chicago gangs, and the actual importance of the connection is very much in doubt. (Our data in Los Angeles indicate similar origins for suburban gangs which carry the same name as the two gangs we have studied. And the suburban Los Angeles gangs are also quite independent.)

In Los Angeles, it may have been a single event—the Sleepy Lagoon case, along with the peculiar media and criminal justice response—that helped precipitate the gangs, followed soon by a brief race riot that also focussed on the gangs. In Milwaukee, there was no single event—at least not one that involved the gangs per se. There had been long-standing problems between minorities and the police, and, more important, a longstanding minority leadership rooted at least in part in the protests of the 1960s, in which police brutality has been a significant theme. And, importantly for our story, the protests were revived during the early 1980s in the aftermath of the killing by Milwaukee police of a young black man. All of the young men and women involved in the gangs were highly aware of this. Then in 1982-1983 there were several "mini-events" that involved one gang after another in substantial conflict, with a sizable police presence. The media publicity about gangs was extensive and highly alarmist.

Thus, to sum up, in Milwaukee as in Los Angeles, the gangs formed in the context of a youthful stylistic fad and substantial inter-group fighting. Again, as in Los Angeles, there was extensive newspaper publicity about the dangers of the new gangs, and in both places the publicity was initially generated by a series of incidents allegedly involving gang violence. Common to both cities was a strong highlighting of race. In Los Angeles, this took the form of the zoot-suit riots. In Milwaukee, the interracial situation was more complicated. It also involved a depressed economic climate that disproportionately affected the minority population. It should also be noted that racial issues were highlighted in Milwaukee by school segregation. As Hagedorn and Macon point out, only blacks were bused for desegregation purposes, and this had a direct impact on the development of gangs.

A major difference between the two cities in the formative stage was the availability in Milwaukee of gang images from Chicago and some limited direct experience with Chicago gangs. This may have accelerated the pace of gang formation in Milwaukee. It almost certainly influenced the particular constellation of the gangs. Unlike the Chicano gangs of Los Angeles, all of the gangs in Milwaukee—black and Hispanic—identify with broad groupings, or "nations," as described by Hagedorn and Macon. The Los Angeles attachment to neighborhood is relatively unknown in Milwaukee.

How Milwaukee gangs got established. The gangs that formed among the children of the 1960s immigrants to Milwaukee are still in the formative stage, with only three cliques. However, there are some indications that the kind of institutionalization that took place in Los Angeles is also under way in Milwaukee.

At the time of their research there was no counterpart in Milwaukee to the heroin subculture that developed so quickly in the Los

Angeles gangs. (Cocaine was being used on a limited scale, but the crack epidemic had not yet hit.) Thus there was no important single illegal subculture which sent gang members to prison. However, a major part of the response to the publicity about gangs involved substantial anti-gang funding to criminal justice system activities. Hagedorn and Macon give specifics: a large influx of money created a gang squad concerned almost entirely with arrests, rather than diversions or referrals. District Attorneys received large grants to speed up the prosecution of violent youth—clearly aiming at gang youth. The Milwaukee Public School system received a large influx of money intended only at security patrols. In an innovative move, Milwaukee police began issuing municipal court citations (or tickets) to gang members for "loitering." While not as extreme as Los Angeles' sweep arrests and conspiracy charges, the practice gives many gang members a first encounter with the courts in municipal, rather than juvenile, court. And it occurs without any crime having been committed. The attendant fines and possible charges for evading fines are often stressful to unemployed men.

As in Los Angeles, the extensive criminal justice activity around the gangs in Milwaukee has not eliminated them, but, instead, added another function. Gangs become support groups in correctional settings.

Milwaukee and Los Angeles: Gangs and the Future

It seems clear that at least some of the Los Angeles and Milwaukee gangs will continue into the future as age-graded structures, well institutionalized in minority communities. The circumstances that marginalized some elements of these communities seem to be persistent features of the late 20th century urban landscape.

There are three points of similarity and difference in the evolution of gangs in these two cities that may have some relevance for people concerned with "new" gangs. First, when we talk about gangs as "institutionalized features of minority communities" we talk about *neighborhoods* in the case of Chicano barrios in Los Angeles and about *broader communities* in the case of black gangs in Milwaukee. Chicano gangs in Los Angeles remain strongly based on neighborhoods, even though, in some cases, the "neighborhoods" cover very large areas. But gang formation in Milwaukee coincided with school desegregation, and this, along with the Chicago concept of gang "nations," appears to have affected the structure of the gangs. While most Milwaukee black male gangs began as neighborhood cliques, Hagedorn and Macon demonstrate in Chapter Six that the concept of neighborhood has ceased to have much importance. These differences, of course, have major implications for intervention strategies.

Second, when we talk about gangs the form of marginalization that comes most readily to mind is the evolution into organized crime. This does not appear to have happened in either city, despite the widespread criminal justice belief that Milwaukee gangs are branches of a criminal conspiracy based in Chicago. As indicated, in Los Angeles individual gang members may become involved in criminal activity, although our data show clearly that by no means *all* of the members do so. There are good reasons for this in Los Angeles. First, there is a strong culture of hostility to hierarchial organization in these Chicano gangs—a hatred for so-called leaders. Second, the gangs we have studied lack the formal structure of Milwaukee gangs: they do not have meetings or dues or jackets or symbols or written rules or rituals. Third, the gang members who might potentially become "soldiers" in an organized crime unit are those very members who become involved with heroin use in Los Angeles Chicano gangs, and heroin addicts are notoriously unreliable. Fourth, the Los Angeles Chicano gangs still retain an ideological ambivalence about *la raza* and the conventional people in the neighborhood: they still tend to consider themselves as "all for the neighborhood" and "all for la raza."

Things are different in Milwaukee, according to the portrait painted by Hagedorn and Macon. Both the black and Hispanic gangs prize strong leadership, and have no hostility to a hierarchical organization. The gang members are spread over large distances which requires that they have formal meetings, including dues. They do not yet have subgroups involved with hard drugs in a serious way. Most interestingly, Milwaukee gangs have no loyalty to the neighborhood or race. In addition, Milwaukee gangs respond to the images of Chicago gangs, and in some cases sustain some kinship ties with members of Chicago gangs where there appears to be a tradition of organized crime. Thus it may be that Milwaukee gangs have the potential for evolution into organized crime unless ameliorative action is taken.

Some writers hold a view of the evolution of gangs that is diametrically opposed to the fear that they are incipient organized crime units. This is the notion that gangs are actually "barrio warriors," or social bandits—rebels against racial oppression whose rebellion takes the form of illegal activity. This concept of the gangs was particularly popular during the days of the egalitarian movements of the 1960s (cf. Cortes 1972; Vigil 1974). And, given the visibility of gang members in change-oriented organizations like the Puerto Rican Young Lords and the Chicano Brown Berets, there were clearly grounds for believing that minority youth gangs are incipient revolutionary organizations. Thus one author found Chicano inner-gang violence to have decreased notably during the days of the Chicano Movement (Erlanger 1979). Some writers still hold to this romanticized view of the gangs (Frias 1982; Mirande 1987), but the data from Milwaukee and Los Angeles give it little support. Erlanger's notion that youthful gang violence and delinquency may be dissipated during epochs of minority protest remains attractive. It is congruent with Curtis' view that youthful minority crime in the 1980s is "a form of slow rioting" (1985). But we find little corroboration for this rosier view of gang membership.

The final point that we can make about gangs in both cities is that they are clearly evolving into a fraction of the growing underclass. The growth of the underclass might seem rather obvious in Milwaukee, with its deindustrialization and loss of primary sector jobs for minorities, combined with the effects of affirmative action in flushing out the stable middle and working class people from the ghettoes. The growth in Los Angeles is less obvious, but the "leftover" syndrome affecting gang members appears to us to be equally clear. The more successful East Los Angeles natives continuously migrate out to the suburbs, and the gang members that remain tend to be "leftovers" from unsuccessful families and/or the children of men and women who return to the barrios after a period of imprisonment. The barrio is familiar and housing (especially with older parents) may be available. Thus the process is more complex in Los Angeles, but the result may be similar.

Gangs in "New" Cities and Old

As I commented at the outset social science has had very little to offer in the way of recent empirical studies of gangs. This is particularly unfortunate in view of the resurgence of the gang phenomenon throughout the United States. Gangs and the emerging underclass are too important to leave to mass media and law enforcement. We need the kind of careful, systematic research represented in this book, done with the active participation of gang members in collaboration with social scientists.

Hagedorn and Macon have done an invaluable service in this study of gangs emerging in Milwaukee. Not only is the study rare in its focus on interviews with actual gang members, but it is virtually unique in its focus on the history both of the gangs and of the communities. The data show clearly that something can be done to ameliorate the situation of these "young" gangs. I have suggested here that one of the most destructive things that can be done is to allow the criminal justice approach to the gangs to prevail. In another "new" city, Phoenix, Marjorie Zatz (1987) has documented the media and police overreaction to the new Chicano gangs, where she sees a "moral panic" without much foundation. I have argued elsewhere that such overreaction further isolates and stigmatizes gang members within their own communities (Moore 1985). What is needed and would be effective in such "new" cities as Milwaukee are programs to reinforce and emphasize the conventional possibilities and linkages open to young men and women who identify with the gangs. Most adolescents in American society walk a tightrope between conventionality and wildness. Gang members are different only because they are tipped toward wildness—and they need most urgently more weight on the other side and more opportunity to become conventional.

1

WHAT WE DON'T KNOW ABOUT GANGS

Q. If the Governor came in here now and said, "Marcus, I'm going to give you a million dollars to deal with the gang situation," what would you do with it?

A. First I'd do some research, like you're doing now, talk to everybody and try to understand.

Marcus, 1-9 Deacons

What do we know about gangs? Aren't all gangs really alike? If you've seen one gang haven't you seen them all? Aren't gangs just groups of young hoodlums terrorizing our cities written about ad infinitum since the 1920s?

In the large U.S. cities, gangs have been around for as long as we can remember. In many smaller cities, like Milwaukee, Columbus, or Minneapolis, there seems to be a recent emergence of youth gang activity. But haven't there always been gangs? Isn't this just another cycle of adolescent gang activity that will come and go along with the mobility of another ethnic group?[1]

There do seem to be a few disturbing details that might merit our investigation. For one thing, gangs just don't seem to be going away like they used to. Moore has traced modern Los Angeles Chicano gangs back to the 1940s (Moore 1978). The "supergangs" in Chicago began in the late fifties and early sixties and the same gangs continue to plague Chicago today. Curiously, the gangs forming in the 1980s in midwestern cities have largely taken the names of the major Chicago gangs. The persistence of gangs in large cities and their apparent diffusion to smaller cities in their regions are new facts that need to be examined. Additionally, in the past gangs have always been seen as a serious adolescent problem. The best advice of the "experts" often was to allow the delinquents to "mature out" of "ganging." Today, however, adults seem to be playing a continuing role in gang life.[2]

If in fact gangs are becoming entrenched in some urban centers and as juveniles mature they are not leaving the gang but assuming an adult role, we may have a new set of problems to face. Perhaps we had better suspend our judgement on whether we are witnessing just a new cycle of familiar youth gang activity. It's time to take a hard look at whether the facts support our old notions.

Scope of the Problem

Our first difficulty in considering the facts is that we don't know too much about the scope of the problem. We do know that in the 1980s, gangs run in the streets in most of our large cities. Sociologist William Kornblum reports that eighteen of this nation's twenty largest cities report gang activity in 1985.[3] But we also know that the gang problem has spread to medium and small cities as well. In a 1983 Justice Department document "Police Handling of Youth Gangs," Needle and Stapleton sampled sixty U.S. cities and surprisingly found that half of the cities with populations between a quarter and a half million reported the presence of youth gangs. More than a third of cities with between 100,000 and a quarter million people also reported gangs on their streets. While Needle and Stapleton's report was only a representative sample of U.S. cities and not a complete survey, it confirms recent findings by Walter B. Miller. Miller's 1975 surveys of twelve U.S. cities and the Justice Department sample of sixty U.S. cities are the only recent scientific nation-wide data collected concerning gang developments.

Neither study looked at the variable nature of gangs nor attempted to look at any differences between cities which reported gang activity and those which did not. We don't know why gangs are forming today in some cities and not others. We don't know how the gangs in smaller cities are similar or different from gangs in the metropolis. There just isn't much data to go on.

Gangs, Denial, and the Images of Modern Cities

At least eleven Midwest cities have seen recent (1980s) gang development and have formed some sort of task force to investigate the problem. But gang activity is almost certainly even more widespread. Many of the task force reports mention a period of denial when city fathers did not want to admit there were gangs in "their" city. For example, in an August 2, 1983, editorial in the Ft. Wayne, Indiana, Journal-Gazette, the police were taken to task for downplaying or denying the existence of a gang problem. "City police clearly prefer that there be no publicity about the problem." In Milwaukee, the Chief of Police actually admitted that police "suppressed" news of gang crimes "for the good of the community."[4]

Some cities prefer to deny that gangs exist at all. The authors of this book called Indianapolis, where reports of gang activity were widespread, only to be greeted with repeated denials. Finally, one official told us: "Look, we do not have a gang problem here. We do have a slight problem in the summer with groups of youths running around with shotguns. But we don't have a gang problem." That must be comforting to Indianapolis residents. Then this official went on to say that Indianapolis was bidding for the 1992 Olympics and "couldn't possibly have a gang problem until 1993."

Indianapolis may or may not have a gang problem. But what it does have in common with other cities in the decaying "rustbelt" of the Midwest is a fear that to admit even the existence of a "gang" problem would damage their cities' images. Rustbelt cities are in a period of transition from an industrial economy into an information based economy. And the transition is proving to be a rough one. City development agencies are busy promoting the virtues of their cities to any business that might bring a boost to their ailing economies. Advertising "gangs" to prospective businesses would be even worse today than advertising a strong union tradition.

While gangs are not appearing in every city, neither do they seem to be just mechanical features of cities with stagnating economies like Milwaukee. In Columbus, Ohio, for example, where public employment, Ohio State, and technological advance have seemed to bring prosperity, gangs have also appeared in the last few years. A closer look at Columbus finds that although unemployment has been dropping in the eighties and median income rising, more than one quarter of the black population in Columbus's Franklin County lives under the poverty line, compared to a little over ten percent of the total population. Spending on human services has seen an absolute decline in the eighties and is expected to decline more in the years ahead.

The planning assumptions for the eighties and nineties for Columbus' Franklin County are telling: while unemployment is expected to decrease, the number of people receiving public assistance and living under the poverty line will increase. A disproportionate number of the poor are expected to be minority. The 1986 Franklin County planning document concludes: "The number of very wealthy and the number of very poor will increase."[5] And this is in a county with a "booming" "high tech" economy.

Apparently, as William Julius Wilson has pointed out, what is important to understand is not just economic growth, but the uneven nature of that growth.[6] While this growth may benefit some, others are left out. To many observers, economic segmentation is creating an "underclass" of mainly urban blacks and Hispanics who are not sharing in the benefits of economic expansion. Coinciding with this economic transformation, we are witnessing a rebirth of youth gangs in many small and medium sized cities and their entrenchment in larger cities. Might there be some relationship between these facts? Could this transition in our economy affect the nature of gangs themselves? What factors are associated with the emergence of gangs in today's urban centers?

Maybe we had better look closer at the nature of today's gangs.

Gangs and the Media

One way to investigate gangs would be to look at media coverage of gang activity.

It appears that the new 1980s gangs are "discovered" by the media well after their actual formation. This "discovery" labels gangs as a social problem and sets off a specific pattern of response. Often a spectacular incident sets off a "Youth Violence Task Force" to determine the nature of the problem and make recommendations. Columbus, Ohio, for example, was unfortunate enough to have gangs of youth assault the daughter of the Governor of Ohio and the son of the Mayor of Columbus in rapid order in the fall of 1985. To no one's surprise, Columbus formed a task force immediately following these incidents.[7] The Minneapolis task force formed the day after a gang murder of a student. Milwaukee's "Youth Initiatives" task force was formed after a local newspaper ran banner headlines discovering the existence of "4,000 Gang Members" in Milwaukee.[8]

But the media only publicizes gangs; it doesn't really tell us much about them. Sociologists who have done empirical research on gangs are unanimous in criticizing media coverage. Klein, for example, after examining the content of newspaper clippings in the Los Angeles area, finds that most of the articles are "negative" in content and serve basically to "form and to reinforce dramatic stereotypes of gang structure and behavior." While most research has pointed out that violence plays only a small role in gang behavior, the media's coverage, according to Klein, is "in almost total disregard of the reality of the streets." He concludes that "the news media are highly suspect as sources of accurate gang information" (Klein 1971, 15-19). Miller emphasizes and reemphasizes in his 1975 survey, "Violence by Youth Gangs and Youth Groups as a Crime Problem in Major American Cities," that the distortions of the media bear little relation to actual cycles of gang activity (Miller 1975, 2, 56-66).

Our own clipping file in Milwaukee bears out Klein's and Miller's allegations. Most accounts of Milwaukee gangs in the media don't resemble anything we found in our research. For example, here's one gem from the July 7, 1986, *Milwaukee Sentinel*: "The reporter found a savage subculture founded on silly signals and chants, witless tenets and unblinking obedience to leaders who were often borderline illiterates."

While this might sell newspapers, it certainly doesn't help us understand today's gangs. It does, however, indicate that gangs have been largely defined to the public with a focus on law enforcement. The public sees gangs as solely "a crime problem," to borrow from Miller. The broader focus of sociologists and reformers of the past is curiously neglected.

This law enforcement focus has been noted by Horowitz (1983) in an article entitled, "The End of the Youth Gang." Horowitz predicts future research on gangs will be dominated by "rightist" assumptions and concerns with individual criminal actions, not group or community dynamics. Spergel (1984, 199) concurs. The Justice Department's study, "Police Handling of Youth Gangs," while emphasizing that gangs are not a serious problem, is entirely devoted to police methods for "handling" gang crime. This publication is the only comprehensive nation-wide treatment of gangs we are aware of published in the 1980s. Klein's work, while openly critical of the accuracy of police knowledge, has been used by some in law enforcement to justify criticism of community-based gang intervention programs (Moore 1978, 46).

What this all adds up to is that media images of gangs are not to be trusted as a true picture of gang behavior; and the media forms and reinforces a law enforcement focus on gangs that may not be the only lens through which to look at today's gang members.

Task Forces, Race, and the Underclass

Another source of questionable knowledge about gangs is the various "Youth Violence Task Forces" that have formed in response to gang problems. In the Midwest, investigation by the authors of this book and data compiled by Needle and Stapleton have found at least eighteen midwestern medium and small sized cities which report 1980s gang activity and eleven separate task force reports. But what do we learn about the nature of today's gangs? The Minneapolis report concluded, somewhat more honestly than some others: "There is no clear picture as to who are the gang members, how the gangs operate, and what are their range of activities."

One reason those reports had "no clear picture" was their methodology. The reports are typically centered on the perceptions of gangs by high school students, police, other professionals, and even suburbanites. All the reports called for more research or investigation, but what was meant by this may not prove to be too helpful. The Minneapolis report called for "A systematic, longitudinal analysis of street gang graffiti...to determine the presence, migration and activities of street gangs...."[9] Did anyone ever think about talking to the people who wrote the graffiti?

If these were task force reports on health care, religion, or business and failed to interview doctors, clergy, or businessmen, how much credence would the reports receive? Task force reports on a city's gang problem merely give us a reading on how severe a social problem gangs are perceived to be by elites, law enforcement, and other interests. They tell us nothing about the actual nature of modern gangs.

One thing we do learn from the task force reports is most cities vociferously deny their gang problem has anything to do with race. "...gang members are typically from a mixture of sexes, ages, and races...." (Racine). "The gang problem...is not a problem of race" (Evanston). Several reports don't even mention race or the ethnicity of gangs (e.g., Cincinnati). But the evidence clearly shows that gangs in the 1980s are overwhelmingly black and Hispanic.[10] The public's fear of gangs is intensified by racial stereotypes and racial antagonism within our divided cities. The important question is not whether race and ethnicity influence gang problems, but what impact has the urban minority experience had on recent gang formation and the public response.

The problem of race in our nation's cities is also becoming increasingly confounded with the problem of class, particularly with the formation of an urban minority underclass. To deny that gangs today are predominantly a minority problem inevitably leads to a failure to analyze the impact of our changing economy on various classes within minority communities. The significance of the formation of a minority urban underclass and the simultaneous emergence and entrenchment of gangs is completely overlooked.[11] What is needed is a new effort in gang research to look more closely at urban gangs in the context of minority communities under current economic and social conditions. Before we explain how we attempted this in Milwaukee, let's look a little closer at the body of academic gang research to see how much it might help us with our task.

Too Much Theory, Too Few Facts

First of all, there is amazingly little recent research. Moore's continuing research on Chicano Los Angeles gangs is focused on earlier gang *klikas*, or age groups, and does not look at today's gangs. Horowitz's (1983) Chicago study is a community study of Chicano gangs in the early 1970s. Campbell's (1984) is a series of biographies of New York female gang members. Klein admitted in 1971 that he'd "had it with gangs." Spergel's current field work appears to emphasize program evaluation. Miller, who still lectures on gangs, has not done original research since the 1950s.[12] We can concur with Spergel (1984, 199): "It is possible that we know less about the current problem than we knew about gangs and gang violence in the 1960s."

The original research of Thrasher and the "Chicago School" of sociology still stands today as touchstones of research compared to any of the writings of the past forty years. Whyte's *Street Corner Society* (1943) is perhaps the single best book since then, with special relevance for today because the research was done during the Great Depression. Although the gangs studied were Italian, the economic conditions in Boston at the time in some ways closely resemble the depression-like conditions facing minorities in cities today.

By the 1960s some new research had been attempted (Miller, Yablonsky, Short, et al.), but the main emphasis was on constructing theories to explain gangs and delinquency. We will examine the utility of the various theoretical approaches for understanding gangs today as we proceed. But observers even during the sixties and seventies pointed out that we had an overabundance of theory and a scarcity of research. Patrick (1973, 155), for example, pointed out that "we are in the absurd position of having very few first hand studies of, but numerous theoretical speculations about, juvenile gangs." Klein makes the point firmly:

"in the past quarter century between Thrasher's Chicago and present day Chicago, New York, Boston, and Los Angeles, there appeared almost no empirical descriptions of juvenile gangs" (1971, 21). The theories developed in the fifties and sixties were rigorously examined by sociologists and for the most part failed to stand the test of empirical verification.[13] In the last forty years U.S. cities and the ethnicity of their poorer residents have changed dramatically. The U.S. economy is sweepingly different. Doesn't it stand to reason that the nature of urban gangs might change as well? We don't know because we haven't done the investigation.

Why not? One reason is that the vast majority of sociologists and researchers are white, and gangs today are overwhelmingly minority. The history of the lack of minority participation in research is a long one (Moore 1973, Takagi 1981). While there are serious ethical and epistemological questions involved, the fact is that sociologists in the 1980s have not considered minority gangs to be subjects of particular scientific interest. For white sociologists, "benign neglect" may be tempered with the difficulties of access. The ghetto has been traditionally suspicious of the motives of university researchers, and for good reason (Blauner and Wellman 1973). For minority academics the failure to confront in print the reality of minority gangs may in part be explained by the "withholding tendencies" described by Sawyer (1973, 367). Fear that an accurate description of some ugly realities of minority gangs may lend credence to racist stereotypes has led some minority academics to "withhold" from any careful investigation of the subject.[14]

Empirical research on urban gangs is out of fashion in academia. The "Chicago School" of sociology that literally forced its students "from the library to the streets"(Kirk and Miller 1986, 39) has fallen into disfavor. While the ethnographic traditions of the Chicago School have a few modern proponents (Liebow 1967, Miller 1986, Valentine 1978) the demise of ethnography and the "Chicago School" has been paralleled by a vast expansion in criminal justice research. As noted earlier, the emphasis on the study of gangs "as a crime problem" allows criminal justice researchers to study gang members as felons, or law violators, and not as part of a community. The major variables of race, sex, age, and class are used solely to explain behavior which violates the law. Broader concerns about social and economic structures or community processes are not seen as important.

Criminal justice research can take place in the safety of a prison or a juvenile detention facility, where information given researchers may be quantifiable but is inherently unreliable.[15] Criminology, despite its preoccupation with race, "has remained a white social science" (Georges-Abeyie 1984, 142). It has not produced any studies of note about modern gangs.

Gangs of course, are accessible only with difficulty by any outsiders, white or minority.[16] Yablonsky points out that "to the gang boy every researcher could be a cop" (Yablonsky 1961, vii). Whyte has detailed for us the long and difficult process through which an academic becomes accepted by a gang. Whyte learned Italian while living in the home of a "Cornerville" resident (Whyte 1943, 279-358). Moore (1978) solved the problem by use of Chicano *pinto*, or gang, collaborators. She explores the deep distrust between minority gang members and academics (1977, 145-46) and concludes that "unless community participants are actively involved in both the research and its uses, as we have done in this study, both the research and its ultimate uses tend to be highly suspect. While this can be termed politicization, the alternative is not very pleasant either. Unless the community is involved, so-called objective research will almost inevitably be politicized beyond the researcher's control" (1978, 10).

Moore's collaborative research became the methodological starting point for our investigation in Milwaukee. We could find no other method to identify the influential gang members, gain access to them, and be reasonably sure our respondents were speaking the truth. Milwaukee gang members were involved with all stages of our research and shared its promise to "tell their story" and perhaps even bring change.

The Milwaukee Gang Research Project

This book is in one sense the product of the intersection of two lives: John Hagedorn's and Perry Macon's.

John Hagedorn, the principal author, has had a long history of social activism and community work. He left the university in the 1960s, swept up in the civil rights and anti-war movements of those times. Born in Milwaukee and raised in a small northern Wisconsin town, Hagedorn spent the late sixties and early seventies organizing welfare rights organizations and anti-war groups in Milwaukee. For five years in the late 1970s he played a role in working class organizing in Boston.

He returned to Milwaukee in 1979 and continued a life of activism, working in several community coalitions concerned with education and police brutality.[17] He took a job as a community organizer in 1982 and while organizing block clubs observed the beginnings of Milwaukee's youth gangs. He then became the director of Milwaukee's first gang intervention program, the Youth Diversion Project. When he left to conduct this research project, he also returned to school, receiving a B.S. in Education and a M.A. in Sociology. He is now enrolled in the University of Wisconsin-Milwaukee's Urban Social Institutions doctoral program.

Perry Macon saw gangs from the other side, as a participant. Raised in Chicago in a Black Gangster Disciple neighborhood, his family moved to Freeport, Illinois, in 1975, when Perry was thirteen. Perry and four of his brothers were in constant trouble with the law and spent time at several Illinois juvenile correctional institutions. Finally, the family moved to Milwaukee in 1978.

It didn't take Macon long to get into trouble in Milwaukee. While he was being arrested and convicted for burglaries no fewer than three times, he also watched the origins of gangs in Milwaukee. In response to pressure from other gangs and to aid his money-making efforts, Perry, known as "Lord Macon," founded the Vicelords in the summer of 1982. It was after his arrest for a third felony burglary charge in the summer of 1983 that Macon and Hagedorn met in the first month of the Youth Diversion Project. Macon is now a student at the Milwaukee Area Technical College.

The Youth Diversion Project (YDP) was both successful and frustrating. It was successful in that we found it was not hard to structure a program that would be accepted by young people in gangs and provide a meaningful alternative to the bleak future of gang life. While drugs, violence, and crime were interwoven with gang life, most gang members, even those usually termed "hard core," seemed to us quite unlike the stereotype of the aspiring "career criminals" promoted by law enforcement and the media.

But the YDP was also frustrating. First, while we could get many young people back into school, get limited employment for a few others, and help a few more with court problems, no half million dollar program could begin to address the gang problem. The emergence of gangs in Milwaukee in the 1980s was clearly tied up with the economic conditions facing the black and Hispanic communities at that time. As much as we could help a few, we could not change the basic conditions that created the gangs and guaranteed their persistence. Second, while we could design workable programs, we did not have a significant impact on public policy or the criminal image into which gangs were cast. While the YDP was able to hire only a few mainly part-time workers, the law enforcement buildup was massive. The police gang squad soon grew to twenty-six full time officers, and other institutions strengthened their security and prosecution capacities. Our penny-ante efforts were overwhelmed by a high stakes law enforcement poker game in which we could hardly get to the table.

The major "experts" on Milwaukee's gang problem were the Chicago Gang Crimes Unit, whose frequent trips to Milwaukee included scary slide shows of murders and a display of gang weapons that would make the U.S. Army run for cover. Their Chicago image of organized crime and recurrent senseless homicide was the image of Milwaukee gangs adopted by elites and the media in Milwaukee. If Milwaukee's gangs weren't like Chicago's today, we were warned, failure to "act" in a hard-line manner would allow Milwaukee's gangs to become like Chicago's in five years or maybe sooner.[18]

Our program did have its rewards and successes. Macon and Hagedorn, along with outreach worker Nancy Diaz, were quickly able to meet and build relationships with most of Milwaukee's still forming youth gangs. Offering part-time employment to gang members on the condition they attend an alternative school, the YDP attracted many of the founding members of Milwaukee's gangs. A major break-dance competition was organized in 1984, followed by a summer mural project in which members of rival gangs worked together on six community murals. The YDP's part-time outreach workers, hired largely from the gangs, went to all the hangouts and playgrounds and allowed the YDP to become influential among the gangs. While our program had formal objectives to satisfy funding sources, our actual goal was to gain influence among the gangs so we could recruit to our education and employment programs and curtail some of the recurrent violence.

And we did develop some influence. For example, a shooting war broke out in the spring of 1985 between the Latin Kings and Spanish Cobras, and each gang began pressing legal charges against members of the other gang for the incidents. When the shooting stepped up and everything else had failed, we used our prestige to organize what we called a "Hill Street Blues" face-to-face meeting between the two gangs. The actual meeting was as much drama as negotiation. Twenty of our security men lined the hall to "guarantee the safety" of the two rival Puerto Rican gang leaders. A deal was cut: the war would be called off if everyone on both sides agreed to drop already pending charges from the prior five or six shootings (fortunately, no one had been injured yet). The District Attorney was furious and considered but eventually decided against filing obstruction of justice charges against Hagedorn. The tactic, after all, had worked; the war and shootings stopped. We gained respect on the streets and our programs gained new recruits.

Our efforts, however, had almost no impact on public policy. The media and local police constantly pictured gang members as "losers" who were not too bright, were intent on violence, and would inevitably become career criminals tied to Chicago-based gang drug sales. The only legitimate response to such people was police and prison. A local Task Force was formed and issued a report that did nothing to change this image, nor did it create a single job nor fund an additional program. It did, however, recommend strengthening current police gang squad efforts.

Talking to the "Top Dogs"

It was at this time that Hagedorn met Joan Moore, author of *Homeboys* and now teaching at the University of Wisconsin-Milwaukee (UWM). She had been a member of Milwaukee's gang task force and had seen similar public processes at work in Los Angeles. Her book *Homeboys* was a collaborative work with Chicano gang members and had explained Los Angeles gangs as an integral part of Chicano communities and the segmentation of Los Angeles' labor markets.

In order to change the public image of gangs and to argue for a less one-sided response, we decided to write an accurate history of Milwaukee's gangs, describe their structure, learn how they were tied to Chicago gangs, and explore what was happening to the founding members as they aged and became adults. The only way to get this kind of information was to interview the founding members themselves.[19] The Milwaukee Foundation decided the project was worthy of a serious attempt and provided $18,000 for a year-long study that would make recommendations for local policy. After more than a few difficulties at

UWM, the interviews began in December 1985 and concluded in June 1986.[20] A two-hour questionnaire was developed, based on Moore's Los Angeles interviews. Forty-seven gang members were interviewed from nineteen of Milwaukee's largest gangs.

Those interviewed were the "top dogs" of Milwaukee's gangs. Forty-two of them participated in the actual "founding" of the nineteen gangs. Eleven are or were the recognized leaders. Two were former high-ranking members in Chicago's Black Gangster Disciples and Latin Kings. Only three joined after their gang formed. Fifteen of the gangs are black, three Hispanic, and one white. Three of the gangs are female. Also interviewed were nine key policymakers in criminal justice and social service agencies. The gang interviews were conducted in the homes of Hagedorn or Macon and a few in Hagedorn's office at the UWM Urban Research Center. Open-ended questions were used, and no interviews were conducted while the respondent was in custody. We paid twenty dollars for each interview.[21]

The key ingredient in this project was the cooperation of the gang members themselves. The interviews started, naturally enough, with those gang founders Hagedorn and Macon had known while working at the YDP.[22] After the early interviews, many of the gang founders helped Macon and Hagedorn locate other key gang members, the "top dogs" in the formation of the other gangs. The interviews took place approximately five years after most of the gangs had formed. The gang founders interviewed were then young adults, most of them in their early twenties. As a part of the interview, the respondent was asked to list the entire group of friends who started the gang and various facts about their present status. The present circumstances of two hundred and sixty founding members were tracked from all nineteen gangs.

Not all the interviews proceeded smoothly. A few people we talked to were found to have little knowledge about events surrounding the founding of the gang and were paid, but not interviewed. Others whom we recruited from the streets were skeptical of us at first, even if we seemed to know a lot of the "top dogs." For example, one interview began slowly; the young man from the "3-4 Mob" obviously did not trust his white interviewer. As we got to the part of the interview where we went through the list of the present circumstances of his fellow founding members, he was especially nervous. These seemed like "police" questions. However, when Hagedorn assured him we did not want real names of the founders, just initials or street names, he agreed to continue. A change in his attitude took place as he went through the list of his friends who founded the gang, realizing how few were employed, how few had graduated, how many had been to jail, and how many were still involved with the gang as adults. He seemed, perhaps for the first time, to grasp what was happening to all his friends from the neighborhood. He had Hagedorn stop the tape, looked at him square in the eye and said, "This is for real, isn't it?" A large majority of interviews turned out to be intense, genuine experiences for the interviewer, but sometimes also for the gang founder.

What Can We Learn From Milwaukee's Gangs?

Our research resulted in a study that was aimed at influencing local policy. We also convened a conference of representatives from fifteen middle and small sized midwestern cities in fall 1987 to compare their city's gang experiences. In the course of organizing that conference, we found that while each city's gangs were in many ways unique, there were many similarities in the way gangs were approached as a law enforcement problem. There was little valid and reliable knowledge about gangs and no research that could be used to counter the simplistic stereotypes used to justify public policy. The theoretical basis for understanding gangs was an eclectic mix of past theories which did not adequately explain the nature of modern gangs.

This book is, on one level, about Milwaukee's gangs, their origins and structure, the adult status of the gang founders, the effect of race and ethnicity on gang formation, and the public response to the gang problem. Our findings challenge the prevalent popular stereotypes of gangs and question much of the current theoretical explanations of their nature. A major conclusion of this study is the uniqueness and variability of modern gangs and the importance of local factors in understanding and fashioning a flexible response. But on another level, this book is a challenge for both sociologists and practitioners to go beyond the law enforcement paradigm in both theory and policy. The development of an urban minority underclass in the last decades, first in large cities and more recently in middle and small sized cities, has altered the nature of gangs and demands new investigation and new policies. The entrenchment of gangs in our cities presents problems that can neither be ignored nor solved by the simple-minded policies of "more police and more prisons."

Truly, here is a void that sociologists should fill. To puncture stereotypes and shape new directions is an appropriate role for academic research. But academia unfortunately has treated gangs from traditional perspectives and has buttressed the popular notion of gangs as merely a "crime problem." Perhaps the dominant role of the Justice Department in funding the research, prevention, and cure of the problem has had some bearing on how gangs are framed by academics. This book looks at academic notions of gangs and subjects them to a trial by the fire of our data from Milwaukee. We have aspired to make our critique of academic theory readable not only for the sociologist, but also for anyone concerned about gangs and urban policy.

How a problem is studied has some bearing on what is discovered. If gangs are studied in a prison, or by perusing police or court files, the conclusions will tend to rationalize the criminal justice response. But if gangs are studied within a community, analyzing the impact of social and economic policies on various classes within those communities and witnessing developments over time, perhaps different conclusions may result. This book needs to be read above all as a method, as a way to look at a pressing social problem; it is not our intention to offer a new set of stereotypes.

Before we turn to a careful description of how Milwaukee's gangs formed, let's look more closely at a few factors historically associated with the emergence of gangs and their relevance today.

2
WHAT HAPPENED TO THE BEER THAT MADE MILWAUKEE FAMOUS?

Q. What's the biggest cause of fights?
A. Ah...I think money.

Q. Money?
A. Not having money and a lot of them be frustrated, and you know they might have just enough money to get them some beer or something. Get drunk and get to going off. Talking about jobs. Everybody always talking about they want a job. Younger fellows you know. "When summer comes I'll get a summer job." Then half of them don't be able to get the summer job. So they got to run around and try to steal and shit."

Tony, Four Corner Hustlers

It is twenty years since rioting and unrest unsettled our nation's cities. The flames that burned on Milwaukee's Third Street in its northside black community have long since died down. But the condition of that street is today much worse than after the flames of 1967.

In place of Gimbels Department Store and the small businesses that hung on in the sixties, boarded-up stores serve as props for junkies and prostitutes. Gang graffiti tells all who can read street writing that this turf has been claimed by black youth called "Vicelords" and "Castlefolks." Though a few new buildings show that downtown is moving into the ghetto, they cannot hide the signs of economic depression. Even Schlitz, the beer that made Milwaukee famous, has moved, its jobs lost and its Third Street brewery remodeled to accommodate new county social service offices. Perhaps the closing of Schlitz best symbolizes Milwaukee's changes over the past twenty years: a large plant closed and converted to house an expanding welfare bureaucracy. Instead of industrial workers bringing home a paycheck, we have social workers mailing out welfare checks.

But isn't this just another retelling of an old story? Aren't the gangs of today basically the same delinquent boys who have plagued U.S. cities for the past sixty years? Or have the social and economic changes of the past decades had an effect on the nature of urban gangs?

Certainly, in examining Milwaukee gangs, we find they are situated in historical circumstances that have both similarities and differences from times past. Unlike those who would assert that gangs today are basically the same as gangs of the past (Miller 1976), we suspect these changed circumstances may play a role in some aspects of gang behavior, notably the process by which young gang members as they grow older "mature out" of the gang into the working class. And unlike those who study generic gangs without ethnicity and from no specific community (Cohen 1955), we believe class, ethnicity, and local community are all key variables in understanding contemporary gang developments. Because of the scarcity of modern research on black and Hispanic gangs, we believe new research is needed in the cities of the eighties. Thrasher's or Suttles' (1959) method of investigation, of emphasizing the variation in gangs and studying them as a part of a specific community, appeals to us.

We need not start without a framework. A good method of investigation would combine direct observation of gangs with a reexamination of factors that have been historically associated with gang development.

Comparing the immigrant European experience of the past with the black and minority experience today may yield some insights into possible changes in the nature of today's gangs. While our data is drawn from only one "rust belt" city, Milwaukee, other cities can readily compare their environments with the Milwaukee experience.

Those who think that "a gang is a gang is a gang" whether in 1920s Chicago or 1980s Milwaukee have the burden to prove their position.

Demographics: From Polka to Breakdance

Gangs in the 1920s for Thrasher and the 1940s for Whyte were youthful European immigrant gangs, jammed into crowded cities. This rapid influx of poor youthful newcomers is one historical condition that led to those youth "milling about" and "ganging."

The large-scale European immigration which ended in the 1920s was seen by many as responsible for the earlier proliferation of youth gangs in Milwaukee (Schlossman 1977, 102) and other urban centers.[1] Frederick Thrasher, who studied 1,313 gangs in 1920s Chicago, provided this classic definition: "The gang is an interstitial group, originally formed spontaneously, then integrated through conflict" (Thrasher 1963, 46). By "interstitial," Thrasher meant gangs were located in the crowded "slums" surrounding the central business district. The ethnicity of gangs might change, but their location didn't. As immigrant groups moved up into better working class jobs and out of the worst housing, the new immigrant groups who took their place spawned new youth gangs who warred with gangs in neighboring areas.

By the 1960s, the ethnicity of gangs had changed. There were fewer European gangs and more black and Hispanic gangs. But the paradigm used by theorists remained the same: the gang experience was the transitory product of the social tensions of immigrant youth newly arrived in a hostile city.

Milwaukee offers a good example of U.S. urban demographic changes over the past sixty years. When Ronald Reagan visited Milwaukee during the 1984 election campaign, his aides insisted that the media event be an ethnic extravaganza, with lederhosen-dressed Herrs and pretty Frauleins and plenty of bratwurst and polish sausage. While some local Republicans objected that the ethnic image no longer fit Milwaukee, they were overruled by Washington campaign staff. To the minds of outsiders, Milwaukee is a hard-working ethnic town, with good Germans and Poles working their eight-hour day in local factories and coming home to Gemütlichkeit and Schlitz.

The President's aides were caught looking backward. Like so many other cities, Milwaukee's ethnic working class is rapidly moving to the suburbs, leaving the decaying central city to blacks and Hispanics. When Eisenhower defeated Stevenson in 1952, more than 96% of the 650,000 residents of the city of Milwaukee were white. By the time of Kennedy's "New Frontier," Milwaukee's population had risen to nearly three quarters of a million and blacks were still less than 10% of that total. By the Nixon years, Milwaukee's population still was over 700,000, but it had begun to fall. The black population topped 100,000 and whites were headed for the suburbs. When President Reagan munched on a bratwurst on his campaign stop in 1984, blacks made up more than one quarter of all city residents. Nearly one of every three Milwaukeeans today is a non-European minority.

And the black and Hispanic newcomers were youthful and poor. While the number of youth overall in Milwaukee County declined in the 1970s, the black and Hispanic youth population jumped by 25%. More importantly, there were nearly double the number of minority youth living under the poverty line in 1980 than in 1970. A majority of black children in Milwaukee now live in poverty. William Julius Wilson summarizes this phenomenon:

> The black migration to New York, Philadelphia, Chicago,
> and other Northern cities—the continual replenishment of
> black populations there by poor newcomers—predictably
> skewed the age profile of the urban black community and
> kept it relatively young. . . . In the nation's inner cities in
> 1977, the median age for whites was 30.3, for blacks 23.9.
> *(Wilson 1984, 96)*

In Milwaukee in 1985, the median white male age was 31.5, while the black male median was 20.8 and the Hispanic male 21.3. Milwaukee population projections forecast an absolute increase in the number of black and Hispanic children under 18 and high birth rates well into the next century.

Like immigrant gangs of the past, Milwaukee's 1980s minority youth gangs crowded on playgrounds, fought with one another, and generally made trouble. On one level all that had really changed for the young people who formed the gangs was ethnicity.

Economics: From White Working Class to Black Underclass

Gangs have been seen by most theorists as "working class" (Cohen) or "lower class" (Miller). The gang has been viewed as a single generation adolescent adaptation with the youthful delinquent eventually "maturing out" of his ganging behavior and getting on with his adult life of work and family.

For the "Chicago School" of Shaw, McKay, and Thrasher, gangs and delinquency were associated with areas of the city containing the foreign-born and black migrants. The relative abundance of industrial jobs provided a way out of poverty for some of the newcomers. Immigrant gang boys were able to mature out of delinquency in part due to an industrial-based economy which continually needed a large supply of low-skill labor. Whyte's 1930s "college boys," who were described as Italians with social mobility, differed from his "corner boys" only in degree. "Doc," the leader of the "Nortons" corner gang, worked his way into a job as a supervisor in a local plant (Kornhauser 1978, 126-30). Immigrant gang boys assimilated into American society at varying rates along with their ethnic group.

In the war years after the Depression, industrial jobs were relatively available for ethnic youth. In Milwaukee and other northern cities, discrimination and segregation restricted black entrance into basic industry in varying degrees until World War II, when the largest growth in black population occurred.[2] The black community was always relatively small in Milwaukee compared to many other Midwestern cities. The effects of the business cycle were more severely felt by Milwaukee blacks, who had a precarious hold on the "good jobs" provided by an industrial city (Trotter 1985, 60). Even the good times weren't always so good. For example, in 1950, despite a growing economy that saw only 2.7% white unemployment, 9.7% of the black workforce were unemployed (Washington and Oliver 1976, 77).

While the sixties and seventies saw their ups and downs, the eighties brought a deepening depression to the black community. It was no longer possible to step up on the industrial ladder of mobility briefly available for some after decades of discrimination. That industrial ladder was suddenly snatched away. Between 1980 and 1985, the Milwaukee area lost 35,900 manufacturing jobs. Projections by the State Department of Industry, Labor, and Human Relations forecasts that this downward trend will continue. Milwaukee now has over 15,000 more service jobs than manufacturing jobs.[3]

Black workers today remain concentrated in those areas of the economy undergoing decline or paying low wages. In 1980 there were twice as many black workers in factory and low paying service jobs than blacks in managerial or professional occupations. The situation for Puerto Ricans and Mexicans was similar (Valdez 1979, 177-78; de Santiago 1980, 66). In contrast, the white ethnic working class has radically changed character. By 1980 two thirds of all white employees who lived in the city of Milwaukee were managers, in sales or other administrative support positions, or in a professional occupation. There were more white managers and supervisors alone than white industrial workers. The number of white managers has tripled since 1970. It's no surprise we could find only one white neighborhood gang in Milwaukee.[4]

The 1980s have been disastrous for the black community. A recent City of Milwaukee report found that in 1984 alone the number of households earning below $10,000 a year increased an astounding 25%. Most of these households are black or Hispanic. The 1985 Milwaukee black unemployment rate was 27.9%, second highest in the nation among larger cities. The ratio of black unemployed to white unemployed was the worst in the nation (see Appendix III).

The significance of these developments is that a large part of the black and Hispanic communities can no longer be considered working class. Minority youth, who formed Milwaukee's 1980s gangs, will not have an industrial ladder to step on in order to "mature out" of the gang. When many black adults find employment today, the job is more likely to be part-time, temporary, and low-wage, more like their youthful jobs than the full-time, unionized stable jobs of the past.

Some sociologists and economists have understood this deindustrialization of the U.S. economy in part as the development of internal "segmented labor markets." In this segmentation, the more skilled, high-wage or primary sectors of the economy exist largely separate from the low-wage secondary sectors. Poor minority youth sell their la-

CHANGE IN EMPLOYMENT STRUCTURE
Manufacturing and Service Jobs
City of Milwaukee: 1975–1985

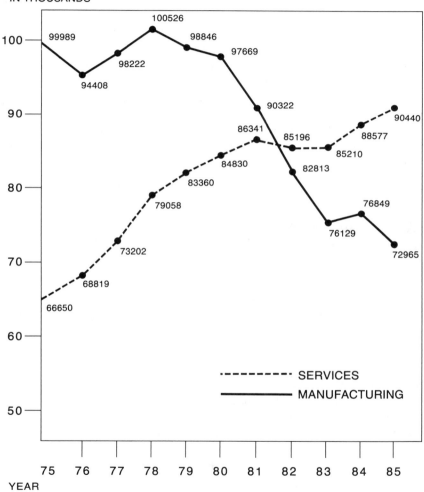

EMPLOYMENT
IN THOUSANDS

SOURCE: Wisconsin Department of Industry, Labor, and Human Relations

bor almost exclusively within this secondary market in the nation's cities (Bullock 1973).

Moore (1978) points out that Los Angeles Chicano gangs exist
within a labor market that consists of low-wage, usually part-time work,
welfare, and the illegal economy. Within poor minority communities, a
combination of the three types of subsistence is often necessary for survival. Chicano gang members in Los Angeles continue their gang life
into adulthood. This closely parallels our findings in Milwaukee.

One "changed circumstance" then, from the immigrant gangs of
the past to the minority gangs of the present, is the structural narrowing of the opportunity to mature out of delinquent and deviant ways of
life. In the 1960s, blacks and Hispanics in large cities like Chicago and
Los Angeles first felt the effects of these conditions. Gangs that formed
in those cities around that time continue to exist today. In the 1980s, cities the size of Milwaukee are experiencing both economic segmentation
and the reemergence of gangs. Gangs today appear to be a permanent
feature of a growing urban minority underclass.[5]

Education: From Learning to Labor, to Not Learning at All

Gangs have always been associated with dropping out of school. Milwaukee's 1980s minority gangs were formed largely from youth who
were on street corners rather than in a classroom. Betsy, a black sopho-
more bused to a southside high school far away from her all-black
northside neighborhood, describes the problem best. She asked us:

"What's the difference between today (a school day in May) and
last September?" She was sitting on the steps of the "Game Room," a
popular local hangout overlooking a busy street. She continued: "How
many buses do you see?" We could see only one yellow school bus, partially filled with black students, making the long return trip to the north
side.

"In September," Betsy explained, "there are five filled buses taking kids home after school. Where are the other four buses?"

But lack of education today has a far more serious consequence
for gang members than it had in the past. Historically, as Colin Greer
(1972) and others have pointed out, the role of the public school was to
assimilate immigrants and prepare them for work in an industrial

United States. Hard work, English, and a little luck were all that was really needed to make it. The actual mobility of the German and other immigrant communities attests to the successful assimilation of these ethnic groups through public education and the long-term growth of the economy from 1920 to 1960 (Steinberg 1981).

Today, minority high school dropouts don't get jobs in factories, but work for minimum wage in fast food and other service jobs. What skills must be taught to qualify someone for such jobs? Listen to Phillip of Milwaukee's 2-4 gang explain what skills are needed to work at McDonalds:

> **A.** You don't have to know how to read to work at McDonalds. You just can't be color blind.
>
> **Q.** How's that? What do you mean?
> **A.** Color blind. You know, on the cash register. Red is for hamburger, yellow is a cheeseburger, green's a fish.

The public schools today apparently don't even need to teach reading to prepare poor youth for available work. Kenneth Polk puts the change in education in perspective.

> In decades past, orderly flows existed whereby the less competent young persons would move directly into the labor market upon departure from school. . . . The availability of work provided such young persons with an alternative to school. . . one that provided both an escape from the pain of schooling and access to a job and income. . . . The fact that enough jobs existed at earlier times gave even the lower status students a sense of rationality. . . . Data from more recent years suggest an ominous change, and a new pattern whereby the lower status channels lead either to no employment, or to entrapment in the lower level of a dual labor market, a level that consists of marginal, low-paid, often part-time jobs that provide little in terms of training for the future or access to advancement. . . . This situation is creating a new class of marginal youth."
>
> (Polk 1984, 467-69).[6]

Good jobs in the modern era obviously demand a much higher level of education.[7] But the new high-tech, skilled occupations are leaving poor minority youth behind. Minority students in large numbers are not only dropping out of the schools, but many of those that remain are doing terribly.

The Milwaukee Public Schools, touted as a national model of a de-segregated school system, long resisted reporting on the relative perfor-mance of its black and white students. Finally, a Governor's study Commission in 1985 drew some devastating conclusions. Among them were the finding that the gap between white and black achievement, rather than narrowing as the child progressed in "desegregated" schools, continued to widen. One third of all grades received by black high school students are "F"s. Forty percent of all black high school freshmen drop out before their senior year. Any "academic progress" was confined to the college bound specialty programs. The average grade-point for black and white students in all but two college prep high schools was an astounding "D." The majority of Milwaukee Public School students, and the vast majority of its black students, were either dropping out of school or graduating with minimal skills.[8]

No black or Hispanic students went to college from Betsy's high school in 1985, but for those blacks and Hispanics who do go on to col-lege, the outlook is also dim. The University of Wisconsin-Milwaukee, the major urban university in Milwaukee, enrolls only 20% of its fresh-man class from the Milwaukee Public Schools. The rest come from the nearly all-white suburbs. Only 6% of UWM's incoming freshmen are black, about the same percentage as in the total student body, but far less than the black 25.3% of Milwaukee's population.

Just as in the public schools, the problem gets worse as black stu-dents advance. Black graduate students today are less than 4% of total graduate enrollment. This reflects disturbing trends nationwide. Since 1976-'77 black graduate enrollment has fallen nearly 20%, from over 65,000 to less than 53,000 in 1984-'85.[9]

Black and Hispanic youth who have had a poor quality education can no longer compete for "good jobs" that could provide meaningful mobility. For a gang member, the gang experience, rather than being a transitory "rite of passage" into an adult role of family and work, con-tinues into adult years filled with joblessness or meaningless part-time work.

From Ethnic Power to Black Powerlessness

Immigrants have always faced discrimination and unequal treatment from those with power. Gangs have always formed from powerless minorities and have often become a part of the political struggle of their ethnic group to achieve equality. Whyte's gangs were part of the political rivalry of Italians and Irish in 1940s Boston. "Doc," the leader of Whyte's "Nortons," even decided at one point to turn his widespread popularity to good use by running for office. Royko writes about the career of one prominent Chicago gang member and future mayor, Richard Daley. Daley's Hamburg Social and Athletic Club played a role in the race riots of 1919 and in Democratic ward politics. Royko describes the Irish gangs as playing an integral part in urban politics of the early 1900s (1971, 35-38).

The black experience of inequality in northern cities is a long one and was punctuated by a series of racial uprisings that shook our cities twenty years ago. The struggle for black political power in our cities has been central to the contemporary urban scene. It would seem foolish to look at the emergence of minority gangs and neglect racism and the minority experience of inequality, but almost all academic studies do just that.[10]

It would also be a mistake to think the level of racial antagonism is the same in all U.S. cities. Some cities have black mayors or police chiefs and substantial black political power, while others have changed little the past twenty years. Racism, like other attitudes, varies between people, communities, institutions, and cities. Milwaukee, compared to other cities, has a unique and persistent pattern of discrimination and racist behavior.[11]

After the disorders in 1967, a fascinating series of "race relations" surveys of elites, professionals, and black communities were taken nationwide (Rossi et al. 1974). Fifteen cities were chosen. Some, including Milwaukee, had experienced "major" disorders in 1967, some had experienced disorders earlier, and some had racial peace. The most striking fact about the surveys in Milwaukee was the agreement between random samples of local elites and members of the black community: both groups believed blacks in Milwaukee had almost no influence on decision-making in city hall. Milwaukee was near the bottom of the list among all cities surveyed on almost every measure of race relations. A

1970 follow-up study by an anti-poverty agency found that black "exclusion" from decision-making in both private enterprise and the city and county administrations was still "glaring." In 1987 there were three black aldermen, but no major city department had a black department head. Another series of surveys of Milwaukee elites in 1987 concurred with past surveys: race relations was still one of the most important unresolved problems in Milwaukee.

Milwaukee is a city that has not seemed to like change.[12] Its recently retired German mayor served seven terms, longer than any urban mayor in history. Its Irish County Executive was in office from 1976 to 1988. Its two white congressmen are seldom challenged and never defeated. Its last school superintendent served longer than any other in the country save one. Until recently, its Police Chief had a life term by state law. City Hall's political base remains the old coalition of white ethnics, big labor, and downtown business (see Appendix IV). The black and Hispanic communities have been essentially locked out of power and decision-making. And when most of a powerless community is poor, control depends upon force.

The police have always been controversial in Milwaukee. The early 1900s socialist movement aimed at control of the police in order to curtail the power of business. A socialist-populist coalition succeeded in passing a state law that gave a life term to the Milwaukee police chief to insulate him from pressure of the industrial barons and the vagaries of machine politics (Harring 1983, Conley et al. 1982).

Harold Breier was handpicked by Mayor Henry Maier to take over a corruption-riddled police department in 1964. Breier was a German cop of the old school. His popularity among whites was immense: A 1982 poll found that 74% of all whites thought he was doing an outstanding job.

But the black community had another view. In the same poll, 74% of blacks thought Breier was doing a lousy job and should resign. In 1984, no black had a rank higher than sergeant in the Milwaukee Police Department. At least ten black youths had been killed by police under suspicious circumstances while Harold Breier was Chief. Hostility to the police permeated the black community and especially its youth.

Two police killings of black youth help us better understand the extent of the black youth-police hostility. In 1958 a black youth, Daniel Bell, was killed by police. The killing was ruled "justifiable homicide." Twenty-one years later, a troubled white police officer came forward and admitted that his partner had murdered young Daniel in cold blood. While an outraged black community demanded justice, the City of Milwaukee fought to the bitter end a just settlement of the matter. In 1981 another black youth, Ernest Lacy, was killed by police as he went to a convenience store for a soda. Lacy supposedly "resembled" a rape suspect, and he died after being brutally subdued. Demonstrations of up to 10,000 for justice were ignored even after an inquest surprisingly indicted three officers for homicide. While one officer was eventually fired for his role in the killing, once again "official" Milwaukee resisted granting a "measure of justice." The killing of Ernest Lacy and the revelation of the murder of Daniel Bell took place coincidentally with the formation of black gangs. The lack of political power and the nearly universal fear of police by black youth were a component part of the Milwaukee black experience of the 1980s.

What effect has this experience of racism had on gang formation? While in the past immigrant gangs played a role within their communities' political life, Milwaukee's 1980s black gangs appear much more alienated. While thousands of their brothers and sisters marched for justice for Ernie Lacy, black gangs hung out on the playgrounds, skeptical of any "movement." The intensity of the experience of racism along with the demonstrated lack of political clout of black middle class leaders contributed to the deep sense of frustration and antagonism of black youth. Today's black gangs, as we will show, are alienated even from their own communities.

Conclusion: The Need for Reexamination

Immigrant gangs were seen by the "Chicago School" and others as products of the disorganization of newly arrived poor immigrant communities. This disorganization was seen to be transitory, usually lasting only a single generation. The new immigrants eventually got jobs, learned English, gained political influence, and moved into stable working class homes. Their youthful immigrant gangs largely disappeared when their communities moved up the economic and social ladder. This paradigm has been the dominant framework for gang theorists.

While the black and Hispanic experience is similar in its origins to the immigrant experience, economic and social changes have altered the "maturing out" process in minority gangs. The interstitial nature of gangs, as explained by Thrasher, no longer appears to be descriptive. Gangs, for the "Chicago School," were interstitial or "in between" ethnic communities, in between youth and adulthood, and in between disorganized and more stable, integrated communities. On the contrary, today's minority gangs have become permanent features of their communities and show signs of persisting over many generations.

Economic segmentation and the development of a new underclass appears to be a general nationwide phenomenon, but the degree of racial integration into power structures clearly varies. How much effect the presence or absence of minority administrative and political officials have had on the development of gangs is a question for comparative research.

In Milwaukee, gang formation took place in a context of a continuing crisis in race relations. The effects of economic segmentation combined with black powerlessness has led to a severe sense of alienation between black underclass youth and their neighborhoods and communities. We'll look closer at the particular form racial oppression has taken in Milwaukee and the role of that city's desegregation plan in Chapter Six. What is important for our discussion at this point is that racism and race relations within various cities must be included as variables in understanding gangs and their behavior.

We need to turn now to another difference between some of today's gangs and gangs of the past. Recently, youth in smaller cities have been forming gangs that have the same names as gangs in larger cities. Does this mean gangs in Milwaukee are products of the diffusion of Chicago gangs? Are gangs in Phoenix "exported" from Los Angeles? Are we witnessing the emergence of "satellite gangs?" It's time to let Milwaukee gang members tell their own story.

3

HOW DO GANGS GET STARTED?

Gangs are increasingly operating outside their neighborhood turf and are showing signs of moving into other parts of the U.S. Although no organized network has emerged, police in at least six western cities have reported visits by L.A. gang members, who come seeking outlets for crack cocaine.

Christian Science Monitor,
June 12, 1987

How did gangs get started? Is it like a virus, did it jump from one city to the next? No, it ain't like no virus.

Darryl, Black Gangster
Disciples

How do groups of youth become a gang? In Milwaukee, just 90 miles north of Chicago, what role do Chicago gangs play in gang developments? Is there a "contagion" factor? Are smaller city gangs merely "satellite gangs" or do they basically have their own identity? Are gangs in cities like Milwaukee one result of organized gang crime expanding their drug markets? How would we find out?

What We Know About How 1980s Gangs Began

Contemporary accounts of gang origins aren't very helpful. Most of the Task Force reports or media articles we have seen either fail to mention how small city Midwest gangs got started or attribute gang origins to migrating gang members from a nearby big city. The Evanston task force report has a brief section, "History of Gangs," which describes black and white groups of youth in the 1970s "hanging out." By 1983, the authors report, the problem "is markedly different." The authors go on to say, without elaboration,"We suspect that these youth delinquency problems changed character during the 1970s" (Rosenbaum 1983, 11).

When gang origins are mentioned in local accounts, it is generally in the context of gang members moving from Chicago or other large cities and starting "satellite" gangs named after their metropolitan gang. This is an important question to consider, since many gangs in midwestern cities are named after Chicago gangs. If these gangs are not "satellites" or "branches" of their metropolitan counterpart, we must explain why they use the same names.

Some accounts, however, strain credibility. In a report to the Minneapolis Gang Task Force, a corrections official blames her city's gang problems on other cities. She states that of the twenty-two gang members in a detention cottage, "at least ten moved here from out of state." The report goes on: "Within this population of ten, some of these offenders report family involvement with Chicago, Milwaukee, or Kansas City gangs." The report ends with the following warning: "I've heard presentations by professionals from Milwaukee and Chicago who have traced the development of gangs in their cities. These great cities have been crippled by gangs. People are no longer free to walk the streets. . . ."[1]

We might be inclined to dismiss this as self-interested hysteria, but the rather questionable data has been apparently repeated by sociologist William Kornblum, author of the excellent volume *Growing Up Poor*. In a recent article Kornblum (1987, 100) mentions that in Minneapolis "half of the youths arrested from a gang called the Disciples had lived previously in Chicago." Citing unnamed "experts," Kornblum speculates that the upsurge in gang violence has been caused by the "urban exposure that poor youths from the rural South received in the 1970s and 1980s in northern cities like Chicago and New York." The gangs then must have somehow spread to Minneapolis and other cities.

If our analysis of the problem is to blame a city's gang problem on the diffusion of big city gang members, solutions become similarly simplistic. One recommendation that has been popping up in various cities, including Minneapolis, is for "computer tracking" of big city gang members. Others propose to treat gangs as organized crime and pass laws that would incarcerate anyone admitting gang involvement.[2]

Rather than say more about this familiar "outside agitator" approach now, let us just mention that once again we have a lack of primary data. How do the "experts" in these cities know that their gangs began as a result of diffusion of Chicago or Los Angeles gang members? We should point out we have more documentation of Chicago police traveling from city to city agitating for a certain type of response to gangs, than we have documentation of traveling gang organizers. Perhaps someone should come forth with more data than "10 of 22 gang members incarcerated in a single juvenile cottage moved from another city."[3]

Can the academic literature shed some light on gang origins?

Thrasher and the Subculturists

First of all, much of the academic literature on gangs is not concerned with the origins of gangs, but with explanations for the origins of juvenile delinquency. What many theorists try to explain is why adolescents become delinquent, why they break the law, retreat into drugs, or become violent. Gangs, to Cloward and Ohlin, Cohen, and others, are delinquent by definition. This practice of seeing the gang as primarily a "law-violating group" has of course been popularly adopted, thanks to a

helping hand from law enforcement agencies, the media, and some contemporary sociologists.

In most of these theories, there are no descriptions of how a gang
originates. It simply is not considered important. According to these
theorists, gangs are a consequence or component of a "subculture"
which enforces delinquent norms of one sort or another on all its members. Where descriptions of gang histories are given, they typically are
brief and attribute gang origins to past conflict.[4]

This is a major difference between much modern gang theory and
the classic descriptions of Thrasher. For Thrasher, forming a gang is
one response of immigrant youth to a disorganized community. Gangs
are of all types, formed spontaneously, and integrated by conflict. Delinquent or criminal behavior for Thrasher's gang members is no more
common than among other adolescents in the slum.[5] As Bordua notes,
Thrasher's gangs are filled with the joy of life, not burdened with "status anxiety," or filled with indignation at the injustices of society, as
subculture theorists would have us believe.[6] Thrasher's accounts, although they describe immigrant Chicago over fifty years ago, still remain the best descriptions of the process of gang formation.

For Thrasher, gangs begin as a "play-group," which was a "gang
in embryo" (1963, 23). Gangs are unique. "No two gangs are just alike"
(36) since they represent variable experience of groups of immigrant
youth adjusting to disorganized life in America. The origin of a gang is
"spontaneous," a natural occurrence of groups of youth as they live in
the crowded slums of Chicago. Some of the groups become "integrated
through conflict" (46) and form a loose structure; many others just disappear almost as fast as they arise. As time passes, the gangs fade
away, to be replaced by new ethnic gangs.

Descriptions of gang formation since Thrasher are rare. The few
we have generally follow Thrasher's well-researched model. Suttles perhaps makes the point most sharply: "The object here is . . . to suggest
that street corner groups can be understood in large part by examining
their place in the local community, rather than in the society at large"
(1958, 4). Keiser, in his history of the origins of Chicago's Vicelords
(1969), relates the words of several informants' accounts of how the Vicelords formed. This chapter, which is by far the most valuable part of
his book, shows the origins of the gang in Lawndale, which "has long
been a breeding ground for 'delinquent' groups." The Vicelords' origins
were traced to groups of boyhood friends. For Keiser, the Vicelords

were just another gang in the Thrasher tradition.[7] Perkins (1987) has a long and interesting section of his book devoted to the origins of black gangs in Chicago dating back to the 1919 race riots. Perkins shows that black gang activity has not been constant, but has varied in nature and intensity. Moore (1978) describes the history of three Chicano gangs in East Los Angeles, as part of the development of three specific communities. Tice (1967) has the only extant academic study of Milwaukee gangs. Like Keiser, he devotes a chapter to the history of the "Rebels," a Puerto Rican gang of the 1950s. His account (the chapter is entitled, "We Were Raised Together") explicitly agrees with Thrasher. The "Rebels" and their adversaries, the "Kings," were the sons of first generation Puerto Rican immigrants and followed the classic pattern of play groups becoming gangs (17-18).

But the small number of studies of the origins of gangs show sociologists' overall lack of interest in the subject. No academic study or popular article we could find explores the origins of so-called "satellite" gangs. Most academic research on gangs is fundamentally concerned with understanding why gang members are delinquent, not with understanding how and why they formed and their function within a community.

If we try to understand how and why gangs form, as well as their delinquent behavior, perhaps we will end up with a different analysis than current stereotypes. Were Milwaukee gangs formed as a result of the "diffusion" of Chicago's gangs, or did they form according to the pattern described by Thrasher? Are they aspiring career criminals or wild neighborhood youth? Who can tell us?

Breakdancing and Fighting: 1980-1983

    Q. How did the gang start?
    A. It was a dance group. They danced against schools.
          And the Timeboys just got a group and got into that.
          And then that's when these other gangs come out.
          We was going to different schools and everything,
          but there was, you know, different groups at different
          schools. And there'd be the Timeboys, and there's

2-7, there was 1-9s and 2-4s. But you see the
Timeboys were not originally a gang. They were a
dance group. But then all the time they would dance,
other guys would get mad and this and that, and
they would go at the Timeboys and they would have
to fight. And that's how the Timeboys got the
reputation they were a gang.

Bill, Timeboys

Milwaukee's gangs had diverse origins. Unlike those who would es-
pouse the "outside agitator" theory of gang development, we found that
influence from Chicago gangs accounted for only a small part of the reasons for Milwaukee's gang development.

Gang founders related four different paths they took toward forming their gangs. Three of the nineteen gangs we studied, like the Timeboys, formed their gang out of a dancing group. Ten more gangs

ORIGINS OF MILWAUKEE'S GANGS

Gangs	Origin
Sheiks	DANCING
Time Boys	DANCING
Cameo 2-7	DANCING
3-4 Mob	CORNER
2-7 (Originals)	CORNER
Punk Alley	CORNER
Hillside Boys	CORNER
1-9	CORNER
7-11	CORNER
2-4	CORNER
6-4	CORNER
Vicelords	CORNER
4 Corner Hustlers	CORNER
Cobras	CHICAGO
Kings	CHICAGO
Cobra Stones	CHICAGO
Castle Folk	CHICAGO
2-7 Syndicates	FEMALE AUXILIARY
V-L Queens	FEMALE AUXILIARY

reported they formed from corner groups of friends who became a gang after conflict with other corner groups. These gangs usually named themselves after the place they hung out: for example "2-7," 27th Street; "Hillside Boys," Hillside Housing Project. Two gangs were primarily female auxiliaries. Four more gangs unquestionably had their direct roots in Chicago. In each of these cases, former Chicago gang members moved to Milwaukee, where their children formed gangs named after their old Chicago gang.

There were a variety of motivations for forming each gang, so each path may have become mixed with another. For example, a dancing group might also have been formed from a corner group of friends. But the nineteen gangs we studied claimed they had taken one of the four paths listed above. Most of the gangs were started by thirteen to sixteen year olds attending middle schools across Milwaukee between 1981 and 1983 and had their roots in groups of friends in a neighborhood. All the gangs, regardless of type, followed similar stages of development.

Breakdancing and drilling were the main social activities of thousands of black and Hispanic youth in the early 1980s.[8] These groups formed "spontaneously":

> Me and my friends were just sitting around and my friend said let's get some names to put on our shirt that no one has. Then, so I said, "I know, the "Sheiks." I'm fixing to look it up in the dictionary and see what it means, and it said, "a strong person." So I said, "That fits me." So we got the "Sheiks" put on the back of our shirts, and then they said, "Who is the Sheiks?" And I said, "It's going be a dancing group."
>
> *Jeanetta, Sheiks*[9]

These groups practiced on street corners and in local gyms, developing fierce rivalries. The transition from dancing groups to gangs came as fights broke out after dancing competitions. For example, the Cameo Boys began as a drill team and fought with the Timeboys after a breakdance competition at a local theater in 1982. They later merged with another group of friends called "2-7 Originals," forming the 2-7 gang. Like Thrasher's groups, not all dance groups went on to form gangs. Some danced out the fad and went on to other things. Milwaukee residents have read the graffiti on their garages listing the names of countless dancing and corner groups that existed for perhaps only a few weeks and then faded away.

Black and Puerto Rican youth all over Milwaukee seemed to be forming groups and taking a name in the early 1980s. Even partying was cited as a cause for naming yourself:

Q. 2-7, How did it start?
A. Through the radio.

Q. What do you mean by that?
A. By when they have parties, they (radio DJs) get to telling there is a party on 1-9 street or on 2-7 street or 0-7 or something like that. That's how it started. If you stay in the neighborhood, that's where they started 2-7 or 0-7 or 1-9.

Jason, Original 2-7s

Ten of the gangs we interviewed reported they began as corner groups, identical in all respects to the classic descriptions of gangs in 1920s Chicago. Groups of teenage friends gathered on corners on their blocks and hung out. Having nothing to do and not in school, they got high, got into trouble, and fought with other corner groups.

Q. Did you start the gang or was it already there?
A. I started it.

Q. How did it start? Explain to me what happened.
A. I was bored. We didn't have nothing to do. We didn't have money to go places. What can you do? So we just made a name for us.

Dick, 1-9s

Q. Why'd you come together?
A. It was a lotta us. 'Cause it was like so many people living in Hillside (Housing Project). And we used to help each other, you know, hang together. We really wasn't about fighting people. It was just about

kicking it, you know, having fun. And we really
didn't ever run in packs. It was just two, three fellas.
And we used to go places and people used to jump us.

Clay, Hillside Boys

You know we were just standing on the corner, then we
got to just getting together every day, and then we came
up with something called the 34th Street Players. And as
we kept going north, the gangs got to coming around and
they got to have gang fights and they got to robbing and
just carrying on.

Rick, 3-4 Mob

Four of Milwaukee's gangs had roots directly in Chicago. But this
should not be seen as a confirmation of a "conspiracy theory" of gang
formation; these gangs appear in their development to be identical in
most aspects to the dancing and corner groups. For example, the Cobra
Stones, also known as Five Alive, originated when two families moved
to Milwaukee to escape gang problems in Chicago. But they found no
escape.

Q.   Were gangs here when you moved up?
A.   Definitely. 2-7s, 1-9s. It worked like this. OK, me and
         my brother we came from Chicago and my cousin
         did. Let's put this to plan before anything jump off
         anyway 'cause we know how it was in Chicago. So we
         just got ourselves together and just named us one
         group. Then we had just three, and I had another
         cousin, that make four, because the only reason I'm
         up here now is just because Chicago too damn rough,
         too many niggas down. I probably see you one day
         and you dead the next day.[10]

The Castlefolks began when the families of teenage friends involved
with the Black Gangster Disciples in Chicago and Gary moved to Milwaukee in the early eighties. They named themselves after an apart-
ment building near Third Street, imaginatively called "the castle,"
where some of the older friends stayed.

Q.   The Castlefolks, you helped start it, right?
A.   This was in '79. I moved to Milwaukee. Now this
         what happened. People from Chicago started moving
         up here. Younger people like me. And people from
         Gary, Indiana, too. Now the Castlefolks, it was like
         twelve of us. All of us lived in this apartment
         building. Didn't have to pay rent. I had all the keys.

Q.   How did it come together, how did you come
         together as a gang?
A.   We started talking and having meetings and stuff.
         We was real serious about this. And we was going
         try to do something for the neighborhood. Well, what
         happened was, they turned out bad.
                                               Mike, Castlefolks

The Latin Kings and Spanish Cobras also were founded by young people with Chicago gang experience. One Latin King related the founding
of his gang to shootings in Milwaukee's "Square Park" and the murder
in Chicago of a Cobra leader.

Q.   How did the Kings and Cobras start here?
A.   Well Jaime was living in Chicago. So when he came
         down to Milwaukee, that's when (he) formed the
         Latin Kings. In '79 shootings were occurring in
         Square Park and so Jaime had pretty many people
         come down from Chicago. KC (a Chicago Cobra
         leader) was shot in Chicago during that time. He was
         not really into gangbanging anymore, since he did
         have a family. So he had his brothers. They came
         here and they organized the Cobras down here.

The murder in the late 1970s of KC, "King Cobra," a leader in Chicago's Cobra gang, did cause tensions between Puerto Rican families in
Milwaukee. But both the Kings and Cobras, while originally composed
of Puerto Rican youth who moved here from Chicago, did not form a
branch gang. Rather they built their gangs by merging with local youth
groups.

The Cobras merged with a group from a Puerto Rican tavern baseball league whom some called "New Yorkers." These young Puerto Ricans hung out like other youths, but were quickly labeled "Cobras" by whites and Mexicans in the neighborhood who didn't like the new Cobra gang or Puerto Ricans.

> No, we didn't call ourselves nothing. It wasn't nothing of a gang or anything, it was just friends. But the Cobras was there, the young ones was doing stuff and we was getting blamed for it. And then you know we was going to fight with them. One day we got together and we started talking, and from there we started hanging out. They started hanging out in Square Park with us so they started calling everybody a Cobra. Even if you wasn't, if you was there, you was a Cobra.
>
> *Julio, Cobras*

The early Kings increased their numbers by recruiting young Puerto Ricans and Mexicans from a school group called the Warlocks.

> **A.** When I was a freshman at South Division, I got jumped by Cobras. They told us to break up or else, you know, they were going to come down on us. And at that time we were small. Everybody went their own way. Then it got different. They started jumping us one by one, and that's when we started the Kings.
>
> **Q.** What happened to the Warlocks, did they fall apart?
> **A.** Yeah, everybody just went their own way. Most of them are in the Kings.
>
> *Edwardo, Latin Kings*

What the four gangs named after their Chicago counterparts had was tradition, a gang identity, and guidance from relatives with gang experience. But aside from the terminology borrowed from their Chicago counterparts, their gangs' formative years looked just like the other corner groups or dancing groups: they were groups of friends who got into conflict with other groups of friends and took a name.

How The Gangs Grew: 1983-1984

By 1983, large numbers of youth were involved with the dancing groups and corner groups as they became popular and competed with one another for followers. As they grew, they attracted the attention of the authorities, and the resulting conflict, far from dispersing the groups, appears to have strengthened their gang identities.

> In the summertime, when school was out, we'll come
> loiter on the corners, you know, nothing wild. Its just we'd
> use to hang there and drink some beer and play basketball
> on the Clarke playground. You know we'd use to get
> together and ante up our little money. So the 1-9s use to
> be with us and we use to all get together and just play
> basketball until like six or seven o'clock. And then the
> police saw that we were having fun, they use to come up
> on the playground and chase us away. And then where did
> that left us? We couldn't play basketball. What else to do?
> So we started stealing. I ain't saying that's why we started
> stealing because we were stealing then. But I'm saying
> that if we couldn't play basketball in our own backyards,
> what else to do but catch the bus and go out stealing?
> *David, 2-7s*

Both the 1-9s and 2-7s, two of Milwaukee's larger gangs, claimed the police had in fact given them their name. The same claim was made of the 3-4 Mob.

> **Q.** You're from 1-9, right?
> **A.** We didn't give ourselves that name, the police gave
> us that name. We called us Deacons. They said we
> was 1-9.
> *Dick, 1-9s*

> **Q.** Do you know how the 3-4 Mob started?
> **A.** They used to be with the drill teams. And then they
> just started hanging out over here, right on 34th and
> Lisbon. They got their name from a cop.

> **Q.** Is that right!

A.   One day a detective drove by and goes, Wow, look at
        the big mob! And one of these guys thought about it.
        And they thought they'd call themselves 3-4 Mob.
                                                    Bill, Timeboys

Conflict with other corner groups and police helped form reputations,
and gangs became "in" among a segment of black youth and a wave of
"choosing up sides" swept the city in 1983.

A.   We had the most best reputation 'cause we had one
        hell of a big crowd with us. We had round three
        hundred niggas or better running with us. They say
        let's go with them, they the best one.

Q.   This was when everybody was dividing up, picking a
        side who to be with?
A.   They hang with you a little while, see how many
        peoples you got with you.
                                            Big Foot, Cobra Stones,

The summer of 1983 was a high point of early gang activity. At this
time the original gang members were high school age and fighting was
the "drama" that attracted youth to the gangs. Certain elements of gang
life were becoming fixed: staying out of school, getting high, and fighting with other gangs. Doris of the 2-7 Syndicates, a female auxiliary
gang, captures the spirit of this phase of gang life.

Q.   When you got together, what did you do most of the
        time?
A.   Ditch school, and get high. Everybody be over
        Jimmy's house. It's like thirty people upstairs getting
        high you know. After we get high, it would be time
        to go to 27th Street. That would be after school time.

Q.   Do you have much time to yourself when you're in a
        gang?
A.   No. The only time you have to yourself is when you
        are sleeping. Because you wake up in the morning
        and get a call saying, "Hey we got to go so-and-so
        and this so-and-so is hopping. Let's go." You get

dressed and go like you're going to school. But you're
not going to school. You get all prettied up to go out
and start a fight.

By the end of the summer of 1983, gangs had become a major social
movement in the black community with over forty different gangs, corner groups, and female groups, and thousands of black youth involved.
For many, gang life was the most exciting thing happening.

For the Puerto Rican gangs, the process was slightly different.
For one thing, the formation of the Kings and Cobras was linked to
Mexican-Puerto Rican tensions. While many people call the Kings and
Cobras "Hispanic," they began as Puerto Rican gangs fiercely resentful
of perceived Mexican dominance, especially within local community
agencies.

(In the late 1970s) we was having shoot outs and that, but
it was with the Mexicans. 'Cause Mexicans and Puerto
Ricans don't mix too much. Well, the thing was, the
Mexicans, they had the programs here and everything.
You would go and they were like turning you down. Right
away they had a spot opening for a Mexican and they
rather give it to them and throw you out the picture. Then
we just started hating them more. So then since we used
to hang out in Square Park, we just started kicking them
out of there. From then after that the shoot outs started.

Julio, Cobras

Gang problems within the Puerto Rican community are also linked to
long-time tensions between different families. Family tensions often
contributed to conflict as much as gang tensions.

Q.   What's the biggest cause of fights here?
A.   It goes way back, way back. If there was a death in
         the family by a group, then it becomes a family feud,
         which means just not the guys or the girls, it's the
         mothers, the aunts, and the uncles, see. It goes and
         keeps going, and that's one of the biggest problems.

Dante, Latin Kings

Just as with black gangs, the two Puerto Rican gangs were "integrated through conflict" with each other and with the police. The perceived discrimination by neighborhood youth agencies added to the gangs' feeling that Puerto Ricans were at the "bottom of the heap" of all ethnic groups in Milwaukee.

But before we explore this further, we must account for one more curious fact. All of the gangs we studied, with the exception of the Sheiks, use the names and symbols of the major Chicago gangs. For example, the 2-7 gang will use the six-pointed star in its graffiti with the pitchforks of the Black Gangster Disciples pointed up. The Four Corner Hustlers use the five-pointed star of the Vicelords with their pitch forks pointed down. Colors of Milwaukee gangs follow the colors used by the super-gangs in Chicago.

Even if the formative process we found occurs in all Milwaukee gangs (including those formed from migrating Chicago families) we should consider whether at some point the gangs are "recruited" to become a branch or satellite gang. Is there some truth to the notion of a modern gang conspiracy?

How Milwaukee's Gangs Came to Identify with Chicago's Gangs

When we began the research, we believed that Milwaukee gang identification with Chicago's gangs was becoming stronger. As a result, we carefully questioned the gang founders about why they considered themselves "People" (the coalition of Chicago gangs including the Vicelords, El Rukn, and Latin Kings, all represented by the five-pointed star) or "Folks" (the coalition that includes the Black Gangster Disciples and Spanish Cobras, represented by the six-pointed star). Consistent with our process-oriented method, we concentrated on understanding how the identification took place. The founders reported to us three ways in which Milwaukee gangs became identified with Chicago gangs.

First and most commonly, when a rival corner group would "represent" Vicelords, using Vicelord colors, hand signals, clothing, etc., the other gang would "represent" the opposite, the Gangster Disciples.

The identification, at least at first, had more to do with who you were against, than who you were for. Many of these gangs, usually the gangs named after street corners (2-7, 3-4), are actually quite hostile to any "Chicago connection." Second, many gangs had members with some Chicago gang experience. As Chicago had a reputation as a city where the gangs were "heavy," identification with a Chicago gang was part of the hype and machismo image of the gang. The "laws and prayers" of Chicago gangs and Chicago gang traditions exerted a strong cultural influence on Milwaukee gang development. And finally, there were the four gangs that were formed directly by gang members who had moved from Chicago. They started a corner group, named it after their Chicago gang, and maintained some nebulous ties.

GANG	IDENTIFICATION	HOW IDENTITY FORMED
Punk Alley	People	FIGHT
Hillside Boys	Folk	FIGHT
Time Boys	Folk	FIGHT
3-4 Mob	Folk	FIGHT
1-9	Folk	FIGHT
2-4	People	FIGHT
6-4	Folk	FIGHT
2-7 (Originals)	Folk	MEMBERS
Vicelords	People	MEMBERS
4 Corner Hustlers	People	MEMBERS
7-11	Folk	MEMBERS
Cobra Stones	People	CHICAGO
Cobras	Folk	CHICAGO
Kings	People	CHICAGO
Castle Folk	Folk	CHICAGO
2-7 Syndicates	Folk	FEMALE
V-L Queens	People	FEMALE
Sheiks	None	NONE

Since we interviewed both sides of all the major warring gangs in the city, we were able to compare different viewpoints on how each gang came to use the colors and symbols of Chicago's Vicelords or Gangster

Disciples. Seven of the gangs reported that they became Vicelords or Black Gangster Disciples primarily because the gang they were fighting was the opposite. Who affiliated first was often in dispute.

> **Q.**   Well, why did you start a Vicelords? Why not just everybody hang out with you?
>
> **A.**   Well, for one, other niggers was coming in the neighborhood and beating up fellas and stuff. And so Westlawn trying to be the opposite of us, so we decided, well it was time for us to blend together too. It started out exactly like this: We were the 6-4 Hustlers and they were 6-4. We came out first. And so that was the name I liked for a team, the 6-4 Hustlers, cause we stayed on 64th Street. And they just tried to get it cause (they lived on) 64th and Westlawn. And then it got so they was talking about Gangsters, and we knew about Vicelords too, so we dropped the 6-4 and just became straight Hustlers: Four Corner Hustlers, which means Vicelords, and then they turn into 6-4 Disciples. Then the little fights got into big fights, and parties started getting broke up and it just took off from there.
>
> *Tony, Four Corner Hustlers*

"Folks" from Westlawn tell a slightly different story.

> 6-4 really started 'cause, you know, the projects, and then it was Silver Spring (Drive). Then on the other side of Silver Spring it use to be, you know, a group up there call theyself Hustlers. We call ourself 6-4 Mad Dogs. And one day they came to us with this dude from Chicago, and he was, like, he was a Vicelord. He was screaming all this "People Love" and all. And I was like, man, I know all about this. He screamed at me, "How do you know?" I just threw some Gangster literature at him, and he wanted to fight me. And and all the fellas in the project said, "No, you ain't messing with our little buddy, you know. We ain't even going for that VL stuff, we gonna become Disciples."
>
> *Darryl, Black Gangster Disciples*

Sometimes the reasons were somewhat comical.

> One of the dudes from Chicago came up and he was a
> Vicelord. So he started showing us the literature and that's
> how it was, and about a week later the Hillside Boys stay
> around the corner. Now fifty to sixty wanting to fight.
> They was calling us the A-1 Boys at first, and we...who
> the hell is the A-1 Boys! And we didn't like that. So we
> called ourselves Vicelords. Nobody want to be known after
> no steak sauce.
>
> *Chuck, Vicelords*

> **Q.** Are Hillside Boys Folks? Are you Gangsters?
> **A.** No, not really. They called us Folks. I think it started
> when we had a fight with them "VLs." That's when
> they started calling us Folks.

> **Q.** So they called you Folks?
> **A.** Yeah.
>
> *Clay, Hillside Boys*

Chuck from the Vicelords best sums up the prime motivation for being
a Vicelord or Gangster:

> Vicelords (was) just something to be calling ourselves
> something, to keep our face from being broken all the
> time. You go around the corner there's a hundred dudes
> sitting there. "We Gangsters, what you be?" "I'll be going
> to the bus stop if you don't mind."

Five of the gangs reported that they became "People" or "Folks" primarily because some of their members had previous gang experience in
Chicago.

> **Q.** When did 2-7 become "Folks"?
> **A.** We never got off into that. Well all I know, when it
> first came out it was a little some of the codes. Like
> I never know how to do it. I just use to come....I'll
> say, "What's up, Folks?"

Q. Why wouldn't you be with the VLs or whatever?
Wasn't that a big issue?

A. Well, all I know from what I can say the reason 2-7s
was Folks riding under the six star was because a lot
of people who were in the 2-7s, they were, you know,
from Chicago and they were under the six-point star.
And they just show us the things of the six-point
star. I guess if it was fives, we would have been
People.

David, 2-7s

Q. Why did you become "VLs?" Why wouldn't you
become Gangsters or just be East Side Boys?

A. I guess because the first person we met was
Vicelords, and we just liked what he was into so
much that we became Vicelords. You is right, if
somebody came up and said we are Gangsters and
read literature, we would have become Gangsters.

Chuck, Vicelords

While four of the gangs we interviewed had their roots directly from
Chicago, all the gangs have remained separate groups with little relationship among themselves. While some in law enforcement have
claimed that Milwaukee has only four gangs with many branches, copy-
ing the super-gang coalitions in Chicago, no such coalition has yet come
into existence in Milwaukee.[11] Some of those we interviewed, who were
heavily into Chicago gang "traditions," did claim that such a Chicago-
style coalition existed. For example, Mike from the Castlefolks saw the
gangs who identify with "Folks" or the Black Gangster Disciples as one
"nation" forming different "camps."

They got different camps. The Castle a camp, Westlawn a
camp, Hillside a camp, Terrortown a camp.

Dan, a Gangster Disciple with roots in both Westlawn and the Castle,
explains further:

Q. Explain to me. I'm trying to make sense of it. You
got 2-7, Westlawn, or whatever and you got the

Gangster organization (all "Folks"). What's the
difference? What's the relationship between all these
different groups and their nation?

A.   They are extremely Gangsters, that is the
relationship there. Number one relationship,
everybody screaming Gangsters, and we know each
other. And as far as the other big relationship would
be, we're black, we're poor, you know that, quite
naturally.

Q.   Do you meet together?
A.   Not really.

Darryl, rather wistfully, wishes the gangs would be more organized:

Most people think gangs is like gangbanging, robbing,
stealing. Yeah, some of 'em like that, but the gangs here in
Milwaukee, they ain't organized. They ain't got enough
knowledge to know about it. And they still got grudges
from when they was knee-high, and they up over the
shoulders now, and still, you know, little grudges here and
there. Oh man, that nigger jumped me when I was nine
years old. Let's whop him. Brr! Bam! That's when 2-7 and
3-4 get to fighting. It's like that. . . . If it was organized,
3-4 and 2-7 (both "Folks") wouldn't disrespect each other.

Interestingly, the one time when several gangs tried to build a "Gangster" coalition, it fell apart because of the arrival in Milwaukee of someone claiming to have authority from Chicago.

The system broke down when a certain "BGD" (Black
Gangster Disciple) from Chicago came up here with a
notebook this big. About a million pages in it. He had a
stack of notes and envelopes and stuff, saying that "I am
your King." And we got to thinking, we're not following.
Ain't nobody gonna come in here and tell us how to run
our shit. 'Cause this ain't Chicago. This is Milwaukee.
                                                      Mike, Castle Folks

Dan continues the story about the Chicago "BGD" who tried to be King
of Milwaukee:

A. And it came to find out he was about trying to take us out. And he called his town "Terrortown," 'cause he said he was going to spread terror throughout the city, you know. And he probably would have, though, but he got put in check.

Q. How did that happen?

A. We just kicked his doors down one day, and came in there. He had to leave. Everybody that was with him we screened out.

One way to look at Milwaukee's gangs is that they all identify with Chicago gangs. But also significant is the gangs' independence and repeated insistence that "this ain't Chicago, this is Milwaukee." There is strong resentment among many of the original founding members of the notion that their gang is in any way tied to Chicago. David, a leader of the 2-7s, for example, gets angry:

Q. The gangs here, are they all starting to take their orders from Chicago? How true do you think that is?

A. They just talking. All these guys here man, they're a bunch of liars and a bunch of wimps. All these gangs even back when we were kicking it. They were liars and wimps. Chicago don't have nothing to do with these gangs. It's just a few guys who lived in Chicago and then come here and show all that shit. A bunch of liars, man.

Dick, a 1-9 leader, is more analytical:

Q. Why are most of the groups going to be one or the other (Vicelords or Gangster Disciples)?

A. They want to be big, they want to be part of something that's real big. The reality is that ain't going to happen. Because I tried explaining to them. If Chicago is so good, why are they coming over here?

Jeanetta from the Sheiks explains her peculiar stance toward the Vicelords and Black Gangster Disciples:

> I always had positive thoughts about a gang. I've always
> said, a gang is not bad. I would say gangs be going around
> just jumping on people, but they don't. You have to do
> something. You know, we don't run under no stars, no
> points or nothing. We're neutral. They say, What Sheiks
> run? I say we run: Five, Six, Four. And that stands for
> money (five letters), hustle, love. That's what we're about.

Some gang members have memorized the rules and regulations (called "laws and prayers") of the Chicago gangs. "Going to Chicago" for support and weapons is bragged about regularly by those gangs most committed to following the "laws and literature" of Chicago gangs. Don said that one Vicelord:

> took us down to Chicago with him, and we stayed down
> there for about two months. Then they turn us on how to
> take their language and everything, their rules, their laws,
> and everything. Then after that mess we got to naming
> and I called us a Vicelord and that's when Hillside said
> they wanted to fight us again. So we went down there and
> got guns and stuff and got to shooting up the place. And
> after that we ain't have no more problems with them.

Visits by Milwaukee gang members to Chicago appear to be commonplace. Some return with "literature" which is avidly read and memorized to add to the gang mystique.[12] While many strongly feel the need to be part of something "big" and follow Chicago gang cultural traditions, an even stronger theme was the fear that Milwaukee's gang violence would get out of control as it has in Chicago. Nowhere is this theme more evident than among the two Puerto Rican gangs, both depicted by the media and by law enforcement as particularly violent. After the formation of the Kings and initial conflict with the Cobras over a playground in the late seventies, the leaders of the gangs met, and the Cobras decided to move to another turf.

> We didn't want the war, because we knew that they were
> from Chicago, and in order for us to keep that (turf), we
> would have to kill one another. We all knew that. So we all

talked and said, This is not it. Not for killing, either. So
we left it. We even moved out. We had to.
Cecil, Cobras

Discussions and meetings between the two gangs have taken place on
nearly every occasion when conflict began to get out of hand or a killing
occurred. One of those meetings was organized by the authors in 1984;
the others were meetings called by the gangs themselves to avoid wider
conflict. For example, after one 1985 homicide falsely labeled by the
press and police as "gang-related," the leaders of the gangs called a
meeting:

> When they killed him a lotta people coming down to us.
> We say, "We didn't do this, don't come down this way."
> And that one time I talked to (the President of the Kings)
> and he said, "If you kill one of us, we'll play it like the
> city (Chicago)." He said, "I don't want it," and I said, "I
> don't want it." (He said:) "Why don't we work together
> somehow and keep the peace." I tell him, "I'm not a fool,
> and don't try to make me one. 'Cause you know that your
> nation and my nation, we can't keep peace. (But) we can
> keep a coolness down, you know."

Two other homicides in the summer of 1986, both labeled "gang-
related," turned out to be intra-gang affairs. The gangs held meetings
on both occasions to cool off any possible wider violence.

While the level of violence between the two Puerto Rican gangs is
indeed a serious problem, a major gang war has so far been averted.
This is mainly due to the self-concept of the older gang members in Milwaukee and the distinction they make between themselves and their
namesake gangs in Chicago. A Cobra leader with family ties to the Chicago Cobra gang explains:

> **Q.** What does being a Cobra mean to you, if you had to
> say it in a few words?
> **A.** Being a Cobra to me means a person that holds back
> a lot. At times he doesn't do things if he doesn't have
> to. And wants to make it in life. That's where I'm at.
> That's why I'm in an organization. That's why I can't
> get nowhere. I know that.

Q.   How are you tied to the Cobras in Chicago?

A.   We go over there once in a great while. When we do,
they ask us what's happening, and when we tell 'em
they get depressed. They wanta come out here and
do what they gotta do. "What the hell are you guys
doing?" They call it dragging, taking your time. I tell
them the best way I could. Because most of the
heads are family too, like blood. And I tell 'em,
"Look, it's like this. If I let you guys do it, if I do it
like you guys want, I'm gonna go to jail."

Q.   Right.

A.   They ask us how do we deal with it. I tell them how
we deal with it (holding back). They freak out and
say, "That works?" I tell them it works.

Similarly, Chicago gangs look down on the Milwaukee gangs as not being up to the standards of Chicago gang traditions. For example, one
King, with deep roots to the leadership of the Latin Kings in Chicago
explains:

Well, in Chicago, to be perfectly honest with you, they
don't like the gangs down here. I mean, I've been up there
a couple of times, and as far as they're concerned they
don't get along with the kids. In Chicago they're much
different than here. They don't just sit around and
threaten.

Dante, Latin Kings

Wilson, a former "general" in the Black Gangster Disciple organization
in Chicago and now living here in Milwaukee, reiterates the contempt
felt in Chicago for Milwaukee gangs:

Believe it or not, a lot of people from Chicago don't like
dealing with Milwaukee. You may have people up here
saying, "Yeah, "I'm a Gangster, and I'm all stoned, and
I'm this," but Illinois really wouldn't recognize him. The
people up here in Milwaukee, as far as gangs, I don't
really see it. But that's basically what it really is then,

gangs like the old movie "West Side Story." That's how I
see them, as the "West Side Story."

"Satellite" Gangs

It is clear from our research that the diffusion of Chicago gangs accounts for only a small part of the reasons for Milwaukee's gang formation. Milwaukee gangs appear to have formed in the classic manner, as
described by Thrasher. Milwaukee gangs also do respond to the image
of the larger Chicago gangs, and some consciously emulate them. While
relationships exist between the satellite and metropolitan gangs, they
vary and appear to be more cultural rather than structural.[13]

There is almost no literature on small town gangs and nothing at
all on gangs in satellite cities.[14] While Kornblum quotes law enforcement officials asserting that small town gangs tend to be "more exclusively criminal" than big city gangs,[15] most of the scant references to
small town gang activity suggest it is less serious than in the metropolis
(Takata and Zevitz 1987).

One obscure 1969 article did try to compare small town gangs in
Illinois and their Chicago counterparts. Hardman's catalog of similarities between small- and big-city gangs is a list of most stereotyped gang
traits: emotional attachment of members, predatory behavior, compul-
sive accumulation of weapons, initiation rituals, disdain of school and so
forth (Hardman 1969, 176-77). Hardman interviewed twenty members
of four gangs in a small Illinois city. Half of the interviews took place
while the respondents were incarcerated, raising questions about their
reliability. Two of the boys had been members of big-city gangs, and
thus Hardman compared their answers to his 107 questions, with the responses of the other gang members. Big-city gangs, according to Hardman, had more formalized structure, more "fascistic" leadership, were
more concerned with profit than "kicks," used narcotics, and were coer-
cive in their recruitment practices (180). Interestingly, he states that fifteen of the twenty "Freeport" gang members he interviewed had
belonged to other gangs (in "Freeport," we presume), "but in no in-
stance was there any evidence of borrowing structure, behavior or other
patterns from previous gangs" (178). Hardman does not explain why
any of the respondents would give reliable responses to an outsider.

A more enlightening article, "Youth Gangs and Black Suburbs," looks at varying gang activity in Chicago suburbs in the recent period (Johnstone, 1981). The author points out, "Many large American cities are afflicted with serious gang problems, but others, inexplicably, are not" (356). After reviewing the scant literature on gangs in nonmetro-politan communities (358), Johnstone surveys 605 black youth in seven suburbs with multiple census tracks of 50% or more black population. He finds gang activity reported in all seven suburbs, and the activity varies by level of poverty. "Gangs are more prevalent in suburbs with large concentrations of poor families, large numbers of youth, high rates of crowding, low proportions of persons in professional and managerial occupations, and, interestingly, higher proportions of blacks" (366). Johnstone concludes, "Ganging seems no longer exclusively a phenom-enon of the 'interstitial' zones of the city, because these neighborhoods no longer hold a monopoly on the social conditions that foster ganging" (367). Johnstone makes no mention of origins of the suburban gangs, whether they were "satellites" of the adjoining Chicago super-gangs or were formed by some local process. His study, however, clearly gives credence to our notion that local conditions are crucial to understanding gang formation and development.

From our Milwaukee interviews we can tentatively draw three conclusions about the development of gangs in satellite cities:

(1) The fundamental causes of small-city gang development are to be found by analyzing local conditions. Gangs still seem to form basi-cally in the Thrasher mold. Those who would see gangs as the result of diffusion and big city corruption of small-city youth are at best looking for an easy answer. "Computer tracking" and "gang history tests" will certainly not arrest gang development.

(2) Gangs in smaller cities tend to follow big-city gang traditions, borrow ideas about big-city gang structure, and respond favorably to the image of the big-city gangs. This seems to be a nationwide pattern. Since big-city gangs of the same name have lasted now nearly thirty years, many families who have had gang experience in those larger cites have moved to "satellite" cities, bringing their gang traditions with them. Gang members in satellite cities like Milwaukee are much like other residents of their own city: they have a love-hate relationship with the metropolis. While defensively asserting they are "just as good as Chicago," or "this ain't Chicago, this is Milwaukee," they are also envi-ous of the larger city and try to emulate some of its traits. There is no

reason to believe that the big-city gangs presently have the strength or willingness to found multi-city branches. The use of satellite gangs as an outlet for an organized distribution of drugs presupposes a level of gang organization that has not yet been proven to exist. The use of big-city names and symbols by local gangs indicates a process of cultural diffusion, rather than structural ties.

(3) Proximity to the metropolis probably plays a role in the intensity of identification with the big-city gang. The closer the smaller city is to the metropolis, the closer the identification may be with the big-city gang. Clearly, if the smaller city is within the suburban area of the metropolis, there is more of a chance that ties of local gangs with the big-city gang would exist. It would make sense that gangs in Joliet, Illinois, only thirty miles or so from Chicago, may have closer ties to Chicago gangs (and to Chicago gangs in the Stateville Penitentiary in Joliet) than would Milwaukee gangs. We doubt, however, that gangs can be "exported." Milwaukee, which is just over an hour drive from Chicago, clearly underwent a basically independent gang development. Research on other types of cities and towns closer to Chicago or other metropolitan areas is lacking and needed.

Even if gangs are formed locally, how are they organized? Is the view of gangs as a "criminal conspiracy" a good lens through which to define gangs and understand gang structure? Are there other ways in which we could better define today's gangs? Let's take a closer look at the nature of Milwaukee gangs, how they are defined, and what they do.

4

HOW DO GANGS GET ORGANIZED?

What started out as more or less of a social club in the late 1950s has grown into a powerful, well-organized, and violent street gang with chapters not only in Chicago, but also in many cities all over the Midwest.

Terrence McCarthy
Chicago Police Dept.

Q. How well organized do you consider your group?

A. Really, we not really organized in a sense. We are good friends. We are together. When a couple us get high, we just spend our last dollars. We'll just think of something to do and get us some more money. Like to hustling, stuff like that. Ain't really organized.

James, Black Gangster
Disciples

Why is it important to know how gangs are structured? Today's dominant law enforcement perspective understands the gang basically as a
criminal conspiracy. According to this view, a gang has many misled followers on the "fringe," but its leaders are a "hard core" of sociopaths or
career criminals. With this perspective, it is easy to believe that gangs
may evolve into "organized crime" or turn into structured "branches"
of metropolitan "supergangs." The job of law enforcement, then, is simply to jail the "hard core career criminals" to get them away from the
more salvageable "fringe."

One minor problem is the gangs we studied in Milwaukee don't really seem to fit this stereotype. Milwaukee gangs don't look anything
like the pictures often painted of them by law enforcement. But what is
a gang?

Many studies spend considerable time discussing the definition of
a gang.[1] Defining a gang has more than a little importance today. Since
gangs are targets for vigorous law enforcement efforts, the current definition of a gang needs logically to reinforce a gang's criminal and violent image. At least one observer (Zatz 1987) has charged that the
criminal image of Chicano gangs has been promoted by law enforcement mainly to justify applications for federal grants to support special
gang units.

Needle and Stapleton (1983) note widespread confusion in definitions. After reviewing past attempts, they decide that "contemporary
usage" of the term by police departments will be their operational definition. This "contemporary usage" is basically borrowed from the
works of criminologists Walter Miller (1975) and Malcolm Klein (1971).
Miller has been most influential in criminalizing the current definition
of gangs. His major monograph, "Violence by Youth Gangs and Youth
Groups as a Crime Problem in Major American Cities" surveys officials
in twelve U.S. cities concerning their definition of a gang. Miller (1975,
9) tells us those surveyed "reserved the use of the term 'gang' for asso-
ciational units which were both more formalized and more seriously
criminal than the more common type of street group." Miller then summarizes his respondents' views and accepts their definition of a gang as:

> "a group of recurrently associating individuals with
> identifiable leadership and internal organization,
> identifying with or claiming control over territory in the
> community, and engaging either individually or collectively
> in violent or other forms of illegal behavior."

What we need to note here is that "gang" is differentiated from a "group" mainly by characteristics that are operationally important to law enforcement. But is this the only way one can define a gang? Community residents, parents, other youth, and the gang members themselves may have a very different way of understanding a gang. In fact Miller's definition is a radical departure from past sociological conceptions. Indeed, while Miller insists U.S. gang activity has not changed much in sixty years, he paradoxically approves of a major change in image and formal definition.

Klein takes Miller's position to its logical conclusion. Beginning his book with a discussion of definitions, he points out that criminal justice agencies and the mass media "use the term gang more to meet their own ends than to achieve disinterested enlightenment" (1971, 7). However, Klein decides in the end a gang should be defined basically by the perceptions of others and fundamentally by the perception of law enforcement officials. For Klein, a gang is:

> any denotable adolescent group of youngsters who: (a) are
> generally perceived as a distinct aggregation by others in
> their neighborhood; (b) recognize themselves as a
> denotable group (almost invariably with a group name)
> and (c) have been involved in a sufficient number of
> delinquent incidents to call forth a consistent negative
> response from neighborhood residents and/or enforcement
> agencies" (1971, 13).

In the final analysis, for Klein, a gang is any group of youth police call a gang. Needle and Stapleton quote Miller and Klein at length. They finally decide Klein's definition is best since, in Klein's own words, it "is nothing more than a confirmation of contemporary lay usage of the term."

While it is certainly important for law enforcement agencies to define "crime problems" and fashion policies appropriate to deal with them, to accept the law enforcement definition as fully descriptive of gangs is another matter. Criminologists leave little room for critical analysis when they ask what a gang is, then tell us how those concerned with law enforcement define "gangs," and finally turn around and say, since this definition is "contemporary usage," we should adopt it too.

The definitions of Klein, Miller, and others are quite different from other contemporary definitions and perspectives on gangs. Richard Cloward and Lloyd Ohlin, for example, although they thought gangs delinquent by definition, also defined them more broadly as part of "delinquent subcultures" spawned by three different types of poor communities. The well-integrated, stable slum with a criminal opportunity structure resulted in criminal gangs. A disintegrated, unstable slum whose residents could not find organized criminal opportunity resulted in fighting gangs. And badly disorganized slums, where nothing but demoralization could be found, led to despair and to drug-using gangs.

While Cloward and Ohlin's typology has major empirical problems,[2] their framework is quite different than Klein's or Miller's. Cloward and Ohlin define gangs within a perspective which tries to understand the influence of certain types of poor communities on the development of gangs. This perspective is more in step with classical sociological theories.

Back to Thrasher, One More Time

When Miller and Klein insist on defining gangs mainly by characteristics operationally significant for law enforcement, they stand in even sharper contrast to the work of Frederick Thrasher. As mentioned previously, for Thrasher, gang youth were neither more nor less criminal than other youth in their disorganized communities, a point supported by some recent research.[3] For Thrasher, and later Suttles and Moore, three aspects of gangs and their structure stand out: variation within a community, process of formation, and age divisions. It is these three characteristics that combine to define a gang.

For Thrasher, above all a gang is unique. "It may vary as to membership, type of leaders, mode of organization, interests and activities, and finally as to its status in the community" (1963, 36). Organizationally, Thrasher describes diffuse types, solidified types, conventionalized and criminal types, and even "the secret society." Thrasher found 1313 different gangs in 1920s Chicago. Moore begins her descriptions of "Three Barrio Gangs" by saying: "Each of the gangs considered here is unique, reflecting the varying factors of the ethnic context of life in Mexican Los Angeles, the institutional structure, and the economic structure" (1978, 55). For Thrasher and Moore, there is no general type of gang, but gangs with collective histories reflecting the communities where they grew up. Suttles' Ph.D. dissertation is devoted to understanding the corner groups as a part of a specific local community, the Addams area in Chicago. For Suttles, the gang is so loosely organized it is seen by its members as no more than "a series of individual histories" or the "happy coincidence" of individual association (1968, 175-77).

Rather than define gangs in terms of their structure or how they are perceived by police, Thrasher defines gangs in terms of the process in which they are formed and their specific activities. His full definition can be sharply contrasted to Klein's and Miller's:

> The gang is an interstitial group originally formed
> spontaneously, and then integrated through conflict. It is
> characterized by the following types of behavior: meeting
> face to face, milling, movement through space as a unit,
> conflict, and planning. The result of this collective
> behavior is the development of tradition, unreflective
> internal structure, esprit de corps, solidarity, morale, group
> awareness, and attachment to a local territory" (1963, 46).

To understand a gang, for Thrasher, Moore, and Suttles, one needs to understand not only specific communities, but the specific processes the gang undergoes in formation. Miller and Klein, while claiming violent and law-breaking conduct is typical of all gangs, make no mention of specific communities or internal process. Following Klein and Miller, most gang research today pays little attention to the wide differences in gang behavior or to how and why gangs are formed. Instead, researchers concentrate on the occasional violent and criminal acts of some gang members. Research is reduced to formulas for figuring out how to identify a gang member, how to prevent others from joining gangs, and how to deter present members from maintaining their gang loyalties. Gangs themselves become nothing more than their media and police stereotype.

Finally, for Thrasher, Suttles, and Moore, gangs are age-graded, not monolithic entities. Rather than a bureaucratic gang, we have a sort of coalition of age-graded groups. Moore has been tracking the history of formal age-graded "klikas" of three Chicano gangs back to the 1940s. Suttles analyzed each of his Addams area gangs in terms of its different age groups. Thrasher, in quoting a field worker, clearly describes the process of the formation of age-graded groups: "A new crop of youngsters in a district plays together and the older groups passes on. . . . One may see as many as four different age groups. . . ." (1963, 59).

Rather than picture the gang as a "core" of violent offenders and a "fringe" of less criminally involved youth, gangs for Thrasher, Suttles and Moore are divided by age, with considerable variation within each age group of friends. To analyze a gang, one must analyze each age-graded group, not merely look at the gang as a criminal structure with older "leaders" on the top and younger "fringe" on the bottom.

Some police departments want to picture the gang in the familiar bureaucratic pyramidal shape. Like a police department, the gang is seen as having a "Chief" on top, and "lieutenants" commanding troops, who are on the bottom of the pyramid.[4] An example is the Phoenix Police Department's chart of Chicano gang structure (see facing page).

If this is how the beat patrolman or social worker is taught to understand the structure of a gang, we need not wonder what kind of policies they will adopt.[5] While we have no knowledge of what Phoenix gangs really look like, we can safely speculate from this police manual that Phoenix police do not know much about their gangs either. But what about Milwaukee gangs? Do they follow the Phoenix "pyramid model" or Thrasher's "age-graded model?"

What Do Milwaukee Gangs Look Like?

Q.   What's 2-7 right now? Where are they?

A.   Well, OK, it's still some, but they're like the younger brothers and sisters . And they're so young, they're like twelve and thirteen and fourteen. It's like they still want to carry on that little stuff.

Q.   Probably doing things that you did back then.

A.   Right!

Doris, 2-7 Syndicates

MILITARY PYRAMID: a comparison of Hispanic gangs and military structure.

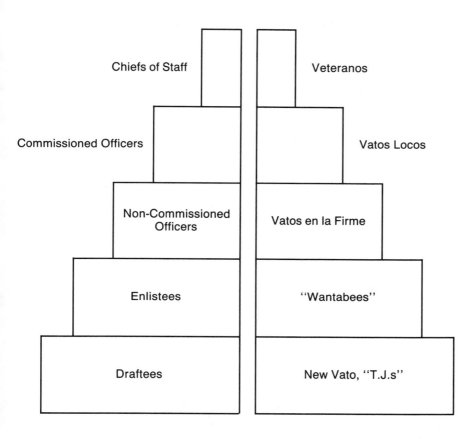

Chiefs of Staff	Veteranos
Commissioned Officers	Vatos Locos
Non-Commissioned Officers	Vatos en la Firme
Enlistees	"Wantabees"
Draftees	New Vato, "T.J.s"

SOURCE: Phoenix Police Dept. 1981.

Milwaukee's gangs come in a variety of forms and shapes, but none that look like a pyramid. They are all age-graded, with the gang beginning as a group of friends and youth roughly the same age. As the group ages, a new age-graded grouping forms from neighbors, acquaintances, and relatives. (See figure on facing page.)

We interviewed young people from nineteen founding groups that formed almost all of the major gangs which continue to function in Milwaukee. Members from six gangs reported three age-graded groups had formed within their gang by spring 1986, and seven reported two distinct groups. One gang, the Hillside Boys, who formed in a large Milwaukee housing project, reported four new groups and a history dating back to the 1960s and perhaps earlier.

> **Q.**   Did you start the Hillside Boys, or was it already there when you joined or what?
>
> **A.**   I think it was already there, 'cause it was like the older fellas that handed it down to us, you know. It was already there, so we just held the name.
>
> **Q.**   The Hillside Warriors, were they the group that was before?
>
> **A.**   Yeah. Them the guys who was there before us. And that's like handed down to us, like if we need backup, if we couldn't handle something, we just give them a call, and they would help us. We like first got running in 1980.
>
> *Clay, Hillside Boys*

The Hillside Boys were the only black gang that reported groups with a history dating back before the 1970s. Punk Alley, the sole white gang interviewed, reported two previous age groups (one named "Teenage Wasteland") which formed beginning in 1973. Every other gang in our study was started by the "founding" group whose members we interviewed.[6]

Each age-graded group has its own internal structure. Far from the stereotyped view of a gang with a "hard core" of criminally-minded leaders on top and a broad "fringe" network of impressionable kids, each age group develops its own sub groups.

> **Q.**   When you joined with the Deacons, how many people would you estimate there were?

THE STRUCTURE OF MILWAUKEE GANGS as described by gang founders

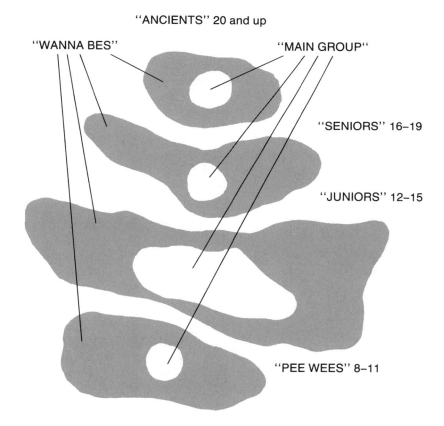

"ANCIENTS" 20 and up

"WANNA BES"

"MAIN GROUP"

"SENIORS" 16–19

"JUNIORS" 12–15

"PEE WEES" 8–11

> **A.** Mainly it's about fifty tough Deacons who always
> beat and wouldn't turn around and run. But then
> there's other Deacons that wanna be Deacons, that
> just bum around with us and get high. It was always
> just like a "main group" and then there's the "wanna
> be's."
>
> **Q.** What's the difference between a "wanna be" and a
> true Deacon?
> **A.** "Wanna bes" are people you can't trust to watch
> your back. Real Deacons are the people that fight.
> I'm here man, any time you need me.
> *Marcus, 1-9s*

Each age-group has its own "main group," its leaders, and its "wanna
be's," to use Marcus' apt phrase. Milwaukee gangs are in fact a combination or coalition of age-graded groups, each with their own "main
groups" and "wanna bes." The makeup of each of these age groups varies between gangs and over time within each gang. A "wanna be" this
week may be in the "main group" next week.

Becoming a member of a Milwaukee gang is usually an informal
process, often related to some act showing courage or commitment. Because the gang is a semi-secret group, trust is necessary to become a
"real member." Seven of those we interviewed answered that initiation
rites included an act of some sort of "fighting," and two said the new
member had to "rip off" something in order to become a member. All
others (36) said either that there was no initiation procedure or that it
varied with circumstance. For the originals who founded the gang,
there did not appear to be any initiation rites whatsoever.

> **Q.** Is there an initiation?
> **A.** It all depends all right. Like for me, for me to go join
> (all it would take would be) saying I'll be in it. But if
> it's somebody that just came out in the street, they
> have to prove themselves. Like steal with one of us or
> something. You know, show that he's "down."
> *Bob, Vicelords*

Q. Is there an initiation?

A. Not really. There would be a time extended to yourself, to prove yourself like.

Q. Probation, huh?

A. More or less. Not to prove yourself to be a tough person, but to prove your trust, you know? Can you be trusted? Are you gonna go, you know, get just information and go talk to the other side. Stuff like that. Nothing like, OK, we wanna see how bad you are—go rob the next corner store you see. Nothing like that.

Q. So what happens once you've passed probation?

A. Then you're trusted and everything. You know, just become one of the fellas, and that's what you are.

Edwardo, Latin Kings

The transition between "juniors" and "seniors" or between different age groups also takes place in a variety of ways. For some gangs, there is no clear transition: it just happens as the group ages. For other gangs this process is formalized with, for example, "JKs" (Junior Kings) or "Peewee Cobras," representing specific age groups and having rituals for transition to the "seniors."

Q. How do you graduate from junior to senior?

A. You could be a LK (senior) at age 14. You have to prove yourself that you're down, that you can do your stuff right, you don't talk in front of nobody if you're going to do some stuff, so you don't get caught for it. Most of the people that be like bragging to girls, and right away, it gets around the street, and the cops already know. So everybody looks at the people that keep their mouths shut, they're down for their nation and all that stuff, they move them up.

Edwardo, Latin Kings

The age of the "originals," or founding members, when the gangs started supports this age-group interpretation of gang organization. Of the forty-four interviews of original gang founders, thirty four were between thirteen and seventeen years old when the gang began. Milwaukee gangs began mainly with similarly aged middle-school youth in the early 1980s. Only four of the gangs were reported as forming before 1980.

Gang leadership varies as well between different gangs. Sixteen of the young people interviewed reported they were primarily responsible for the formation of their gang. Eleven are or were the recognized "leaders" of the gang. One third of all those interviewed said reputation or ability to fight was the main criterion for a leader. A few (8) said someone was the leader because they knew most about gangs, usually meaning they knew rules and regulations from Chicago gangs. Some even disputed there ever was a leader:

> **Q.** Was there a leader when you came together? A leader of Hillside?
>
> **A.** No. Hillside is like, you know, you do what you want to do. Something like that. But if you need some help, you always got some backup. That's all.
>
> *Clay, Hillside Boys*

> **Q.** Was there a leader?
>
> **A.** Nope. Not as far as I was concerned. If there was one, I didn't listen to him.
>
> *Chuck, Vicelords*

For most age groups, however, there was a leader or leaders who had the most respect from his or her peers.

> **Q.** Did you have a leader when it started out?
>
> **A.** Well, when we first started out, it was like the most visible. Which, that was me and one of my buddies. And, you know, since we was the ones mostly doing all the fighting, we was like elected the leaders.

> **Q.** What do you mean by "most visible"?
>
> **A.** Well, say like when they come down in our neighborhood, we'd be the first ones to jump at 'em,

> you know, while everybody else—once we got
> fighting, everybody else would get into it, you know.
>
> *Tony, Four Corner Hustlers*

Q. Why was RB the leader?

A. He knew the most, and he knew people in Chicago.
Being from Chicago, you have connections there. And
he was daring. Daring, dangerous, and not afraid.
And that's what it takes to become a leader.

> *Dante, Latin Kings*

For many groups, "titles" for the leader are nonexistent. In the past,
"titles" were often taken from gang social workers who endeavored to
re-direct the gang's delinquent energies by helping it become positively
organized (Suttles 1968, 176-77). In Milwaukee, where there are titles,
they are borrowed most often from the "literature" of Chicago gangs.
"Elites," "Lords," "Kings," and other titles mimic Chicago gang names
and customs. Seven of those interviewed reported a system of "ranks"
or a semi-formal hierarchy. Specialized functions of "treasurer" or "war
counselor" were reported by two gangs, but most of those interviewed
emphasized the informal nature of the structure in each age group and
in the gang.

Seventeen of forty-seven interviewed reported they paid dues
while twenty seven claimed there were no dues in the gang. Interestingly, of the fifteen interviewed who thought their gang was well organized, only seven reported they also paid dues, suggesting
"well-organized" for many might mean something other than a structured organization. For all those who claimed they paid dues, the
amount was less than five dollars per week.

Q. You got dues?

A. Oh yeah.

Q. Everyone always pay?

A. Not always. And it's like . . . we had it like everybody
pay two dollars a week, and we get up two hundred
to three hundred dollars and we buy weed. And we
have parties to make the money back and certain
persons go to jail and we bail him out.

When we asked how things had changed since the gangs began, we received a wide variety of answers. Most responses were related to "getting older" (3), "more hustling" (5), "more fear of jail" (4), "more members" (5), or "more guns" (4). Only one person said gangs today were "more organized" and only three said things were the same.[7]

The Activities of a Gang

What does a gang do everyday? Crime occupies only a small portion of the daily existence of a gang, a point made throughout the academic literature.[8] When we look at what one does while he or she is in a gang, we have to differentiate between ages. Clearly, a fifteen year old does different things each day than does a twenty-one year old. Following Whyte, we also want to look at routines, the daily life of a gang member. How do Milwaukee's gang founders describe what they did everyday when they were sixteen to eighteen and Milwaukee gang activity was at its height? Nearly everyone we interviewed (thirty-four of forty) was in agreement about the main activity of gangs—partying and hanging out. Only four responded "fighting," one "ripping off," and one "going places."

> **Q.** When you were together, what did you do most?
> **A.** Well, in the summertime, we'd come loiter on the corners, you know, and not anything wild. It's just we use to hang there and get everybody together so we can go drink some beer and play basketball on the Clarke playground.
> *David, 2-7s*

> **A.** On Fridays we'd all meet up on Reservoir Park. sit down, get high, talk. See if anybody know any good, you know, good ways to make any money. That was it.
> *Ben, Vicelords*

> **A.** Getting high. Getting high, and the higher you got the more devilish things got on your mind. If we could work we would, but whenever we got off work

and got paid we would always come back there and
do what we had to do, you know, let each other know
we was OK.

Dan, Castlefolks

When the founding group was in its mid-teens, aside from hanging out,
the gang was structured around fighting. We saw earlier how corner
groups came in conflict with one another. David explains the structure
of the 2-7s, strongly disavowing a military-like organization:

Q. Did you have ranks?
A. It wasn't an organization, it was a gang. We was
     organized enough that if one throw down, all throw
     down, you know, fight.

As the gangs expanded, as we've noted, they became involved with conflicts with other corner groups. Constant fighting occurs at a particular
stage in the evolution of a gang. It helps shape the structure of the gang
and lasts through the mid-teenage years. Gang structure, for these teenagers, enabled them to fight other gangs and not much more, a point
emphasized by Suttles (1968, 181). One 2-7 told us:

Q. How well organized do you consider your gang?
A. It wasn't organized until a fight came upon, and
     everybody wanted to fight! That's the only time it
     was organized, when a fight came. And, when
     everybody was getting high and most of the people
     who didn't have money was getting high free! That
     was the only organized time if you ask me.

Another form of conflict pits the gangs against authorities, especially
the police. We should not underemphasize the significance of how authorities define and treat gangs. Hostility between police and other authorities and gang members plays a crucial role in how the gang is
formed and how its members see themselves and acquire a delinquent
or deviant identity. We'd like to illustrate this process with an edited interview with David, one of the leaders of the 2-7 gang. David explains,
more clearly than most, how conflict with authorities affects gang formation and how the gang member feels the impact of police harassment
and labeling. The interviewer is Hagedorn.[9]

David's Story

Q. Explain how the 2-7s started.

A. We began as just the Cameo Boys. That's how it started off. One day they had a competition for drill teams at the Uptown Theater, near your house. And the Time Boys was there. We had a grudge against them and they had a grudge against us from school. And we had it out with the Time Boys and that's when the gang started.

Q. How did you get the name, Cameo Boys?

A. Because we idolized the Cameos. Its a group called Cameo, so we just took the name "Cameo Boys" (laughter).

Q. After the fight, how did the Cameo Boys get so popular? What happened next?

A. By that time gangs got so known that everybody thought, "Hey, this is cool" to be in a gang. And plus they saw we had so much reputation. Someone might see you with this girl and that girl and really think you were cool.

Q. Was there a leader?

A. Well, everybody looked up to me and Dan. But the way I look at it, I never was the leader, even though everybody called me that because of the publicity that I had. When I got waived to adult court and all those newspaper articles appeared calling me the leader, everyone just thought I was. But the reason I actually became the leader was because of the policemen. They called me the leader first and they just spreaded it around. But that was because I stood up more than everyone else. We had a fight. There was about fifty people coming to fight. All my buddies ran, but I just stood there. I figured I just got to take that little whipping and whatever.

Because I was always bold. I never considered myself as a leader and no one else considered me as a leader. But after that fight the police called me a leader so I guess I was. But I can go out right now today and go to the younger generation and I can go call the shots over them because they think I'm the leader. But the older organization would look at me like, "Is you crazy? You ain't no leader to me."

Q. Let's talk about the police a little. How did they react when you started getting a reputation?

A. They just started arresting as many people as they can so they can move up as quick as possible. You know, they don't want to listen to you. And if you are on probation you might as well forget it because you not going to make it through probation in Milwaukee. They are going to make sure you get revoked and go to jail. OK, just say a person with no record at all, you know nothing, got caught for being out after curfew (Milwaukee has an eleven o'clock juvenile curfew). He gets labeled down whatever neighborhood he get caught in. If he was in the 1-9s neighborhood, he's going to be a 1-9. And if he was in the 2-7s, he's a 2-7, and on and on. And they'll take his picture and post it up on this board and say, "Hmm, that's another gang member. Watch out for him. We're going to label him as this and we're going to give him a record. We're going to make sure that we get paid. And we're going to keep this little commotion going." The gang squad is the biggest gang.

Q. Frankie from the 1-9s told me how they got named by the police because they got arrested on 19th street.

A. They put ideas in your head. You know they actually yelled out from the loudspeaker in the police car in my neighborhood that I was the "leader of the 2-7s" and everybody heard. At the time I liked that. I was

young. And you know I knew I was going to get a lot
of props (support). And so, I just start saying I was
the leader you know. And I started getting lots of
props. And so they really put stuff in your head,
instead of helping you.

Q. Do you remember any turning point when shit got a
whole lot worse? Between the kids or from the police
or anything? Was there anything that marked a
change?

A. I can't really say. I got arrested for a lot of shit.
Bullshit, you know, like curfew tickets. They used to
arrest me like this: I was washing my clothes at the
laundromat on 26th and Center in our neighborhood.
And I was washing my clothes and the cops came in
and said if you're here in another fifteen minutes
when we come back, we're going to arrest you. I
didn't leave, so they arrested me. Left my clothes in
the dryer and everything. And I'm like, "Man how
can you guys arrest me?" "Because we told you we
going to get you every time you smart mouth us.
We're going to get you." And they arrested me for
loitering. But you know I was so young a man, I
used to just tear the tickets up when they give them
and throw them away. I never did go to court for
them.

Q. Give me a rating on the Gang Squad. One to five.
One they are doing a great job, five is total bullshit.

A. Five.

Q. Why is it I could've guessed that score? OK, now
here I'm going to give you a job. The Chief of Police
walks right in that door and he says you are going to
run the Gang Squad. He's going to give you the job,
Captain of the Gang Squad. All right, what do you
have them doing?

A. Well, I don't want them out there harassing the
gangs, you know, stirring up more and more. I want

them to be out there, at least be like a counselor to
them, you know. Get out there and talk to them.
Don't get out there and start all types of things,
driving on the sidewalk, just stopping them just to
get their names. All that, making them look like
criminals, even though they haven't done nothing.
But suppose a bus passed and your school teacher
was on that bus and she sees you getting stopped by
the police. What is she going to think? She don't
know they just want to stop you just to fuck with
you. She probably thinks you're getting arrested
because her bus is going to keep on going. She ain't
going to see what else happened. You know, that
fucks with a person too, man, just getting stopped for
no reason.

Are there "Fighting Gangs," "Criminal Gangs," and "Drug-using Gangs"?

Not all theorists share the classical age-graded view of gang structure.
Cloward and Ohlin, in postulating different "types" of gangs based on
types of communities but disregarding age, have confused many empirical researchers (Hardman 1967). Spergel's (1964) attempts to fit gangs
of his "eastern city" into these types is only the most notable example
of the harm done by Cloward and Ohlin's typology. Recent studies of
gangs in the Midwest have also at times dogmatically followed the Cloward and Ohlin typology. The Evanston study, for example, seemed surprised to have found that some gangs have "split into an older group . . .
and a younger group" (Rosenbaum 17). Despite this observation, the
study did not try to analyze Evanston gangs in terms of age divisions.
Evanston gangs were described, Cloward and Ohlin style, as divided
into "fighting street gangs" and "money-making gangs" (21), again a
typology that can be meaningful only for law enforcement.

To understand most gangs as coalitions of age-graded groups
clears up some of the confusion of Cloward and Ohlin's ideal types. All
gangs we studied in Milwaukee were "fighting gangs," but the fighting
period was generally when the gang members were "juniors" or in their

early teens. As the gang matured, their interests turned more to fundamental problems of survival.

One gang we found in our Milwaukee interviews at first did appear to be a prototype of the Cloward and Ohlin "criminal gang":

> **Q.** When you were all together with the fellas. What did you do most of the time ?
> **A.** Plot on stealing something to make some money if we hadn't already stole it. Yeah. It was like all the other gangs was out there fighting amongst each other, but the Vicelords worked downtown at the money. They fighting. We making money.
>
> **Q.** Did you try to recruit other people?
> **A.** No
>
> **Q.** Why not?
> **A.** We didn't need to share no more money with nobody.
> *Chuck, Vicelords*

Further interviews, however, with other members disputed Chuck's emphasis on money-making. The others interviewed pointed out that the escapades Chuck was referring to took place during a very short period of time when the Vicelords regularly went to downtown Milwaukee and "ripped off" stores, snatched purses, and went on a crime spree. While this was undoubtedly the most exciting and memorable period for the Vicelords, it was a comparatively short time in the history of the gang.

Rather than a formal "type" of gang, based in a particular kind of community, we have a specific gang concentrating for a specific period of time on one kind of activity. Chuck and his friends stopped their criminal activities soon after police seriously turned their attentions to the Vicelords' antics. The gang dissolved after the Youth Diversion Project referred all the active members to jobs during 1984.

Milwaukee gangs vary, not only among themselves, but also between age groups within each gang, within the age groups, and over time. Rather than seeing the Vicelords as a "criminal gang" for once and always, we should see their criminal activities as one phase of a varied life of one age group in the gang.

Hustling, Drugs, and Survival

> **Q.** How important was the gang to you during the time
> you were most into it?
>
> **A.** I feel it was real important, 'cause you know when I
> was in the gang, it was about hustling. That's all we
> did was hustle at the time of the gang. We really
> didn't do a lot of fighting, but when we had fights it
> was about the hustling. I used to have new clothes
> every day, money in my pocket every day. I felt gangs
> was important to me at that time.

Corner life can be exciting, the drama of conflict with other gangs and
with the authorities adds to their appeal to many young people. But life
on the corner also means the need to have some money, especially as
one gets older. With few jobs available, "hustling" is how a gang member might put a few dollars in his pocket. "Hustling" means surviving
any way one can, "getting over" on someone, making a buck just to
make it day by day. Because of the lack of good jobs, the hustling mentality has grown particularly among young males, and everything, including work, begins to be seen as a "hustle."

The need to hustle is accepted as legitimate, as necessary to survive. Don tries to "neutralize" the "wrongness" of stealing:

> **Q.** Do you think stealing is wrong?
>
> **A.** Yeah, you know something, I feel that stealing is
> wrong, but you know, stealing to try to either help
> yourself or your parents or something is OK, but it's
> not right. I wouldn't say it's right, it's, you know, OK
> if you're trying to help somebody. But if you're just
> trying to steal just to steal something, then I figure,
> you know, it's all the way wrong. If you taking
> something from the rich and giving it to the poor,
> then you know you're doing a good deed. But you're
> still doing something wrong.

As the gang members age, the need to support themselves becomes
most important. One twenty-two year old rationalizes how he sees the
gang and stealing:

Q.   Do you consider doing something like robbing. You consider it wrong?

A.   No. I consider it like this here. At the time, ain't no jobs, and I'm not starving for nobody, you understand? I feel that if I gotta starve, I'd rather take than starve. Hey, if you gotta eat, and keep some clothes on your back, and take care of your bills, I don't think stealing is wrong. Less they gonna give you a job, that's all. And then, you know, I see if you got anything you need, you don't gotta steal, but if you ain't got it, you need to steal. That's how the organization came in effect. It stopped me from stealing. It was like, they gave me their support when I was feeling pretty bad myself.

Q.   What does being in an organization mean to you?

A.   Well, organizations is like, you don't gotta worry about starving. You can always go to your nation and ask and get. You've got support when you need it. You ain't gotta worry about nobody snatching your mama's purse.

"Hustling" by definition is unplanned, spontaneous money-making anyway you can.

Q.   I got a job for you, a full-time job. I'm going to let you run the Gang Squad and you can be Captain tomorrow and they're all saluting you. What are you going to tell them to do differently than they are doing now?

A.   I'd try to understand really more or less where they come from. What makes them commit these crimes? Why do they do it? What makes them do it? How do they do it. I was reading the paper one time that they (the police) was wondering how (the gangs) get together to just go out and steal. It's not more or less planned. You don't plan that. You just all get together, you all have a little money, and you all talk about getting some more money. And you get high,

> and we play basketball and they say we want to get
> some money. We get away from there, split up,
> everybody going their own way. Check in later on in
> the night. It's more or less spontaneous, not just
> planned.

Selling drugs, especially marijuana, is a common hustle within the gangs. It is an easy way to make money and has "enjoyable" fringe benefits. Thirty of those interviewed reported their gang sold regularly, and eleven said the gang sold now and then. One person said her gang never sold illegal drugs, but an admitted cocaine problem that resulted in her imprisonment casts some doubt on her contention. Eight of those interviewed reported they presently sold drugs regularly, and twenty-one said they sold now and then. Only two persons interviewed, however, could be called "dealers," obtaining quantities of drugs for others to sell. Fourteen said they did not sell anymore. While four persons said they got their supplies from someone else in the gang, most (20) reported that the main suppliers were not in gangs, but contacts known on the street.

> You want to know where the drugs come from? Sure, we
> got a dealer (in the gang), but look at this block. There's a
> dealer here, there, there, there. and that just on one block.
> *Diego, Latin Kings[10]*

As gang members age, the sales of drugs and other petty crime becomes one means of securing their survival. As one of the Black Gangster Disciples put it: "Its all about survival now." But it is not much more than survival. Drug sales for most gang members are just another low-paying job—one that might guarantee "survival," but not much else.[11]

Organized Crime and Milwaukee Gangs

What are the consequences of "hustling," drug sales, and other criminal ventures of older gang members? Does the gang inevitably mature into an organized criminal form? This is a serious question since we do have some precedent for gangs turning to organized crime. Thrasher described the process in some of his 1313 gangs as they took up careers in organized crime, but they were clearly a small minority of all gangs. More recently, Moore (1978) has described the growth of Mexican "state-raised youth" (prisoners who have spent their entire lives in correctional facilities) forming organized crime networks within California prisons and barrios. She points out, however, that while the three gangs she studied all use heroin, they are not part of this "Mexican Mafia" nor could possibly be considered "organized crime."

The "super-gangs" in Chicago are widely considered to have organized a vast network of drug sales. While non-law enforcement research is lacking concerning today's Chicago gangs, we can reasonably believe that many of the founding groups of those gangs have stayed together and followed career paths of organized crime. To generalize, however, about all gangs in Chicago, even those of the same name, and consider them all "soldiers" in a vast drug empire, probably takes the issue too far.

When we look at Milwaukee, certain other factors stand out in suggesting organized drug sales may not be an easy path of development. In Chicago, gangs carved out turf in large high-rise housing projects, where a small organized group could control drug sales and reap enormous profits by simply controlling the housing project elevators by armed force. No such housing projects exist in Milwaukee.

Milwaukee gang drug sales, despite the clear intentions of some "entrepreneurs," have largely remained at an individual, "street" level. One Milwaukee gang founder had a clear notion of why Milwaukee gangs would not turn into organized crime:

Q.   Are the gangs here like Chicago? Do you think things
         are going to go that way here?

A.   No. Too much free enterprise. Ain't no brother gonna
         mess up no free enterprise. See in the neighborhood
         I know well, within two blocks about four people
         selling dope.

Indeed, those gang members whom we interviewed and we knew were considered "major dealers" hardly led a life of luxury. The ladder up the criminal opportunity structure is not readily available to many within the gangs. One gang we interviewed described a drug house they had set up to organize their distribution of drugs. The house was a "drive-in" where buyers drove their car up to the corner, a "waiter" or "waitress" came out and took the order and the gang filled it in a jiffy. But the house only lasted a few months and the gang discontinued organized drug sales. Why did they stop when they were making money? The reason the gang members gave was simple: It was too much of a hassle. This gang was not cut out to become an organized criminal venture. The police did not really bother their sales, but the organization necessary to pull off an on-going drug house was too much for this gang, whose members were concerned with "making it" day by day. While many of the adult members of this gang still sell cocaine and marijuana, it is done, as in most other gangs, individually and sporadically.

This is not to deny the possibility that some gangs or individuals may follow a career path in large scale drug sales. The existence of a leadership tradition and the formation of gangs based on Chicago style "nations," not neighborhoods (see Chapter Six) may reinforce tendencies for some gang leaders to pursue careers in organized drug sales. The organized crime model is tempting, if difficult. The lack of full-time jobs certainly heightens the probability that some unemployed gang members will try to organize and expand drug sales into a major venture.

Law enforcement and community agencies need to differentiate between the very common street sale of marijuana that is nearly universal within the gang, and those "entrepreneurs" who wish to transform the gang into a network for drug sales. Given the variety of factors operating, the growth of Milwaukee's street gangs into organized crime at this time is far from inevitable and unlikely to be widespread.[12]

Conclusion: The Formation Process of Milwaukee's Gangs

Rather than define gangs by describing a generic organizational structure, or define them by the occasional violent acts of some of their members, we have chosen to follow Thrasher and others whose focus is on age divisions, the wide variations between and within gangs in the context of a specific community, and the formation process. This formation process can be summarized in five stages:

1. Milwaukee gangs typically began as groups of thirteen- to sixteen-year old friends hanging out together and forming a social network for one another. This social network usually condones use of marijuana, alcohol and various delinquent acts.

2. The group conflicts with other similar groups and begins to form an identity in opposition to a rival group. The gang is usually named after the place where its members hang out. Within the group, some persons assume a degree of leadership, generally because of fighting ability.

3. Conflict with police, school officials, and other authorities over fighting and other delinquent acts helps shape a delinquent and deviant identity about and within the group.

4. As the group of friends ages, a new younger group of friends emerges and emulates the original or older group. The younger age group has its own "structure" and "leaders" and relates to the older age group in a variety of formal and/or informal ways.

5. The older group, as its members reach age eighteen or so, turns from constant fighting and getting arrested to more adult concerns of survival.

It should now be clear why we spent so much time describing how Milwaukee gangs formed in Chapter Three. The law enforcement paradigm defines gangs in a narrow and unchanging manner, which neglects the process of development which different age groups within gangs undergo and ignore or undervalue variations of all sorts. Gangs are not seen as young people struggling to adapt, often destructively, to a specific economic and social environment. Rather, gangs are treated as a major criminal problem and their members dehumanized as no more than aspiring "career criminals." Where data exists to support these stereotypes, it often consists of generalizations in the media from the acts of a few to all "hard core" gang members. The fact that gangs today are overwhelmingly minority and most police departments overwhelmingly white, allows for racism to contribute to these stereotypes and results in even greater hostility on the street.

Our process-oriented definition is not a snapshot of a gang standing still; it attempts to describe different gangs in motion, as their members grow, change, conflict with others, and try to survive. But what happens to these young men as they grow older? How do they relate to the gang and what do they do? What effect has Milwaukee's changing economy had on the maturing out process? Its time to turn to a more complete description of the adult status of the founding group of Milwaukee gangs.

5

POOR, BLACK AND TWENTY-ONE

If I steal, it's for a reason. I gotta live like everyone else. I can make it for two or three more years. But after that, what's gonna happen?

Don, 1-9 Deacons

The term underclass suggests that changes have taken place in ghetto neighborhoods, and the groups that have been left behind are collectively different from those that lived in these neighborhoods in earlier years.

William Julius Wilson,
The Truly Disadvantaged

How do we explain the increasing adult participation in gangs? Much of the recent academic literature on gangs has noted this increase in adult gang participation (Horowitz 1983, Moore 1978, Spergel 1984). Their accounts sharply differ from most studies in the past, which have treated gangs as fundamentally an adolescent problem (e.g., Cohen 1955, Geis 1965, and Yablonsky 1966). As late as 1975, Miller's surveys found the bulk of all gang members nationally to be between the ages of ten and twenty-one (1975, 45).

There are only a few references to adults in gangs in past studies, and they portray the adults quite differently from the situation today. Thrasher described a few gangs who held together and became adult criminals (297). But Thrasher's gangs were quintessentially adolescent: they were "interstitial" between childhood and adulthood. The adult gangs were a small minority of the 1313 gangs he studied. More interestingly, Whyte's "Nortons" were a Depression-era Italian gang whose members were not juveniles, but young adults in their twenties (1943, 35). Joblessness in the depression apparently held these Italian juvenile corner groups together well into adulthood, unlike previous gangs in poor communities, which dissolved as gang members aged and their members were forced to solve the problems of work and family.

In other cases, adults are treated in popular accounts as "Fagins," or older criminals using juveniles to do their evil bidding. For example, the 1983 Evanston report on gangs sees adult gang participation in this traditional "Fagin" perspective: The older members are described by the author of this report (without citing any supporting data) as the more consciously criminal, while "youngsters are sent out into the neighborhoods to identify vacant homes for burglaries and to commit thefts" (Rosenbaum 1983, 17-18).

This view of adults as manipulating juvenile gang members appears in many media accounts and has only surface validity. The lack of effective sanctions by the juvenile justice system for young delinquents may lend itself to this type of relationship in certain types of criminal behavior (for example, carrying drugs, burglaries, etc.). However, the "Fagin" stereotype does not in any way explain the widespread increase in adult participation in gangs. This stereotype is often based on a pyramidal understanding of gang structure that we contend is highly questionable.[1]

Most studies typically have found the gang member "maturing out" of the gang as he ages. For example, Tice (1967, 48) in his look at

Milwaukee's Puerto Rican gangs in the 1950s, quotes an adult Jose looking back: "We don't do it in gangs anymore. We depend on best friends." The gang is something Jose left behind with adolescence. The former "homeboys" went their own ways, and old friendships usually continued only when based on common residence or work.

However, the more perceptive accounts in recent years have raised some questions about the process of "maturing out." Moore (1978) takes a hard look at adult Chicanos within "institutionalized" gangs in East Los Angeles. She shows how "klikas" (age-divided groups within Chicano gangs) continue on for decades after adolescence. Some Los Angeles gangs even hold "reunions." Horowitz confronts the question frankly in her study of Chicago's Hispanic gangs: "Most core gang members who are still in a gang at eighteen remain in a gang as Seniors" (1983, 178). For Moore, the changed labor markets in Los Angeles have contributed to the maintenance of gang identity and traditions into adulthood.

Spergel notes the adult presence in Chicago gangs and attributes violence mainly to young adults by a careful comparison of homicide rates: "The violent gang is essentially a young adult adaption" (1983, 202).[2] Perkins, who is one of the few to pay attention to variation in gang behavior over long periods of time, finds that significant adult participation in black Chicago gangs began only in the 1960s. Most studies, however, agree with Klein that the gang is still "a caricature of adolescence" (1971, 81). Most would also conclude with Klein: "Though the need is great, there has been no careful study of gang members as they move on into adult status" (136).

The Underclass and the Liberal-Conservative Debate

It is the contention of our study that increased gang involvement by adults is largely due to the drastically changed economic conditions in poor minority urban neighborhoods. These changed economic conditions have altered the maturing out process and have contributed to the institutionalization of gangs as a means for young adults to cope with economic distress and social isolation. Today's Milwaukee gangs, we believe, are basically a fraction of the underclass. But before we look at the data from our Milwaukee study, we will review the liberal and conservative perspectives on poverty and gangs. Can they explain the relationship between the emerging underclass and today's urban gangs?

William Julius Wilson (1987) gives an insightful analysis of liberal and conservative perspectives on the formation of an underclass. Liberals have seen poverty as a result of "the consequence of restricted opportunities" (1987, 14). This, the dominant philosophy in the 1960s, has fallen into disrepute today. Liberal analysts simply could not account for the growth of an underclass despite the massive 1960s "War on Poverty." Some liberal analysis was flawed since, in Wilson's words, it saw "increasing black joblessness.........as a problem of poverty and discrimination, not of American economic organization" (130). Another flaw, according to Wilson, was the fear of liberals "to discuss openly or, in some instances, even to acknowledge the sharp increase in social pathologies in ghetto communities" (6). Prominent liberals dismissed the significance of anti-social ghetto behavior and accused those who described the more ugly features of ghetto life as "blaming the victim" or "racist."

Ironically, this failure by liberals to confront the actual conditions of the underclass contributed to the resurrection of a discredited, but classic conservative theory—the "culture of poverty." This view, that poverty can be explained by the individual characteristics of the poor and by a self-perpetuating "tangle of pathology," became the dominant theoretical and political perspective in the 1970s. In other words, conservatives such as Charles Murray (*Losing Ground,* 1984) have filled a void in popular thinking and taken advantage of the lack of cogent liberal analysis. The eighties have seen nationwide acceptance of the conservative agenda of dismantling social programs and spending more on the criminal justice system as a response to the growth of the urban underclass (including gangs).

This liberal-conservative debate on poverty has been represented in theoretical discussions on gangs by Walter E. Miller on the one hand, and Richard Cloward and Lloyd Ohlin on the other.

Walter Miller's classic study of the "culture of poverty," "Lower Class Culture as a Generating Milieu of Gang Delinquency" (1958), is the clearest example of this conservative perspective. For Miller, gang delinquency is not a characteristic of youthful rebellion to oppressive conditions as it is for Cohen or Cloward and Ohlin; it is, instead, the unchanging reflection of certain lower class focal concerns: "trouble, toughness, smartness, excitement, fate, and autonomy" (Miller 1969). These are cultural traits of a distinctively American lower class characterized, by, among other things, a preponderance of female heads of households (Bordua 1961, 130). Gangs persist, Miller says, because "they are a product of conditions basic to our social order" (1974, 320).

We need to point out two concerns. First, Miller's lower class culture is not ethnically specific; it is a true melting pot. Since gangs are generically "lower class," Miller is thus relieved of any responsibility to analyze ethnic or local community variables, an approach as foreign to ours as it was to Thrasher, Suttles, or Moore. More important still is Miller's view of class. For Miller, as for most "culture of poverty" theorists, class is a subjective variable, a reflection of the outlook of certain people, not a specific place within social structure. Someone is lower class not because of how he or she makes a living or how much money he or she makes, but solely by what he or she thinks, by his or her "culture." Miller's theoretical framework is a conscious evasion of the changing consequences of social structure for various ethnic groups and classes within those groups. This is why Miller sees gangs today as basically the same as gangs in the past. The changing class structure in our central cities has no importance for an ethnically neutral, culturally unchanging, but for some perplexing reason increasing, American lower class.

This analysis has been popular, particularly in today's government circles, in part because it attributes gang crime and violence to persisting individual cultural traits, instead of analyzing destructive behavior in terms of changing social and economic structures. But it has also been popular because Miller is one of the few recent scholars who has actually done empirical research on gangs, and his descriptions of gang behavior are life-like and lend credence to his conservative theory.[3]

Cloward and Ohlin, on the other hand, despite the title of their book *Delinquency and Opportunity: A Theory of Delinquent Gangs,* have very little to say about gangs. They are, instead, basically concerned with the origins of delinquency in different kinds of communities (see our Chapter Four). But, as Moore has pointed out (1987), the data on which Cloward and Ohlin based their influential theory was drawn from classic "Chicago School" research that was already thirty and forty years old at the time. Despite their important theory of "differential opportunity," Cloward and Ohlin's descriptions of gangs, drawn from

1920s ethnographies, are simply not believable today[4] and give greater credibility to Miller and other conservative theorists who have looked concretely at actual gang behavior. As Wilson has pointed out:

> It is not enough simply to recognize the need to relate
> many of the woes of truly disadvantaged blacks to the
> problems of societal organization: it is also important to
> describe the problems of the ghetto underclass candidly
> and openly so that they can be fully explained and
> appropriate policy programs can be devised (1987, 149).

Neither the liberal nor conservative theories on poverty and gangs can explain the way gangs were affected by the economic transformation of U.S. cities in the last few decades. Miller dismisses any notion that gangs have changed: lower class people always have such "focal concerns," and he refuses to analyze social structure or the changing U.S. economy. Cloward and Ohlin, though properly concerned with mobility and "opportunity structures," give us only a general theory, which fails to describe or adequately explain the forms or persistence of modern gangs.

The formation of an underclass, or a category of people permanently excluded from participation in mainstream occupations (see Moore, introduction, pp. 6-8), changes the way we should think about gangs. Our interviews in Milwaukee suggest that gangs are a fraction of the underclass in two ways: First, our family histories of the forty-seven gang founders we interviewed are like a snapshot catching these families beginning a decline, and not a picture of temporary distress within long term upward mobility. Second, our data on the present circumstances of the 260 young people who founded Milwaukee's nineteen major gangs suggests a positive relationship between unemployment, lack of education, and continued gang involvement as adults.

Family Decline

Deindustrialization and the segmentation of Milwaukee's economy (described in Chapter Two) has had a powerful effect on the lives of Milwaukee gang members and their families in the 1980s. Those gang founders we interviewed[5] are clearly facing bleaker economic prospects than their parents. While in some ways they resemble gang members in the past, vastly different economic and social conditions are changing the way these young adults are forced to adapt to their environment.

The parents of Milwaukee's gang founders were not recent migrants to the city. Most had moved to Milwaukee between 1970 and 1981 for economic reasons, and following other family members. For most of the black families, Milwaukee was the second step in their move north. An earlier migration to Chicago or Gary to find industrial work had led to a 1970s move north when jobs began to get scarce in the Chicago area.[6] They also left Chicago because of the deteriorating conditions in that city's ghetto by the end of the 1960s. Of the black families, one third reported some gang involvement by family members in another city (mainly Chicago) and one in ten listed gang problems as one reason their families moved to Milwaukee. These families moved from Chicago's black ghetto into predominantly black or Hispanic working class neighborhoods in Milwaukee.[7]

The parents of the Milwaukee gang founders we interviewed were working regularly in somewhat marginal, but full-time jobs and were fairly well-educated. Half of the families had at least one parent who graduated from high school, and two had a parent who had attended college. Less than one in ten founders reported welfare as the main source of their income while they were growing up. Nearly nine out of ten founders interviewed reported their families as having had at least one parent who held a relatively stable working class job during their childhood.

The family life of the gang founders was not typically the "broken home" of the stereotyped juvenile delinquent. While a third of the gang founders reported serious domestic violence while they were growing up, a third reported only sporadic fighting at home and a third reported a healthy and tranquil home life. Nearly half of those interviewed reported one of their parents drank heavily, but more than half reported no one in their family had a drinking problem. Three founders reported that someone in their immediate family had been at one time addicted to narcotics. Dante summarizes the family situation of Milwaukee's gang founders well:

> Because what's important to them, especially at that early age, is they are confused. A lot of them come from broken

families, a lot of them come from good families, so it's not
always, you know, mama's a junkie or daddy's an
alcoholic. It's not true that almost all gang members come
from a broken family. That's not true. I didn't come from
a broken family. I came from a very good mother who
raised us.

The picture we have formed of the parents of Milwaukee's gang founders is a traditional American image of poor families migrating to relative opportunity to give their children a better life. But Milwaukee's
changed economic and educational conditions in the seventies and
eighties provided not the next step upward for their children, but the
first step downward into the underclass.

The Gang Founders

The forty-seven gang founders were between eighteen and thirty years
old when we interviewed them. While half of their parents had a high
school diploma, all of the founders had dropped out of school, most
kicked out for "fighting." Only five had subsequently entered an alternative education program and received a General Equivalency Diploma
(G.E.D.) or high school diploma, and four more reporting they were currently enrolled in some education program. None attended post high
school classes. None of the founders held a job three months before and
three months after our interviews with them. The founders were also
becoming conditioned to accepting current economic conditions. When
asked what kind of job they wanted when they were thirty, a third said a
professional or business occupation, but almost all of those admitted
their aspiration was not realistic. "Success" for most of the founders
meant simply "being in school" or "having a full-time job."

The founders were well aware that they were not living up to the
aspirations of their parents. Asked who they considered a failure in
their family, nearly two thirds answered either themselves or a brother
or sister. On the contrary, less than one in ten thought that their parents
had been failures. J. J. expresses vividly this sense of decline:

> **Q.**   Who in your family would you say has had the
>   biggest influence on you?

A. No one. I always did what I wanted to do. I was the
first in my family ever started stealing. In my
immediate family. I was the first in my family ever to
go to jail. I was the first one in my family ever do
some time. You know, everybody just did their own
thing. It wasn't like one person was trying to fall
behind the other ones.

While gangs are often thought of as replacing family ties, the deteriorating economic conditions seemed to make family values quite important to the founders. Asked what about their family they were most
proud, half answered "how the family sticks together." Though in their
early twenties, many of the gang founders still lived at home with their
parent(s) on an irregular basis. Half of the male founders reported they
had already fathered children, but none were married and very few living with the mother of their children.

Comparing our gang founders and their parents to a similar portrait of gang members and their families in the 1950s by Spergel (1964)
yields some interesting comparisons. Spergel studied gangs in three
different communities in an "eastern city" in an attempt to support the
Cloward and Ohlin's theory of gang delinquency.

Spergel's delinquent's parents were more poorly educated than
the parents of our gang founders. They were also foreign-born, recent
European and Puerto Rican immigrants. They tended to be employed in
craft or industrial jobs which were more plentiful in the 1950s, rather
than in the more marginal occupations of our Milwaukee gang founder's
parents. As with the Milwaukee families, Spergel reports the families of
"eastern city" delinquents tended not to be "broken homes" and had
similar aspirations as our founders.[8]

While Spergel's delinquents were younger than our founders and
had similar educational experiences, their positive work experience as
teenagers is quite different than gang members in Milwaukee. Spergel
reports, "Several of the youths had obtained jobs through family connections and were working with a father, an uncle, or some other relative on the docks or in the construction industry" (10). Street workers in
traditional YMCA detached workers programs also were able to find
jobs for gang members (10-11). A comparison of the economic conditions between Spergel's "Eastern City" and Milwaukee reveals some
fundamental changes gang members face today.

**OCCUPATION AND UNEMPLOYMENT
1980s BLACK MILWAUKEE COMPARED TO THREE 1960
COMMUNITIES IN AN "EASTERN CITY"**

City	White Collat	Craft	Blue Collar	Service	Laborer	Unem-ployed
RACKETVILLE	22.4%	20.5%	22.3%	14.8%	14.6%	6.9%
SLUMTOWN	22.2%	10.3%	29.4%	22.1%	5.4%	10.0%
HAULBERG	50.9%	14.0%	11.6%	12.0%	3.2%	4.6%
MILWAUKEE	22.5%	13.7%	37.4%	15.6%	10.4%	27.9%

The occupational rates are for all employed males. Milwaukee data are
from "U.S. Bureau of the Census, Social and Economic Characteristics of
the Population, 1980." The Milwaukee unemployment rate is for June
1987.

Two statistics stand out in this comparison. First, the percentage of
Milwaukee blacks working in industrial occupations ("blue collar") is
three times as high as in the "criminal subculture" of Italian
"Haulberg" and significantly higher than in the "violent" Puerto Rican
community of "Slumtown." But while Milwaukee blacks were more
concentrated in heavy industry, we have seen that in the 1980s it is precisely these industrial occupations that are experiencing the greatest
decline.

Second, while Spergel called attention to what he said was the
"high" 10% (p. 3) unemployment in "Slumtown," Milwaukee's 27.9%
black unemployment rate presents a sobering picture of the future for
all young black adults, not only gang members. An unemployment rate
of "only" 10% would be an economic miracle for the Milwaukee black
community today.

The picture we are presenting shows our gang founders caught in
economic conditions that that lead to very different choices from those
available to gang members in the past. In order to bring this portrait
more to life, here is another one of our edited interviews with a leader
of one of Milwaukee's major gangs. This excerpt looks at his family
history and captures some of themes we've touched and also how his
circumstances and outlook differ from his parents'. Hagedorn again is
the interviewer.

> **Q.** Let's talk a little about your family, OK? Where was
> your father born?

A. He was born down South in Monroe, Louisiana. New Orleans, Louisiana.

Q. Do you know what your father was doing when you were growing up?
A. Shit.

Q. Shit? What do you mean?
A. Put it down. Shit.

Q. I got it on tape, too. What do you mean by that?
A. Well, I hardly ever saw him. Moms didn't marry my Pops. So when I got eleven, we came up here.

Q. Do you know how far in school your father went?
A. I heard he was pretty good, my Moms said. I ain't seen him since I was like sixteen.

Q. Did he graduate from High School?
A. I don't know. They went to the same school. Probably did, 'cause I know she did and everything.

Q. Where was your mother born, same place?
A. Yeah. She got pregnant with me when she was eighteen.

Q. And was she working?
A. Yeah, 'cause our auntie down there, they pretty wealthy and shit.

Q. What was she doing?
A. I don't know. She was into something down there. What did she tell me? Like a little factory or something. I told her probably picking cotton.

Q. When did your family move to Milwaukee? Do you remember the year?
A. Let me see, '71, '72. Yeah, I was eleven, '72.

Q. And no one in your family was involved in a gang before you moved here, right? Or were they?

A. No.

Q. What was the specific reason you moved here?

A. Um, well, we had a lotta relatives up here in Milwaukee. So we came here. When we first moved up, we was on 6th and Locust. Scandalous! I ain't never seen no houses like those. I'm used to the country and shit. Seeing tall ass weeds and shacks standing there. This was terrible.

Q. Everybody feels proud about something in their family. What are you proud of in your family?

A. Think I'm most proud that everybody mostly still living in our family. I got to watch my little sisters grow up. 'Cause she's fourteen now, damn, near big as me. I remember when she was like six or seven how she used to get into stuff and always had a big mouth. And my little brother, he's bigger than me. Boy! About the most pride I have is him, 'cause he graduated from school. Well, I wish I coulda stayed in school like him. I never knew he was that smart, you know. I'm proud of that. He's pretty smart.

Q. Everybody feels ashamed of something in their family too. Is there anything you're ashamed of?

A. Only thing I can call ashamed of was I was messing up a lot, man. For a while. I was ashamed when I got that whuppin' (from his stepfather). Dude put them scars on me. That's what I was ashamed of. Everybody knew about it—about everything. I still look back on that. I was pretty tough, man. I couldn't get over that for a long time. That's why I don't really go see the dude now. He tried to offer me jobs and shit. You know, he got plenty money. But it just ain't there. It got to where I told him, "You ain't my daddy." And that hurt him. And ever since then, it ain't been, you know. . . .

Q. Who's the most successful person in your family?

A. Um, I'd have to say Mama. She's been through a lot. She's still going through a lot with me. I think she kinda felt like I kinda let her down: problems, no job and shit. We talked about it. You know, my brother got a job, and he been doing all right. But by me dropping outa school and messing up and getting into this shit and that. . . .

Q. How is she successful?

A. She always working. She's laid off now. We got laid off together. She got me that job that just was over. Yeah, she always had her job, and she was like movin' up to somethin' better, all the time. She went from one factory to another, making a extra dollar and something an hour. Then went to another one, 'til she finally went to this place where she was bringing like $300 home a week! And she got laid off from there, you know. She was working there for about two and a half years.

Q. She going to get called back?

A. I don't know. She been laid off for a while. February'll be a year. So, can't say. This job we have now, we just worked before Christmas. That was the best job I ever had in my life. Two hundred dollar check every week, you know. I was happy. She was kinda proud of me 'cause I wasn't in no trouble in work. I was being quiet, doing my job, you know. Then they started laying people off there, and nobody expected the whole company to move to Arkansas. That kinda took a lot out of her again. She kinda be working like at this bar. But he pays her out of his hand. So, part-time, and stuff.

Q. Who's the biggest failure in your family?

A. I think I was. I think me.

Q. How come?

A.   'Cause a lotta people in the family was kinda looking up to me, and for a minute I was doing all right. And it went all down hill.

Q.   OK, let's do some education. Highest grade you completed in school was what?

A.   Tenth.

Q.   You said you mainly had fighting problems in school. Did you have other kinds of problems? You had good grades up until a point and then. . . .

A.   Yeah, well, it got so man, ninth grade was all right. Everybody was talking about basketball. So I made it for awhile. Then just slacked off, started losing interest, started skipping and shit. Kicking with motherfuckers and slick cars and shit. Just fell apart. Start going for like, you know, I was like just making average grades like 1.4, 1.5 (grade point average, roughly a D+). 'Til it went down to .6 ("F") and shit.

Q.   You get suspended?

A.   Yeah. Not too much. six, seven times. Usually for fighting. No, all of them for fighting.

Q.   How old were you when you first started using drugs and started to drink?

A.   I was about fifteen, sixteen.

Q.   That late, really?

A.   Well, way it is now, they starting younger. Shit don't really make no difference now, 'cause I know little niggas thirteen and twelve that be smoking weed and selling joints and shit.

Q.   Ever used a needle?

A.   Nope. I ain't got offered it, but, that's one thing I ain't never gonna try. Don't wanta mess with them needles. I already have enough problems with the doctors.

Q. When do you get high now?

A. Well, damn near everyday. Practically. 'Cause if I ain't got it, one of the fellas got it, or one of the girls got it. Selling it, you know. It's out there.

Q. How often do you sell?

A. Well, I used to be pretty high up in it. But getting to be too much hassle. Too many people come to the house. My Mom's house, you know. So I was staying with somebody else. So I had to stop 'cause I couldn't handle it when I was at my mother's house.

Q. How often does the gang sell marijuana?

A. Regularly. Every day, twenty-four hours.

Q. And where do you get the shit? Other dealers here? How do you get the stuff?

A. Yep, other dealers. They gonna get they money back, anyway, see. We can get it for how much it's worth, and then once we sell it, we give back how much it's worth and then make the profit.

Q. And these people aren't in the gang that you buy it from?

A. No. Some are, some not. And if you got a supplier who's a gang member too, you don't have to pay nothing upfront. Split this, split that. You know, you might get a dollar for every bag you sell, or two dollars for this much bags you sell.

Q. What about Chicago? Do you ever get the stuff from gangs in Chicago?

A. Sometimes. But most of the stuff is right here. Ain't no sense of going way over there for that shit.

Profile of the Founding Group

Our conception of gangs as a fraction of a forming underclass finds further support in the current status of the 260 young men and women
who founded Milwaukee's nineteen major gangs. We asked the forty
seven founders to carefully list all their friends who formed the gang.
We did not want them to list the entire "main group" of the gang when
it was largest, but the specific group of friends who founded the gang:
the "ancients," as Phillip of the 2-4s called them. Those interviewed
took this very seriously. Since all those listed were their best friends at
the time the group formed, at ages thirteen to seventeen, it was not
hard for them to list each one and report whether they were working,
had graduated, had been to jail, and whether they were still "hanging
out" and involved with the gang. The original gang founders were generally still close to one another. Our interviews took place at least five
years after the gang was formed and the 260 gang founders were then
mostly young adults in their early twenties.[9]

EMPLOYMENT AND GANG INVOLVEMENT: ALL GANG FOUNDERS

Employment	Bl. Male	Hisp. Male	Wh. Male	Female
FULL-TIME	9.7%	10%	10%	8.6%
PART-TIME	14.3%	0%	40%	11.4%
UNEMPLOYED	70.3%	82.5%	40%	63.0%

Gang Involvement

	Bl. Male	Hisp. Male	Wh. Male	Female
Involved As Adults	81.1%	70%	100%	8.6%
TOTALS 100% = 260	N = 175	N = 40	N = 10	N = 35

NOTE: Totals may not add up to 100% due to deceased and unknowns.

The entire group of 260 gang founders, nearly all between eighteen and
twenty-five at the time of the interviews, were still hanging out on the
same corners where they began the gang five to eight years before.
While only ten percent were reported to us as employed full-time,

nearly three quarters were reported to us to be still involved with the gang. Of those reported employed, no one was reported as earning more than $5.00 per hour. In fact, we have good reason to believe that the number of gang founders reported to us as working full- or part-time substantially overestimates actual employment. After the interviews were over we spoke to one gang founder. He had reported in the interview most of his fellow founders were working "part-time." It turned out that what he meant was the founders were on general assistance, a welfare program that pays $175 per month and has a work requirement. For him, this was "work." Most gang founders we interviewed were regularly on and off general assistance, so the percentage of gang founders actually working is likely to be even lower than what was reported to us.[10]

We did not expect to find such high levels of continuing adult male gang involvement. The gang founders, faced with harsh economic conditions, have maintained their gang ties and continued to hang out together. Fighting has been replaced by a focus on survival. Rather than maturing out of the gang into a job, or raising a family, Milwaukee gang founders have just kept hanging out together.

We asked the founders what the gang meant to them in their own words. Most told us the gang was now like their family, a means of support or survival. While more of the gang founders will certainly break away from the gang as the years go by, for a vast majority of these young adult gang founders, time appears to be standing still.

The thirty five female founders presented a different story. Less than ten percent (3) were reported to be involved with their female gang at all and fewer (2) involved "the same or more" with the gang. The young women, once they turned eighteen seemed to no longer identify with their female gang. One reason may be that more than half of them (18) already had a family. None of the women were married, and those with children were all reported to be on AFDC. It could not be determined how many of the female originals had boy friends in a male gang, or if they continued their involvement with a male gang. Involvement with the female gang, unlike male adult gang involvement, appeared to cease after the women turned eighteen or became mothers.

Clearly, Milwaukee's economic conditions have made continued gang involvement likely for unemployed adult males. In the absence of work and the family that steady work would support, the gang helps Milwaukee gang founders survive emotionally, and, sometimes, economically.

Education

When we examine the educational backgrounds of the gang founders, we find more support for our position that gangs are a fraction of the underclass.

BLACK MALE FOUNDERS:
GANG INVOLVEMENT AND EMPLOYMENT BY EDUCATION

GANG INVOLVEMENT	Graduated	Dropped Out Back In School	Not In School	College
SAME/MORE	66.7%	66.7%	62%	33.3%
LESS	19.6%	19%	22%	33.3%
NOT AT ALL	13.7%	14.2%	16%	33.3%

EMPLOYMENT	Graduated	Dropped Out Back In School	Not In School	College
FULL-TIME	25.5%	4.8%	4%	0%
PART-TIME/ UNEMPLOYED	72.5%	95.2%	89%	66.7%
TOTAL = 175	N = 51	N = 21	N = 100	N = 3

NOTE: Totals may not add up to 100% due to deceased and unknowns. "Back in school" refers to alternative GED program.

Looking at the black male founders, we find that less than a third graduated from high school or received a GED.[11] More than half were not pursuing any educational programs at all. Only two were attending a junior college, and one was in college. Compared to all 1985 U.S. high school graduates, a full 58% of whom attended college, Milwaukee's gang founders find themselves unequipped to face today's more educationally demanding "good jobs."

What does a high school diploma do for the job chances or gang involvement of Milwaukee's gang founders? Those who did get a high school diploma were reported to be no more likely to have left the gang than those who dropped out of school. Of those who graduated or received a GED, nearly nine of ten were reported to be still hanging out with the gang. Of those who dropped out, nearly the same percentage was reported to be still involved with the gang. In other words, high school education, by itself, does not seem to influence continued gang involvement for black males. While those black male founders who graduated from high school were more likely to get a full-time job than those who did not, still, nearly three quarters of those black male gang founders who graduated found themselves unemployed.

Having a diploma did not seem to keep black males out of jail, either. While two thirds of those who dropped out of school spent more than a few weeks in jail, two thirds of those who did graduate spent some time in jail as well. (See Chapter Seven, p. 163.)

Today's "good" job market simply demands more skills than a high school diploma. One person reported in our Milwaukee interviews:

> I ain't never had a job. I ain't never even had a summer
> job. They don't even wanta give me one of them, and
> them the easiest ones to get.
>
> *J. J., Black Gangster Disciples*

While not typical of the job histories of others interviewed, J.J. was one of the five who had a diploma. High school education or a GED do not appear to have a significant impact on gang involvement, or likelihood of going to jail, nor does it sharply increase chances for a full-time job.

The only factor we found that decreases gang involvement for the gang founders is a full-time job. While about half of all gang founders who were working full-time stayed involved with the gang, more than nine of ten of those who worked no more than part-time remained involved with the gang as adults.

Summary: A Generation On Its Way Down

Forty years ago, Whyte remarked about Boston Italian gangs: "Our society places a high value on social mobility. According to tradition, the workingman starts in at the bottom and by means of intelligence and hard work climbs the ladder of success. It is difficult for the Cornerville man to get onto the ladder, even on the bottom rung" (Whyte 1943, 273). Whyte was premature. The war ended the depression, the economy boomed, and the Italian "Cornervilleman" did get on the ladder and climb out into the colleges and factories of Boston.

Things are different for black and Hispanic gang members today. While the parents of our gang founders migrated to Milwaukee to find the jobs and mobility Milwaukee's somewhat better economy could provide, the 1980s dashed their hopes. The deindustrialization and segmentation of Milwaukee's economy snatched away the ladder of mobility. Gangs are becoming "institutionalized" in poor black and Hispanic neighborhoods, not only as an adolescent adaption, but as a means for young adults to cope with a jobless reality as well.

This first generation of Milwaukee's gangs may resemble gangs of the past, but when the gang ages and reproduces itself as a multigenerational phenomenon, other changes may result as well. The children of Milwaukee's gang founders, rather than having a relatively healthy family life and parents who are working steadily, will grow up in a different kind of home. What effect these conditions may have is uncertain but we can find few reasons for hope.

Wilson's view, quoted at the beginning of our chapter, that the underclass was made up of people who are "collectively different" from poor people in the past, is based on his research in Chicago, where the underclass, and its gangs, have had several decades to become entrenched. That process, we suggest, is beginning in Milwaukee and in other smaller cities. Gangs today in small cities are a red flag telling us the underclass is not just a problem for the New Yorks and Chicagos.

Economic variables, however, are not the only ones in operation. Milwaukee's black gangs have been powerfully influenced by the black experience in Milwaukee, as we shall see in the next chapter. Milwaukee's institutions, especially its public schools, have played a major role in alienating black youth from their neighborhoods.

6
DESEGREGATION ALIENATION AND GANGS IN MILWAUKEE

That sense of community is gone. Like one young dude looked at this mural with Martin Luther King on it and said: "He can't do nothing for me. He ain't on a dollar bill."

Hubert Canfield
Milwaukee Black Community
Activist

Q. What does being in a gang mean to you?
A. Being in a gang to me means if I didn't have no family I'll think that's where I'll be. If I didn't have no job that's where I'd be. To me it's like community help without all the community. They'll understand better than my mother and father. It's just like a community group, but it's together, you know. You don't see it, but it's there.

Tony, Four Corner Hustlers

What has been the impact of the minority experience on the formation of contemporary gangs? In Chapter Two we compared the minority experience in the 1980s with earlier immigrant experience and found both similarities and differences. Most notably, we looked at the consequences of the segmentation of the economy on black youth. The continuing adult participation in gang life, as we hypothesized in Chapter Five, is directly related to these economic changes. Continued adult participation in gangs has contributed to what Moore calls the "institutionalization" of gangs in poor minority communities. While gang activity varies over time, what has become constant in many cities is the persistence of gangs. Gangs are becoming a permanent "institution" within certain poor minority communities, attracting both juveniles and young adults to their traditions, protection, and social life.

New institutions arise when old ones disintegrate. Thrasher believed his 1920s Chicago gangs were formed for immigrant youth to "establish order and secondarily fulfill human needs" (Kornhauser 1978, 52). After a period of initial disorganization, the economic and spatial mobility of European immigrants allowed the institutions of community social control to dissolve or transform their neighborhood gangs. Even during the depression, community institutions continued to function as a means of social control within poor communities. Whyte's *Street Corner Society* (1943) is basically a description of the lively and complex institutional life within a poor Italian community during the 1930s.

But along with massive economic changes, contemporary institutions in poor minority communities that once had functioned to "establish order" and "fulfill human needs "have seriously declined. A major void has arisen and gangs, we believe, are one method by which some young people fill this vacuum. Wilson has remarked that "unlike the present period, inner-city communities prior to 1960 exhibited the features of social organization—including a sense of community, positive neighborhood identification, and explicit norms and sanctions against aberrant behavior" (Wilson 1987, 3). Wilson accounts for the loss of a "sense of community and positive neighborhood identification" in two ways: by the increase in the number of youthful poor, and also by the flight of the black middle and working class from the poorest areas (1987, 50-56). But it is not only the exodus of the black non-poor that has been responsible for the alienation of black underclass youth. Institutional policies as well have contributed to the erosion of positive community spirit and an increase in socially destructive behavior. The nature and outlook of black gangs in Milwaukee have been altered not only by economic changes, but also by some of these institutional policies. The impact of school desegregation on the formation of black gangs has been a major factor in alienating black gangs from their neighborhood and from the black community as a whole.

Desegregation and Milwaukee Gangs

The positive and negative effects of desegregation plans in particular cities have come under increasing scrutiny. Rather than accepting the dogma that any kind of desegregated education will bring a qualitative improvement, many black educators have carefully examined the actual results of various plans. Led by Derrick Bell (1980) and others, many black scholars have seen some desegregation plans as a new form of discrimination. Nowhere is this criticism more valid than in Milwaukee.

Milwaukee's schools carried out a court ordered desegregation plan in 1977, when the founding group of Milwaukee's gangs were largely in Milwaukee elementary and middle schools. From the beginning, school administrators feared a repetition of the racist violence that struck Boston and Louisville in the 1970s. As a result of their fear of white violence, Milwaukee school administrators fashioned a desegregation plan with mandatory busing only for blacks, thereby minimizing white opposition. They also constructed a specialty or magnet school program that gave opportunities to the white and black middle class, while leaving inferior schools for the black lower class. This plan won middle class support among both traditional black civil rights organizations and white liberals.[1]

While the "forced busing" of only black students reduced white opposition to the plan, some black leaders organized popular protests and boycotts within the black community. The burden of desegregation, it was pointed out, had been unfairly placed on black students and black academic achievement had continued to fall. Milwaukee's black children were literally scattered out of their communities. In one all-black neighborhood, children were bused to 95 of the Milwaukee Public School's 108 elementary schools.

And at the same time, the gangs formed. Our study traced the origins of Milwaukee's gangs to corner groups and breakdancing groups

formed from middle and high school youth. The process of gang formation was very similar to the classic patterns of the development of a
gang from a neighborhood play group, as described by Thrasher. But
desegregation brought one change in the process of gang formation. After initially gathering as groups of friends, most black gangs did not
maintain themselves as neighborhood-based corner groups. Neighborhood ceased to have a positive meaning for most black gangs.[2]

Gangs and Neighborhoods

There has always been a relationship between gangs and neighborhoods and there has always been a relationship between neighborhoods
and ethnicity. Our understanding of gangs has been shaped by understanding them as "corner groups" of youth of a certain ethnic background, from the same block or neighborhood, who come together,
fight with other corner groups, and generally make trouble.

Both Thrasher and Whyte viewed the gang as basically a group of
neighborhood youth who stay together until "the families of the boys
move to other neighborhoods" (Thrasher 1963, 31). Suttles viewed the
gang as a functional part of the neighborhood (1968, 173). For Keiser, in
his study of Chicago's black Vicelords, the neighborhood is equally un-
problematic. "We all go to school together, and we all live on the same
street," he quotes a Vicelord as saying (1969, 57). Recently, Moore
(1978) has commented that for Los Angeles Chicano gang members,
"the word for gang and for neighborhood is identical. 'Mi barrio' refers
equally to 'my gang' and 'my neighborhood' " (1978, 35). Campbell
adds: in New York "it is one neighborhood against another, as the gangs
see it. Class solidarity is an alien concept. . . . Gangs remain
neighborhood-based" (1984, 236).

But some factors have more recently acted to weaken this tie between gang and neighborhood. Cloward and Ohlin predicted that "delinquency will become increasingly aggressive and violent in the future
as a result of the disintegration of slum organization" (1960, 203). They
go on to note, with other observers (e.g., Katznelson 1981), that the welfare state has shifted power away from the local political machine. This
loss of patronage and local power has made it harder for minority city
politicians to coopt youth gangs into conventional neighborhood politics, as did their immigrant predecessors.

Walter Miller has pointed out that modern transportation has also influenced gang concepts of territoriality. While traditional gang "rumbles" continue, he explains, "forays by small bands, armed and often motorized, appear to have become the dominant form of inter-gang violence" (1975, 76). Gangs are no longer confined to defending a turf where they live never going elsewhere. While urban gangs today may not roam the suburbs and other places "off limits" for minorities, they are no longer the corner boys Whyte quoted Doc describing: "Fellows around here don't know what to do except within a radius of about three hundred yards. That's the truth, Bill. . . . It's only rarely that a fellow will change his corner" (1943, 256).

Modern transportation and other factors have led to a more spatially mobile population. Moore, Vigil, and Garcia have explored the question of "fictive residence" in Los Angeles gangs (1983). In their interesting analysis, they show that where gang members live is often different than their "barrio," or where their gang is based. Territoriality and residence are two different things for many L.A. Chicano gang members due, among other factors, to frequent relocation of gang family residence. But, for Moore and others, allegiance to the barrio, a specific neighborhood, remains strong even if the gang member no longer lives there.

Most black Milwaukee gangs are clearly different. The "neighborhood" has ceased to be a common place for gang members to live, nor is it particularly valued. While the factors mentioned above played a role in this loosening of identity between black gangs and neighborhoods, the desegregation of the Milwaukee Public Schools has been the principle culprit.

Kids Without Neighborhoods

Q. Did you have to be from the neighborhood to join the 2-4s?

A. Well, back in '78 they had to be, but now they don't have to be. 2-4s are all scattered; there are so many 2-4s now, I run across some I don't even know. If they got together, this would be a good large group.

Phillip, 2-4s

Some observers claimed desegregation itself laid a basis for the development of gangs in Milwaukee. The congregation of groups of black kids at bus stops for self-defense was cited by some black school officials as a possible precursor of the gangs. Other black community activists, like Hubert Canfield from the United Black Community Council, are even more emphatic:

> You don't have a sense of community because of the
> busing situation. People hanging together because they
> know somebody from riding the bus with them or they're
> supposed to be going to a certain school. When people
> started getting transferred all over the city, they started,
> and out of necessity they started, you know, clinging and
> collecting people. Like they were forcing them to be
> organized like that.

While incidents of racial tension in some schools in all-white neighborhoods in the late seventies and early eighties do not seem to be directly related to the emergence of black gangs, it is clear that black students formed themselves into groups for self-protection during the late seventies when large-scale busing began. Among those elementary and middle school black students who were first bused were Milwaukee's gang founders.

Most conflict was not inter-racial. Instead of attending a neighborhood school with their friends, most black corner group founders were bused all over the city and engaged in conflict with other black youth from rival corner groups. This conflict occurred both within the schools and on buses which picked black students up from different neighborhoods. Naturally, the gang founders recruited to protect themselves, and recruitment was not based on neighborhood, but on the need for protection.

> **A.** We used to go to school, right? And like they might
> be controlling this school, and we might be
> controlling that school, and then we might have
> friends who might get put out of that school and
> transfer to their school. And then, some of them
> might not be too cool with them. They might not like
> 'em.

Q.   Did you recruit at the schools? How did you run into them?

A.   Hanging out. Calling. Making phone calls, going out to Westlawn, going over to Hillside, going over on 27th street. Going over here, going over there, meeting people that you know. Seeing people on the bus that you going to school with. People that was your age.

Mike, Black Gangster
Disciples

More than 80% of the black male founders interviewed reported that those who began the gang grew up in the same neighborhood together. At the time of our interviews about five years after the gang formed, a clear majority reported that most of the current youthful members of the gang were no longer recruited from the same neighborhood. Less than a third of the black male gang members interviewed thought that what "neighborhood" a recruit came from was very important for recruitment to the gang. The only black male gangs who reported "membership" as synonymous with neighborhood residence were youth living in the Westlawn and Hillside Housing Projects. With only isolated exceptions, however, black gangs remained all-black and recruitment was not extended to other ethnic groups. The neighborhood, far from being a place to defend, became merely a place to hangout. The question, "How many times in the past month have you had to defend your neighborhood?" which we borrowed from previous Los Angeles research, was not understood by most of those we interviewed and subsequently dropped from our questionnaire.

In contrast, the Hispanic gangs both had clearly defined "turf" where most gang members lived at one time. For the white boys in Punk Alley, the gang and the neighborhood were completely identical. In fact, the white members of Punk Alley strongly resisted labeling as a "gang," claiming gangs are only black and Puerto Rican.

In summary, desegregation in Milwaukee was not the "forward step" hoped for by the civil rights movement. Instead, it increased the alienation of black youth from their neighborhoods. The scattering of black students in schools throughout the city reduced the ability of parents and neighbors to participate in the schools and help control the emerging youth gang problem. The gangs felt no allegiance to school or neighborhood. The public schools, no longer community institutions of training and control, had no relationship to the neighborhoods and were ineffective for both education and social control for the emerging black underclass.

We believe desegregation combined with many other factors to weaken local institutions within the black community. The net result of these institutional and economic changes has been to create a class of young people with an outlook markedly different compared to black youth in the past.

Al Capone and Martin Luther King

A. 'Cause most of it is based on Al Capone, how the gangs come out.
Q. What do you mean, based on Al Capone?
A. 'Cause they saw most pictures about Al Capone. they be shooting up niggers and they thought that was nice, dealing cocaine, making money.

Big Foot, Cobra Stones

For poor black youth in the 1980s, the best adjective to describe Milwaukee might be "hostile": black youth faced a "hostile" future with few available good jobs. A "hostile" educational process left them ill-equipped for any but minimum wage employment. A "hostile" police force was ever present. Their own "hostile" outlook was matched by the equally "hostile" outlook of other black youth, and "hostilities" broke out on a regular basis.

Back in the 1960s, this "hostility" was organized and channeled toward protest and rebellion. The civil rights movement of that day has become "institutionalized," with many of the 1960s civil rights leaders in Milwaukee now heads of the poverty agencies which deliver services to the black poor. In our Milwaukee interviews we talked to several black gang members of the fifties and sixties who had not only "matured out of the gang," but vividly described the impact the civil rights movement had on their lives.[3]

Black gang members in the past appeared to be closely tied to their communities. Short and Strodtbeck, in their mid-sixties gang study, looked at the relationship between white and black gang members and their respective communities. They concluded that black gang members at that time were similar by a variety of measures to the black lower and middle class. On the other hand, sixties white gang members differed by the same measures sharply from the white middle and lower class. "As compared with lower class white communities, delinquency among lower class Negroes is more a part of a total life pattern. . . ." (1965, 108). Black gang members of the sixties, according to Short and Strodtbeck, were hardly distinguishable from other working and middle class black youth.

The years since the Short and Strodtbeck studies, however, have witnessed sharp class differentiation within black communities. In Milwaukee, the black middle class grew from 2% of the black work force in 1970 to 10% of all black workers in 1980. But with deindustrialization occurring at the same time, most of the black community was headed downhill: the gap between an expanding middle class and the bulk of the black community widened dramatically.

This increasing economic polarization has predictably influenced the outlook of underclass gang members. Their alienation and bitterness is directed not only against white society, but also toward institutions within the black community controlled by the black middle class. Indeed, when we asked the gang founders how much influence community agencies had in their lives, nearly three quarters of the black founders said "little or none." The black church was practically unmentioned.

Milwaukee's black underclass gangs are both a part of the black community and yet extremely alienated from it. While all black males we interviewed told us they were proud to be black, they did not see their gangs as a positive part of the black community. Two thirds of the black males interviewed insisted that their gang was "not at all" trying to help the black community.

> **Q.** How much do you see Westlawn Folks as trying to
> help the black community?
> **A.** What?
>
> **Q.** Some people say that they see their gang as trying to
> help the community.
> **A.** Nope. Not at all! No!
>
> *Thomas, Westlawn*

> **Q.** How much do you see your gang as trying to help
> the black community?
> **A.** Everybody for themselves. To be truthful, it's every
> man for himself.
>
> *George, Black Gangster*
> *Disciples*

> **Q.** How much do you see Five Alive as trying to help
> the black community?
> **A.** It ain't trying to help the community in no kind of
> way.
>
> *Leonard, Five Alive*

Those interviewed saw the gang more as a means of excitement or "drama" for the young, and as a means of survival for those older. The gang is clearly separated from the community and from any past black freedom movement. Only about half of those interviewed said that if they saw someone breaking into a house in the neighborhood, they would "stop them."

> **Q.** What if you saw someone breaking into a car in your
> neighborhood. What would you do?
> **A.** Some fellas used to say, "Go on, make their money."
> Some of 'em used to say, "This is our territory. We
> don't let nobody do nothing. We make the only
> money around here."
>
> *George, Black Gangster*
> *Disciples*

The values espoused by the new gangs are centered on "survival" and "hustling," especially as the gang members age and face an uncertain future. Unlike the politics of survival advocated by the Black Panther Party twenty years ago, today's gang values are more individually centered and seldom take the interests of any beyond the gang into account. Hubert Canfield painfully compares his commitment with today's gang youth:

> There's definitely no sense of community, because, when I
> was thinking when I was coming down here about what
> we'd be discussing, I was very active in the Black Panther
> Party. And I guess folks would have considered us a gang,
> but we had another purpose. We was all about trying to do
> things for our community.

While the perception of discrimination was a major impetus to racial organization in the 1960s, Milwaukee's gang founders today thought there
is little or no discrimination against blacks. They believed their experiences in the secondary labor market, for example in applying for a job
at a McDonalds, had nothing to do with discrimination. The problem is
not competition from whites, who don't compete with black youth for
work at a ghetto McDonalds anyway, but the lack of skills needed to advance from a dead-end job to a "good job." In the absence of "good
jobs," the "hustling" outlook is entrenching itself among poor minority
youth.

The polarization of economic classes within the black community
has had a major effect on the outlook of Milwaukee's black gangs. Today's gangs see themselves as largely separate from the needs and
struggles of their own communities and the traditions of the black
movement for social justice. On the other hand, the aspirations of the
middle class within the black community are seen to have little relevance for an underclass struggling to survive.[4]

With an outlook of survival "by any means necessary," it is not
surprising that the gangs would find new heroes. Had we searched in
the thousand or so pages of our transcripts of our forty seven interviews
we might find one or two references to Dr. Martin Luther King. If we
looked a second time for references to Al Capone, we would have found
Capone's name scattered throughout the interviews.

Gangs and Drugs

Along with the decline in positive community spirit, another sign of increasing alienation is the widespread use of drugs. Cloward and Ohlin
(1960), who hypothesized an entire "drug subculture," saw drug-using

gangs as a symptom of total demoralization and despair. Their typology of a separate "drug subculture" has been rejected by most theorists, and it was widely believed that drug use had wiped out gangs in the sixties and seventies (Miller 1975). But rather than wiping the gangs out, drugs became incorporated into the contemporary gang lifestyle.

The importance of drugs to the gang lifestyle is underscored by our study. Sixty percent of those interviewed admitted they used drugs (mainly marijuana) most or all of the time, meaning at least every other day. Nearly a third said they used drugs every day. Less than 5% of those interviewed said that at this time they "never" used drugs. This Cobra's comment is typical:

> **Q.**   How often do you fire up a joint?
> **A.**   Joints? Probably smoke every day. Somewhere along
>   the line somebody fires one up.

Twenty years ago, in comparing white and black gangs, Short and Strodtbeck found that "drug use among these Negro boys seems to be part of the 'normal' pattern of street life and to have much in common in this respect with adults" (1965, 109). While we found no difference in drug use between the black, Hispanic, and the one white gang we studied, one Milwaukee black gang member might correct Short and Strodtbeck:

> You know, I use drugs because right now that's really one
> of the biggest ways for me to get money. The black
> society today is drugs. You know, and it's strange, cause
> there ain't that many jobs, but you notice it's always
> drugs. There's always money, but there ain't that many
> jobs, so how is that?

Drugs are both a means of "partying" for all and a modest means of income for some of the older members. Nearly half of those we interviewed admitted they sold drugs at least "now and then" as a "hustle." Nearly one in five founders said they sold drugs regularly. Over two thirds said that members of the main group of their gang sold drugs "regularly" and nearly all said someone in the main group sold at least "now and then."[5]

Gang Violence

Another indicator of the increasing alienation of gang youth is the level of violence. Walter Miller has summarized the changing extent and severity of violence over the years, concluding that "youth gang violence is more lethal today then ever before" (1975, 76). Although in 1966, Miller found "midcity" white gangs more violent than their black counterparts, this contrast is clearly not true today.[6]

Violence is an all too common part of the urban experience for youthful black males. Black homicide rates are as much as fourteen times greater than white rates for males in their early twenties (Dennis 1979, 20). But gang homicide rates indicate that at least in Chicago and Los Angeles, gang homicide is predominantly a Hispanic problem (Spergel 1984, Moore 1987).

While numerous studies have looked at causes of violence,[7] and gangs for many are associated with violence, some observers point to considerable variation in homicide rates within and between gangs. Moore cites numerous factors influencing homicide rates in two Los Angeles gangs. She concludes that it is important to recognize violence as a variable, not a constant attribute of gang behavior—a fact often unrecognized by law enforcement. Yablonsky's conception of the gang as a violent "near-group" is a stereotyped myth. Two examples from Milwaukee illustrate Moore's concern. First, while many observers have looked at the comparatively high Hispanic homicide rates, we have noted in Milwaukee that Puerto Rican gangs have gone to great lengths to avoid "Chicago-style" violence. They have in fact largely succeeded in preventing large-scale gang warfare. Second, the three Hispanic gang-related homicides that have been reported in Milwaukee since 1986 were all the result of intra-gang conflict, not inter-gang warfare. The extent of intra-gang homicide and violence has not been explored by any serious study.[8]

Gang homicide statistics, however, are unreliable, partly because of the manner in which different cities define a "gang-related homicide."[9] Regardless, a look at gang-related homicides over the last twenty years in many cities fails to find much of a pattern, except overall change for the worse. A major factor, we believe with Miller and Silberman (1978), is the increase in number of guns.

In our interviews, we expected gang members to either brag about their weapons and try to conceal the number and types of guns each person had. We were unprepared for their responses, indicating gang members had many more guns than we imagined. Nearly half of the black males we interviewed said they possessed "more than one" firearm. A large majority said they possessed at least one handgun. None of those who admitted to the possession of a firearm said they purchased the gun legally, raising questions as to the value of gun control legislation. Most said they "bought it off the streets" and over a third said the gun was "stolen." While many admitted using the guns at some time, only a small percentage acknowledged shooting someone and hitting them. The increasing use of guns is a legitimate cause for alarm within poor urban communities.[10]

Alienation and Community-Based Institutions

The increasing alienation of the gangs and the bitterness of the black gang founders toward community institutions demonstrates the weakness of social controls within the black community. But along with bitterness, it seemed to us, the founders also expressed a strong need for such controls and a willingness to respond to genuine community-based programming.

Gang programs have always been initiated in response to the inflexibility of traditional youth programs. Geis (1960, 43) cites the history of the New York City Youth Board as an example of the need for innovative programming to replace the traditional agencies which are unable "to respond readily to new ideas and approaches." The history of the Chicago Area Project is another example of a non-traditional approach, setting up community organizations which employed "indigenous workers" (in reality influential gang members) to cope with gang problems and serve as advocates to traditional agencies (Schlossman 1984). But gangs have almost everywhere remained outside the influence of the poverty programs, agencies, and community organizations that claim to be "on the front lines." In Minnesota, the 1986 Twin Cities Task Force Report commented "that a number of gang youth had preferred the streets to the agencies in the community." Perkins notes that there is no evidence to confirm that traditional youth agencies have been effective in working with black Chicago street gangs (1987, 67).

In Milwaukee few of the gang founders could give any positive examples of community programs. Their major complaint was that the community programs did not listen to them and excluded them from participation.

> **Q.** If you were head of an agency, a community organization, what would you do to deal with the gangs? What would you do differently than they do now?
>
> **A.** I would see how they (gang members) would run it, what ideas they would have. Not so much as me sitting up there and saying, well, OK, this is the way I want it. No, I would want to know what they want.
>
> *Dante, Latin Kings*

> **Q.** What do you think about agencies like Silver Spring Neighborhood Center? Do you think there are things they could be doing better to help kids in gangs?
>
> **A.** Yeah, they could have a meeting or something, like what you're doing, and talk to them and it might help too.
>
> *Felix, Westlawn*

While community programs are often cited as part of the solution in working with gang youth, the gangs more often see the agencies as part of the problem. Parading "gang members" in front of funding panels and self-serving claims that the agency has "resolved gang disputes" may play in the board rooms and with the media, but are often greeted with scorn on the streets. Some of the gang founders are quite bitter about the role of the social agencies and openly call out for new "role models":

> **Q.** If the Governor gave you a million dollars to deal with the gang problem, what do you do with the money?
>
> **A.** First thing I do, I'd probably open up a center. Well, I'd open up some type of business dedicated strictly to gangs. Two, I'd give them (the gang members) the

jobs to work in the place, doing security and all that. I'd buy out that agency I work for now and burn it down, 'cause they ain't doing a good job. To me, they setting a bad example.

Q.   Bad example, how?
A.   'Cause they ain't helping nobody. They sitting on they butts. Man, they suppose to be one of the first ones that got started? They ain't doing nothing. Half the motherfuckers in there's alcoholic. Sitting back drinking and shit. They ain't thinking about us. They thinking about waiting for that paycheck and go buy them some alcohol. I don't feel that's a good example to nobody. All this money they be getting for running them programs and grants. . . . Ain't no telling how much they be using.

Q.   So shut down the phoney agencies?
A.   Yep, I'd shut down them phoney agencies and get to the real ones.

Some years back when the principal author was negotiating a contract with a Hispanic agency who claimed to "work with gangs" for use of their gym for the Cobras, the Cobra leadership poured out a litany of complaints about the agency. They believed the agency would merely harass Cobras and was not serious about the contract. To deal with the problem, the Cobras were invited, by Hagedorn, to attend the contract negotiations. They showed up, about fifty strong, much to the horror of the local agency director. The contract was negotiated with the Cobras present and to their satisfaction. The response of the agency director? "Never do this to me again." The gym, sad to say, was shut down when the contract expired, and the Cobras were once again excluded from agency programming.

Despite the alienation and bitterness, the gang founders we interviewed clearly wanted and needed a "sense of community." This is why Tony talked of his gang as "community help without all the community. It's just like a community group, but it's together." He'll take what he can get. In the absence of effective local institutions, Milwaukee youth have adapted and developed their own.

When Community Controls Are Lacking,
The Police Are Never Far Away

One consequence of the alienation of black gangs from their neighborhoods has been a changed emphasis in methods of social control. In the past when groups of neighborhood "corner boys" got into trouble, they were often held responsible by parents and other older people on their block. Local churches and agencies could provide help and services. The school was nearby and parents were quickly called when trouble arose. Many problems could be straightened out by parental intervention before they became problems for police.

In Milwaukee, desegregation has meant that the corner where many gangs hang out is not in their neighborhood. Instead of a corner group of the children of families on the block, we have a gang whom frightened residents do not know and so police are called when trouble erupts. Similarly, the lack of effective community agencies within Milwaukee's minority communities has led to the filling of this void by the expansion of police, prisons, and other criminal justice institutions.

Gangs of the 1980s are rebellious, but they are quite unlike the civil rights organizations of the 1960s. Milwaukee gangs have caused some serious harm to their communities, but to say this does not imply that we accept the popular criminal justice conception of gangs. To describe what is ugly about a social problem is a necessary part of telling the truth. The truth, we believe, will help us reframe the problem of gangs, so that instead of seeing them fundamentally as a problem of law enforcement, we can see them fundamentally as a problem of a growing minority underclass.

How we frame the problem of gangs conceptually will in the end determine how we act. But the reframing of a social problem is not merely a question of words. It is a political process that often has had less to do with the actual nature and extent of the problem than it does with needs of powerful economic and political forces. In our final chapter, we will look at how the gang problem has been framed in Milwaukee and other cities, and then draw some final conclusions from our study.

7

OUT OF SIGHT OUT OF MIND

Q. How do you define the gang problem now?

A. I see it as a serious problem. I see it as a threat to our city and to our society, like various other times, various other decades we went through, maybe the sixties with the civil disobedience and maybe the riots and things like that in the various cities in the seventies. Right now I think the eighties is the decade of the street gangs, not only here in Milwaukee. . . .

Sgt. Thomas Saye,
Milwaukee Gang Squad

We began this book by asking what do we know about gangs? If this book has accomplished anything in its first six chapters, perhaps it has been to suggest that we know less than we thought. But even if that is true, gangs do not have to remain unexamined. Our research is certainly not impossible to replicate or improve on.[1] While access to the gangs is not easy, it can be gained. Determined efforts, if honest and unexploitative, are likely to succeed.

But lack of facts has not deterred policy makers from proceeding full speed ahead. Nor should they "wait until the research is done." After all, elected officials have an obligation to their constituencies and certainly will act when pressure mounts. Particularly in the middle- and smaller-cities now facing a reemergence of gang activity, and where chances at successful interventions may be best, local officials have taken a cue from larger cities and treated the problem of gangs as principally a law enforcement matter. The basic strategy for coping with gangs remains the iron fist, a strategy that moves the problem from visibility in the community to the invisibility of the prison.

This is not to say that all cities have responded to gangs in the same manner. In Columbus, Ohio, police and social service agencies established a good working relationship and the local gang unit of the police has demonstrated an unusual capability to make a concrete and unstereotyped analysis of local gangs. The police have shown an interest in research and have cooperated with Ron Huff from Ohio State University in his statewide research efforts. On the other hand, the Phoenix, Arizona, Police Department has shown no such sophistication. Its Juvenile Gang Reduction Unit has published a "Latin Gang Member Recognition Guide," with racist cartoon depictions of Hispanics and a text filled with misinformation. Other small cities uncritically rely on information from big city police departments which may not accurately describe local gangs. Attributing local gang development to the "diffusion" of Chicago or other big city gang members, other cities simplistically call for computer tracking of gang members to "protect" their own cities.

Our experience in Milwaukee has been that the gang problem is best described as "disturbing" to several different interest groups.[2] First, as we've pointed out, it is disturbing to the Chamber of Commerce and other powerful economic and political forces who are trying to revitalize and attract new business. Second, it is disturbing to those in law enforcement and youth service who deal directly with youth: gangs represent a new and disrespectful population. Finally, it is disturbing to many in the middle class within minority communities. They see the gangs as an excuse for continued racism by whites and for white labeling of all black youth as gang members.

The immediate interests of each of these groups is served by a strategy of removing the problem from sight. And there's only one place to which the problem can be safely removed: the prisons.

Stages in Milwaukee

The response to Milwaukee's gang problem has gone through three distinct stages: from denial to recognition to repression. These stages occurred for reasons that had little to do with actual developments on the streets, yet each stage has had major repercussions within the gangs. While many would say that the movement of the gang problem from the streets to the prisons is a positive development, our data questions that position.

Stage I. "We Couldn't Have Gangs Here": 1981-1984

Milwaukee, like most small- and middle-sized cities, went through a prolonged period of denial that there was any gang problem. Some cities, like Indianapolis or Cleveland, seem to have been unable to move from this initial stage of public response. Police in Fort Wayne, Indiana, as well stubbornly insisted on denying the existence of gangs for years, despite ample evidence.[3] Denial seems to be a common stage of public response in all midwestern cities which have seen a recent emergence of gang activity.

In Milwaukee very little can be found in the pages of the local newspapers about gangs before 1983. The first major series about gangs was written by black reporter Greg Stanford in May 1983 for the Milwaukee Journal. "Black Gangs, Smoke or Fire?" reflected the lack of clarity about whether gangs even existed.[4] After a series of shootings and problems in the local parks, a black alderman blasted the media for encouraging gang activity by glamorizing it.[5] Our interviews, however, reveal that seventeen of the nineteen major gangs had already formed before 1983 news reports and eight even before 1981. Some of the gangs existed for more than ten years before they were "discovered" by any in the media or by local officials. Rather than prompting serious investigation, the early publicity about gangs brought a torrent of denial from both social service agencies and the police.[6] While there were a few voices from both law enforcement and grass roots community leaders calling attention to the development of gangs, the dominant response as late as 1983-'84 was to vociferously deny the existence of any "gang" problem.

For Milwaukee Police Chief Harold Breier, admitting a growing gang problem was admitting weakness in a Police Department besieged by community opposition. Breier had successfully dealt with other problems by brash denial. He had declared for some years to the astonishment of many that Milwaukee had "no organized crime" and therefore no special organized crime efforts were needed. However he dealt with organized crime, the Milwaukee Chief of Police was not going to ignore the formation of minority gangs operationally. He merely denied their existence publicly and blasted all who disagreed.[7] Unorganized minority youth gangs would get the full attention of the Milwaukee Police Department.

On June 10, 1982 a special seven-man Milwaukee Police Gang Crimes Unit was formed in response to problems in the black community. A second Gang Crimes Unit specializing in Hispanic gangs was formed August 2, 1983. From our interviews with Milwaukee police, it is clear that the formation of the gang units came very soon after police became aware of the existence of gangs. Klein's comment on the inaccuracy of police intelligence (1971, 19) is borne out by our interviews. Like the media, police only became aware of youth gangs several years after most of the major gangs had formed.

Lost in the swirl of controversy over the nature and extent of the gang problem in the city was the realization that few people were doing anything about it except law enforcement officials. The gang problem was defined in the public mind as a minor criminal matter, best handled by the police. While public denials vociferously came from the Chief of Police, in reality a major law enforcement buildup was underway in minority communities. The Police gang unit which began as a seven-member squad expanded into a twenty-six member squad with two sergeants and two administrative personnel. It had made over 20,000 arrests by 1986 and is permanently attached to the Metro Division. The District Attorney's office secured in 1984 a two-year $600,000 federal grant to speed up prosecution of violent youth. Assistant District Attorney Don Jackson explained that the grant was "aimed at juveniles who were career criminals and who were violent. However, we all knew that a number of gang members, gang leaders, and their underlings would also fall within that category, and we knew we would be prosecuting a lot of gang members."

District Attorney McCann initiated a policy of telling judges about the gang ties of defendants, regardless of whether the crime was gang-related. "It's another way of breaking down gangs," McCann said.[8]

The Milwaukee Public Schools responded to gangs in their schools with a $359,584 beefed up security effort.[9] Willie Little, Assistant Administrative Specialist for the public schools, pointed out to the authors that instead of treating the gang problem as one for the Human Relations Department or as a prevention problem, the schools only "reacted" and saw gang growth as basically a problem of "security." Even the Sheriff's Department got into the act by securing a special $100,000 appropriation from the county board to "counter youth gangs."[10]

Liberals and Denial

While law enforcement quietly built up its response capability, some liberal community leaders surprisingly agreed that there was no gang problem. In a letter to the Milwaukee Journal, two prominent liberals, who otherwise disagreed with the right-wing Police Chief on all major issues, praised him for his denial of the existence of a gang problem.[11]

Some community leaders alleged the problem was "invented" by other community agencies solely to grab funds. Although the turf of the Kings and Cobras was within blocks of the United Community Center for over eight years, former Director Jude Pansini reported to United Way: "The first written note we made of a 'gang problem' was on May 5, 1983, when it was pointed out that Milwaukee's Social Development Commission was expecting to receive a sizable grant for anti-gang activity."[12] Why did Pansini and other liberals deny the seriousness of the gang problem and even the existence of gangs?

First, they feared that law enforcement would take advantage of any "gang problems" to increase surveillance and harassment in poor and minority communities. Pansini went so far as to call gangs an "imagined" threat. While increased police pressure did in fact result from the formation of a special gang squad, the denial of a gang problem from many community agencies did nothing for local residents trying to come to grips with the real problems gangs created. The early inaction of community-based programs allowed police to be the only agency "doing something" about gangs. The liberals who were so concerned about the results of a law enforcement buildup did not see it happening under their very noses.

Second, admitting a minority gang problem was seen as fueling the fires of racism.[13] Many within community agencies and minority professionals took exception to descriptions of the gang problem as a "minority problem." They went to great lengths to insist that whites had gangs too and were fearful that admitting there were minority gangs would reinforce racist stereotypes of "unemployed, vicious, and criminal" minorities. The denial that gangs were a particular minority problem had serious consequences. Instead of a careful analysis of the conditions within minority communities that had led to the formation of youth gangs and the beginnings of an underclass, gangs were labeled a problem of "law-violating" youth regardless of race or class. Therefore the problem was seen within the province of the police and juvenile justice system. By denying the minority nature of the problem, organizations and services within minority communities were denied resources to combat the problem in its early stages.

Neither were the growth of severe class contradictions within the black community a welcome development for some of the black elite. The existence of seemingly antagonistic classes raised questions about the ability of the established black leadership to represent "the entire black community" and questioned the effectiveness of middle class-led black agencies. "Black gangs," therefore, was an issue better denied than confronted.

Finally, competition for scarce social service resources prompted some agencies to deny the problem and others to exaggerate it. Gangs clearly could become a source of new money for strapped social agencies. Much of the fight over whether gangs existed could be charted by understanding which agencies were applying for gang intervention money and which ones were not. In today's world of social service cut-backs, any issue can become a source of battle between "human service" agencies. Ohio State's Ron Huff has commented that youth in gangs could take lessons in warfare from watching neighborhood agencies fight over money. In fact, in Milwaukee, the agency most vociferous in denying the existence of gangs reversed its position when a new director was appointed and they were given gang intervention funds.

Characteristic of the denial stage is the refusal to do any objective investigation. It served the interests of many powerful actors not to study the problem and uncover the facts, but rather to attack those talking about gangs as "rabble-rousers" or "racists" and hope the problem would go away.

Stage II. "We Do Have Gangs!": 1984-1985

But some problems cannot be wished away, and once discovered may seem larger than they really are.

The "discovery" of gangs often occurs in spectacular fashion. We reported in Chapter One how Columbus, Ohio, discovered gangs after assaults on the daughter of the Governor of Ohio and the son of the Mayor of Columbus. In Fort Wayne, Indiana, the Chief Probation Officer called a press conference and dumped a box of weapons, including firearms seized from gang members, on a table and suggested the media investigate what was happening on Fort Wayne's streets.

In an important article, Marjorie Zatz (1987) analyzed the reactions of the Phoenix Police Department and local media to the discovery of gangs. She concludes that "it is the social imagery of Chicano youth gangs, rather than their actual behavior, that lies at the root of the gang problem in Phoenix." Police estimates of gang activity jumped almost overnight from five or six gangs to one hundred or more. Zatz decided that three factors converged in creating a "moral panic" in Phoenix: (1) the interests of the police in acquiring federal funds; (2) the imagery of Chicano gangs as "violent"; and (3) the imagery of Mexicans and Chicanos as "different." Her skepticism about police claims of increasing gang violence is based on a careful analysis of data on gang versus a control group of non-gang juvenile offenders. She found few significant differences between the two groups and no major changes in crime rates. She concludes: "It is not at all clear that Phoenix truly faced a major problem of gang-related crime. What is clear, however, is that Chicano youth gangs became defined as a serious social problem—a problem to which the media and law enforcement agencies responded vociferously and vigorously. In so doing, a 'moral panic' was created."[14]

In Milwaukee, newspaper headlines discovering "4000 Gang Members" were quickly followed by TV interviews with hooded gang members, follow up stories on gang violence and heavy newspaper coverage of gang incidents. Zatz's use of the term "moral panic" does not unfairly describe Milwaukee in the winter of 1984. Within a few days, the "gang problem" that so many had previously denied, became a major social problem.

Perhaps the main result of the publicity was the convening of the Youth Initiatives Tack Force on April 12, 1984, by Mayor Henry Maier, to look at the gang problem and examine existing youth services.[15] While the Task Force looked at crime statistics, police reports, and other criminal justice indicators, no analysis of the actual nature and extent of gang problems in Milwaukee was attempted. The methodology of the Task Force was to solicit opinions and reach a consensus among important policy makers. Nothing would be said or recommended that might be critical of a major institution.

The Task Force Final Report (February 1985) confirmed that gangs were indeed a social problem, something now no one could deny. But the Task Force accomplished little else. It failed to set up a single new program or create one additional job. Its main recommendation was for the establishment of a county wide "Youth Commission" to continue its work.[16] Without any criticism of existing practices or policies and without any analysis of gangs that told policy makers anything new, no reform could be initiated. But more serious, the Youth Initiatives Task Force legitimized the existing definitions and criminal justice framework for responding to gangs.

These definitions were largely imported from Chicago and portrayed the problem as a criminal conspiracy. The head of the Milwaukee Police gang squad comments:

Q.   In trying to understand the problem and in
         developing policies, who do you rely on the most in

looking for help? Who have you gone to, to try to get some help?

A.   Well, again, we are a law enforcement agency, and we had to base some of our policies and procedures and some of the things we've done on people who've dealt with this before us. And our main source of information, without a doubt, has been the Chicago Police Department Gangs Crimes Unit, with whom we have a close working relationship. That I will say.

Sgt. Thomas Saye

It was not just the Police who imported their analysis from Chicago. The Milwaukee Public Schools formulated their initial gang policy after an August 17, 1983, seminar with Chicago Gang Crimes Unit personnel. At that meeting a decision was made to treat gangs as a criminal and police matter and to refuse to recognize them within the schools. Utilizing Chicago's police experience with gangs is certainly necessary, even if Chicago's less than successful results are recognized. But the resulting definitions left no room for any response to gangs but police and prison.

Prison officials as well were acting on definitions that were exported without change from Chicago. At a 1985 Wisconsin Correctional Association workshop in Waupun, Illinois, prison officials called gangs the beginnings of a Mafia and claimed that drug dealing had brought gang ties between Chicago and Milwaukee closer. Edward Knight, Superintendent of the Cook County Department of Corrections, said, "The only way we can deal with gang leaders is lock them up and keep them locked up."[17]

In Milwaukee, the stage of recognition was characterized by labeling gangs a public problem that needed urgent law enforcement attention. While denial was no longer feasible, what replaced denial resembled a "moral panic" that frightened the public and justified an on-going and massive criminal justice buildup. Instead of facts guiding policy, policy reacted to the images and definitions of gangs by the media and some in law enforcement. Traveling "gang experts" from Chicago and other large cities added an unhealthy dose of terror tactics. The only viable public policy became getting the problem off the streets and into the jails and prisons.

Stage III. Out of Sight, Out of Mind: 1985-?

> **Q.** Why wouldn't it be a good strategy for the police to
> decide "we're going to find out who the leaders are
> and we're going to lock them all up in jail?"
>
> **A.** 'Cause after you've been with a group and they have
> seen what you're about, they're (the younger ones)
> going to try to be leaders and try to build up the
> group even bigger.
>
> *Julio, Spanish Cobras*

In the third stage, the strategy of the authorities has been to make the
the gang problem invisible. Except for publicizing a few serious incidents, the media seem to be willing to down play gang problems,
agency gang programs become routinized with funding often slowly reduced, the Task Force loses its focus, and police become efficient in
putting pressure on the gangs and "getting the leaders." It is in the interest of almost all local elites to down play the gang problem in public
while continuing the strategy of repression.

The strategy of police pressure and moving the gang problem into
the prisons is a risky one, however. It is based on the assumption that
the gang is a criminal conspiracy that one can break by arresting and in-
carcerating the leaders. Klein summarizes this viewpoint well: "Police
see the structure of the gang as revolving around a few central leaders,
usually older boys who 'call the shots' on what will and will not be done.
This latter premise in turn leads to one of the primary police tactics in
dealing with gangs—to 'get the leaders'" (1971, 18). Piliavin and
Werthman report that police often see all juvenile residents of "bad
neighborhoods" as suspicious and "weakly committed to...moral order" (1967, 76). The tactic of harassment is one that gives officers satisfaction, since the gang member, to their mind, has probably done
something wrong, anyway. It is assumed that these policies deter gang
youth from violating the law.

What have been the results of this approach? While liberals and
conservatives often come to different answers regardless of the facts,
we decided to ask the gang members interviewed to give us their opinions. We also tracked the effect of incarceration on gang involvement for
the entire founding group.[18]

If there was one subject nearly all gang members interviewed agreed on, not surprisingly, it was police harassment. Less than five percent of those interviewed, when asked to grade the Milwaukee Police Department Gang Squad's performance, gave them passing marks. Seventy-five percent gave them "D"s or "F"s.

It will be argued, of course gang members will grade the police that way. But it was not the legitimate law enforcement functions of the police that were so strongly criticized. In fact, five of the forty seven we interviewed wanted to pursue careers in law enforcement. The gang founders believed the police should be carrying out their duties in a different manner. One in five said the police should "go after the real criminals." Another one in four said the police ought to "stop harassing" kids who have not committed a crime.[19] And one in four said the police ought to "talk to kids more," get to know who they are dealing with rather than see the gang as "just a bunch of criminals."

Some pointed out the negative consequences of police harassment both for individuals and minority communities.

Q. What does being in a gang mean to you today?

A. I don't know. It's just that a lotta my friends are into it, and I'm into it. And what got me into the gangs was SH (gang squad officer).

Q. Why do you say that?

A. OK. I would be walking with (two of my friends) and he says, "Oh three 'Folks,' huh." I told him, "Man, I ain't gang-related, man." And then he goes, "Oh, *who you walk with is who you are.*" I said, "Do whatever you want, man, it's your job. And if you're doing it wrong, that's your fault." And then they put me in the book—in his book, with the criminals and stuff.
                    Bill, Timeboys

Q. So let me give you another job. The Police Chief comes in here and he says, "All right, Dante, I'll make you the head of the Gang Squad tomorrow." What would you tell them to do, different than they do now?

A.   I think I would probably be less abusive than what
they are now. And instead of riding them all the
time, why not walk and talk and get to know the kids
before you label them. I mean a lot of them are being
pulled away before they're Kings or Cobras or
anything, and they're being leaned up against the
cars, searched. Get to know the community and
really find out what it's about

Dante, Latin Kings

Though some of those interviewed exhibited hostility toward police,
most had clear opinions about police priorities.

Q.   If the Chief made you Captain of the Gang Squad,
what would you tell them to do differently?
A.   Stop arresting people for that petty stuff. Like for
loitering. And they might be picking on people over
here for loitering, and they fighting right over there.
And that's how come people are getting killed and
stuff, 'cause they starting over here with a little petty
tickets, and people over there stabbing each other.

Tiny, Cobra Stones

While there is understandable resentment of police tactics of harassment, we should not underestimate the effect police policies play in
strengthening and forming gang identities. We should recall the process
of gang formation we explored in Chapter Four. The gang forms itself in
response to conflict not only with other groups, but with police as well.
This conflict is what shapes and organizes the gang and its delinquent
identity. And, as in the case with Bill above, police tactics can even help
to recruit new members. When special harassment policies aimed at
gangs are added to already existing police hostility to minority communities, we can see how the response to police from minority youth labeled as "gang members" can reinforce, rather than weaken anti-social
tendencies.

What happens then when the police are "successful" and a gang
member is incarcerated? Does the prison or jail experience deter gang
members from gang activity?

The literature on gangs and prisons prompts us to be quite cautious about the incarceration approach. As far back as the 1920s

Thrasher warns "that sending a gang boy away to an institution turns out to be little more than one method of evading the real problem—that of adjusting him in his actual social world" (1963, 350).

But today is much different than Thrasher's 1920s. Jacobs points out that the "actual social world" of gang members is no longer a gang life on the streets and a separate institutional world. His study of Stateville, Illinois, prison gangs suggests that "the inmate organization is best understood as an extension of an identical organization imported from the streets of Chicago" (1974, 397). The organization of prison gangs has transformed the prison experience for gang members and other inmates. Wisconsin prisons today, in our informants' reports, are similar to Stateville as Jacobs describes it: "The gang thing is the most significant reality behind the walls" (399).

Instead of a separation from their "homeboys," prison often reinforces gang ties. Moore explores the "continuities" between the prison and the barrio as a support network for Chicano gang members. But she also points out a second phenomenon within California's prison, the growth of the "Mexican Mafia" and "La Familia" as organized crime networks. The social role of "continuities" of the gang in prison needs to be differentiated from the purely economic role of the organized prison gangs in controlling the prison's illegal economy.

Our informants have described a different pattern in Wisconsin's prisons. The formation of Wisconsin prison gangs seems to have developed separately and parallel with gang formation on the streets of Milwaukee and other Wisconsin cities. The injection of 1980s Milwaukee street gangs into the Wisconsin State prison system is just beginning to have an effect. No studies of prison gangs in Wisconsin have looked clearly at the problem. Our method in our interviews was simply to ask whether gang members share the belief that incarceration will break up their gangs. Those interviewed largely believed that prison strengthens gang involvement.

Most of the gang members interviewed held fairly conventional views concerning prison. Most felt that "prison was a good thing because it punished people who have done wrong." Most also felt that prison has a "good effect" because one could learn a trade. But almost two thirds felt more strongly that prison had a "bad effect" because "people learn how to become better criminals." Nearly four in five felt that prison had a "bad effect" because it "dehumanized" prisoners. Nearly nine of ten black males thought prison "dehumanized" prisoners. Over 80% of all those interviewed felt that juvenile or adult prison experience had had no effect or had made the institutionalized gang members more involved with the gang. For example, we asked two Vicelords how gang members are affected by incarceration in Wales, a juvenile correction facility:

> **A.** They be more thirsty for gang activity. Come out thinking they key man or somebody and knock them out immediately. If a dude got out of Wales today, within a week he be in a fight already.
> *Chuck, Vicelords*

> **Q.** Are juveniles in the gang afraid of being taken to Wales?
> **A.** Well, they don't wanta go, but when they get there they don't seem to mind too much to me. 'Cause they come out doing the same old thing. Come out and seems like they're stronger. (You) get more respect 'cause you been in jail.
> *Steve, Vicelords*

These opinions that jail serves to strengthen gang involvement could be considered self-serving in our interviews. However, when we looked at the 147 male gang founders who had been to prison, we received strong confirmation of our respondents' opinions.

While sending a gang member to prison is thought to be a deterrent for gang membership, jail time seems to have had little effect on male gang involvement for the founding group of Milwaukee's gangs. Seventy percent of all black male gang members who founded the gang had been incarcerated or institutionalized for more than a few weeks. Less than 10% of those black youth ended their gang involvement after their release from confinement. While in jail, involvement is clearly deepened, consistent with what Jacobs or Moore would predict. Ninety percent of those incarcerated remained involved, and over 80% were involved at least as much, according to those we interviewed.

Incarceration as a method of breaking up gangs is perhaps the worst single policy at the disposal of public officials. Yet it remains the chosen policy, even though our data and other research strongly suggests that use of incarceration to deter gang participation can easily backfire. Elliot Currie has pointed out that nearly 40% of state prison

MALE GANG INVOLVEMENT AFTER INCARCERATION

Involved With Gang After Incarceration	All Males	Black Males	Hisp. Males	White Males
SAME/MORE	66%	69.7%	52%	33.3%
LESS	17%	15.1%	20%	66.7%
NOT AT ALL	14.3%	12.6%	24%	0%
UK/DECEASED	2.7%	2.5%	4%	0%
	N = 147	N = 119	N = 25	N = 3

inmates and 55% of inmates in local jails had not been working full-time in the months before they went to prison (Currie 1985, 105). An even greater percentage of gang members in our study were unemployed. The pressure to stay with the gang after prison and find illegal ways to survive appears as a rational alternative for gang ex-cons.

The stages Milwaukee and other cities have gone through have two factors in common. First, they are stages that confirm a law enforcement framework for confronting the problem of youth gangs. Second, each stage is marked by strong opinions based on very few facts. Research is absent or is poorly done and has served merely to confirm existing opinion and leave established policy unchallenged.

The strategy of making gangs invisible is unlikely to work. The economic, demographic, and institutional trends that have produced the new underclass gangs will not be altered by large-scale incarceration of gang members. Not only will gangs continue in the communities, but the impact of prison on existing gangs is likely to create even more difficulties.

So Where Do We Go from Here?

First, we might summarize, in sociological fashion, a few of the conclusions of this book. Modern gangs have been largely framed as a "crime problem," but we have taken a somewhat broader focus. We believe the recent emergence of gangs in middle and smaller-sized cities is tied up with demographic trends, deindustrialization, the continuing problem of race in our cities, as well as other variables. Our study, somewhat eclectically, has tried to pick and choose from past theories, while standing firmly on the ground of our own research.

Like Thrasher, Suttles, Moore, and others, we believe gangs are spontaneous products of local communities, best understood by analyzing local conditions and group process. Those who look to "diffusion" or conspiracy theories of gang development or who hope to find easy "solutions" from outside gang "experts" are mistaken.

Unlike Cohen and most others, we found gangs today to be composed of both juveniles and adults. The reasons for this altering of the maturing out process are to be found in the contemporary division of the U.S. economy into largely separate, segmented labor markets. The collapse of public education for poor urban minority youth has segregated an entire generation within a labor market that promises a bleak future.

With Cohen, we believe gangs have a rebellious aspect, but the rebellion, unlike the "class consciousness" or "racial solidarity" predicted by Cloward and Ohlin, is often cynical and directed against the gang's own community. Unlike Whyte, Suttles and others, we find some of today's gangs have become estranged from their neighborhoods and have not played a functional role within them. In some places, black gangs have become alienated from their neighborhood at least partly because of the discriminatory effects of desegregation. We share with Miller his concern about the serious consequences of the greater availability of guns today.

With Moore, we see "hustling" and petty crime as endemic to minority gangs and their depressed communities under present economic conditions. The development of organized crime, especially the organized sales of drugs, is one of many possible paths for some of today's gangs. To label all gangs "organized crime" because some are, however, is unscientific and wrong.

With Yablonsky we see most gangs as not very organized. But unlike Yablonsky, we do not see the gangs as "near-groups" of sociopaths, or as a "core" of sociopaths and a "fringe" of impressionable youth. With Thrasher and others, we see gangs as unique coalitions of age-graded groups, often no more nor less criminal than others similar to them in their communities. Gangs will have their share of sociopaths as well as many well-rounded, "normal" youth.

Gangs are a major problem for minority communities today, but to label them above all a "crime problem" is one-sided and points to answers that may lead to greater problems. With Jacobs, we find prison to be a response to gang activity that can lead to more organized gangs with a more deviant and criminal nature. With Moore, we find gangs are extremely receptive to community programming. We find that most cities have not balanced their law enforcement emphasis with equal resources spent on genuine community programs. We share Currie's perspective that while full, meaningful employment will not solve all the problems, it would solve most of them.

This book is a call for more research devoted to the realities of modern gangs within each city. We find sociology has been neglectful of late to the important social fact of urban minority gangs. Too often academia has slipped into viewing gangs solely from a generic criminal justice perspective and has forgotten the university's role as critical analyst. Research has become professionalized, quantified, and, all too often, sterilized. Moore's collaborative methodology deserves praise and replication.

The result and ultimate meaning of research lies for us not in "disinterested enlightenment," however, but in recommendations for policy. We hope this book contributes to the formulation of policy in each city based on facts, not stereotypes.

With Wilson, we believe that a minority underclass is becoming entrenched in our nation's cities. This underclass is the result of the changing structure of the U.S. economy accompanied by a weakening of institutions within poor minority communities. Gangs have become institutionalized within some minority ghettos as one means for juveniles and young adults to cope with present conditions.

Finally, with Moore, we call for participation of the gangs and the underclass in research and in the formulation of policy. To see this class as capable only of welfare, meaningless work, or prison is profoundly reactionary. We believe this society is capable of making its promise available for the underclass, thus abolishing it. We believe, however, that this will happen only if pressure is brought for change, and the underclass itself becomes organized.

Like most of our readers, we suspect, we are not terribly optimistic for the immediate future. But for us "struggle" is a constant; only the forms of struggle are variable. We encourage all who read this book to struggle against ignorance and for a more humane and knowledgeable social policy towards gangs and the underclass.

A Practical Agenda

While these remarks may summarize the place of our perspective within sociological traditions, the reader might suspect we have a more concrete agenda on our minds. This book has been somewhat schizophrenic, trying to be comprehensible to the policy maker or community leader and at the same time to formulate an argument within sociological theory. If we have failed in our efforts to reach either group of readers, we can only say we have tried.

The conclusions of a book like this one are often its worst part, usually because the authors are academics who have little to do with their "research subjects" except exploit them for a book. Many authors have no practical experience and their conclusions often prove that point. This book was written not only to better explain the realities of today's gangs, but also in the hope that we might influence public policy. Change, however, has proven to be harder than we thought. Gangs are not a sympathetic social problem, like the homeless. The image of gangs inspires fear, not pity. No Hollywood entertainer has organized a "Gang-Aid" concert, and none are likely to do so. Our sympathies are not often extended to those who actively rebel against their station in life, especially those who do so non-politically and destructively.

When we asked the gang founders what should be done, they answered straightforwardly:

> **Q.** OK, we're at the end here. The Governor comes in.
> He says, Darryl, I'm gonna give you a million dollars
> to work with gangs. Do what you want with it.
> **A.** Give 'em all jobs.

The lack of "good jobs" is clearly the major factor that has transformed the gang problem in the past decades. But just as the "easy answer" of prison is not one we favor as a final solution to the gang problem, the "easy answer" of jobs is also not so easy. The transforming of our economy to one of full employment and the abolition of the underclass is not on the nation's immediate agenda, no matter how urgent the need.

We face two additional problems in trying to give direction to those concerned with policy and program for gangs outside Milwaukee. First, our own local recommendations have not met with favor from those with institutional power. Our analysis seemed to alienate everyone—city hall, the police, schools, and community based agencies alike. The conservatives thought we were bleeding hearts and the liberals called us racists and worse. While we have certainly not given up, we have not yet been able to accomplish much for those still hanging out on street corners across Milwaukee.

A second reason we are cautious about listing recommendations flows from our analysis of gangs. Even a cursory reading of our book must impress anyone that while this is a book about gangs, it is also a book about Milwaukee. To understand gangs, one must understand the cities and local communities where gangs are found. Gangs vary not only between cities, but within cities, between ethnic groups and sexes, and over time. And as we have shown in Chapter Four, even the age groups within each gang vary as well. Public policy needs to take all these factors into account. Our recommendations in Milwaukee could hardly fit the gang problem in New Haven, Phoenix, or Miami. Our book is meant to be read more as a method than as an answer.

But with these two disclaimers, we can share with our readers three practical lessons from our experience in trying to "do something" about gangs:

(1) Gang members must participate in any meaningful programs. By "participate" we mean gang programs need to train and hire former local gang members as staff, utilize older gang members as consultants in developing new programs, and make sure input from the gang "clients" takes place and is genuine. Everyone is trying to figure out how to "manage" the underclass, while the crucial problem is how to organize it in a positive way. The social service and community-based agencies that have existed since the 1960s have mostly given up the task of organizing their clients and have concentrated on providing services for the "hard to reach" populations. They have become cost-effective "shock absorbers" for the welfare state.

But it is possible to involve gang members in staffing existing agencies and programs, perhaps helping to rejuvenate them. In Milwaukee, thanks to a grant from the National Center for Neighborhood Enterprises, we conducted a training session for influential adult gang members to prepare them to work in youth or other social service programs. The training concentrated on giving the gang members advocacy skills that could be practically used to get someone out of jail, help with welfare, or get someone a scholarship for vocational training. These are simple skills that can be taught and are useful to the day to day experiences of the gang member. Former local adult gang members are by far the best persons to staff gang programs and are best able to implement a strategy of coopting the gangs. The perennial question of "what works" in gang programs might be the wrong question. The more important question may be "who" is doing the "working."

(2) The main emphasis for dealing with gangs needs to be on creating jobs and improving education, not rationalizing the criminal justice system. This book will not be particularly helpful for those who wish to improve the criminal justice system. While a variety of "diversion" or other kinds of probation or parole programs would be welcome, our emphasis obviously is elsewhere. Indeed, we share with the gang founders a belief in harsh sanctions for serious and violent behavior. We believe, however, it is the criminal act which should merit punishment. The gang member should not be punished merely for who he is.

Too much emphasis has been put on criminal justice programs, and even constructing new "better" programs means shifting more resources to an already top-heavy part of our economy. If the gang problem today is part and parcel of the underclass, then solutions need to stress jobs and education, not merely better means of social control. The problem of full employment with a wage that can support a family is fundamentally a problem of national policy. We suggest support for those politicians who advocate such positions, but urge caution that such advocacy may often be more words than substance. A more tangible objective in Milwaukee has been educational reform, an issue to which many black community leaders, parents, students, and far-sighted business and civic leaders have devoted considerable energy.

The Milwaukee battle over education is a story in itself: as we write, serious consideration is being given to a proposal to separate much of the poorest sector of the black community into its own school district. This battle for the future of our youth, while highlighting the significance of race in today's crisis in education, has been centered on the need to provide a quality education for the largely black underclass. In addition to improving the quality of education, some Milwaukee black leaders have stressed the importance of neighborhood involvement in the schools, of rebuilding the school as a community institution. The best issue for uniting the most people around improving the life chances of the underclass in Milwaukee has been the issue of education.

(3) Good research on gangs is necessary if we are to go beyond the law enforcement paradigm in understanding or policy. Emphasis here is on "good" research. So much that passes for research on gangs is in reality surveys of the perceptions of community leaders, students, and others, along with a recitation of crime statistics to demonstrate how bad the problem is. We have tried to point out in these pages how little we actually know about gangs today. Why have gangs formed in some cities and not others? Does political power of blacks and Hispanics within a city affect gang formation or behavior? Are our findings of continued adult participation in Milwaukee's gangs valid for other cities of similar size? How do we measure the influence of minority institutions and whether that influence is declining? What are the causes for the extreme variation in rates of homicides among gangs? What role is prison playing in gang development in cities where gangs have emerged within the last ten years?

One purpose of this book is to stimulate real gang research in other cities, so we can increase what we know and therefore increase what we know should be done. But just as programs need to include gang members, so should the research. The collaborative method we have learned from Joan Moore and Robert Garcia deserves replication. Without participation from the underclass, there will be no guarantees gang research will help anything but the researcher's career.

The starting place for research on gangs must be the gangs themselves. Zatz (1987) has shown that a careful analysis of crime statistics can demystify popular notions of a "gang crime wave." But while the social reaction to gangs must be soberly analyzed, these conclusions will have little effect without an analysis of the realities of gangs. Those who would pretend there is "no problem" will not be listened to by those in underclass communities who know better or by concerned policymakers. The gang problem must be described honestly, no matter whom it offends, if we are to find workable and humane solutions.

Our research in Milwaukee was aimed at influencing policy in that city, and this book unabashedly tries to use research to influence policy elsewhere. Those who can see no practical answers but more prisons and more police will not easily be convinced otherwise. Though this road of persuasion is surely uphill, we really have no choice but to continue climbing it.

Some others have said research is of no use because the rich don't care and the poor already know the truth. We do not believe reality is quite so simplistic. Books such as this aspire to speak not to gang members and the underclass, but for them. We have tried our best to explain contemporary gangs in a manner that will help the reader understand them as part of an underclass, not merely as a "crime problem." How one poses a problem, we have pointed out, will define how that problem can be solved.

The role of research is to describe a problem honestly so the forward path can clearly be seen by those who wish to find it. It is in this spirit that we began our research and have offered this book.

8

WHAT HAPPENED TO THE PEOPLE AND FOLKS?
POSTSCRIPT 1997

Q.   Do you consider it a job, selling dope?

A.   I consider it a job. A risky job, but yeah a good job is very hard to find. Mostly all the jobs you look for, either they want a high school diploma and if you ain't got a high school diploma, what kinda job are you going to find? Fucked-up job working for what, three-twenty-five an hour, four twenty-five an hour? That ain't going to take you through a month or a week.

Interview with male gang member (1992)

Q.   Some girls feel that when they were teenagers they were angels at home and devils outside. Is that true for you?

A.   Very true. At home I would do as I was told. I was always polite and tried to do as I was told, I didn't want to get whipped again. So once I would hit the streets, I changed.

Q.   Were there any turning points in your teenage years? Things that happened that changed your life for the better or worse?

A.   When I got pregnant, I think that changed my life for better.

Interview with female gang member (1994)

So what happened? Did the people and folks of these pages settle down, or did they stay in the gang? Did the guys "mature out" of the gang and get legitimate jobs—or did they become drug-dealing gangsters? Did female gang members become mothers more concerned for their families than the gang—or did they become new "liberated" criminals? This chapter continues our story of how young male and female gang members lived and tried to find meaning in new, post-industrial conditions.

The fundamental argument of this book is that economic restructuring has had far-reaching implications for central city gangs and their members. Deindustrialization, we speculated, might mean that rather than mature out of the gang, as young boys and girls did in the past, some gang members would stay in a new type of adult gang and try to survive "by any means necessary." We ended the first edition of *People and Folks* with a plea (1) for understanding gang members as part of an underclass, not just as a "crime problem"; and (2) for a public policy that stressed jobs and education more than prisons.

Unfortunately, the economic and social picture we painted in 1988 did not improve as the 1990s began. Wilson's (1987; 1996) analysis of the impact of economic restructuring on the central city proved to be tragically accurate for rustbelt cities like Milwaukee. By 1990 most Milwaukee metropolitan area jobs were for the first time located outside the city (McMahon et al. 1992) and there was no mass transit system to get the central city jobless to the job-rich suburbs. In 1990 African American male unemployment rates exceeded 45% compared to less than 3.7% for all Milwaukee area workers. As African American men entered their twenties, more than half of all jobs they had lasted less than six weeks. Average *annual* incomes in retail trade, where most black men aged 20–24 held jobs, was $2,023; for jobs in service $1,697, and in education $3,084 (Rose et al., 1992).

Reformers came and went in the Milwaukee Public Schools, but the low quality of education remained. More African Americans held responsible positions in local government, but there is no evidence that the elevation of African Americans to sheriff, superintendent of schools, police chief and other top positions translated into much improvement for the black poor. Welfare "reform" succeeded in pushing many young mothers off the rolls and into the low-wage labor market. At the same time child neglect and abuse referrals hit all-time highs (see Hagedorn 1995).

To make matters worse, as the number of jobs in factories declined, the numbers of jobs selling drugs increased. In city after city, gangs were getting involved with the drug trade (Hamid 1990; Fagan 1996) and drug-related violence escalated (Blumstein 1993). Just as our interviews for *People and Folks* ended, the price of cocaine dropped, helping fuel the creation of a mass market. At the same time homicides skyrocketed and Wisconsin's prisons began to overflow with unemployed minority males. The poorly educated young men and women we interviewed in *People and Folks* had few legitimate job opportunities. But dangling in front of them was the tantalizing lure of wildly profitable, albeit dangerous, jobs selling drugs. What would they do?

This chapter seeks to sketch answers to three questions. First, what did happen to these male and female gang members as they became adults? Second, how did they understand their own situation? Finally, in what ways was our "underclass" analysis accurate and what were its limitations? I'll end this final chapter with a short outline of the implications for public policy of what I've learned about gangs.

The Milwaukee Drug Posse and Homegirl Studies

The lives of our original collaborators, John Hagedorn and Perry Macon, diverged as this book was published. As the page proofs for the first edition of *People and Folks* went to press, I accepted a job designing a community-based, family-focused child welfare system for Milwaukee County. Three years later our reforms were frustrated, but my book based on our struggle, *Forsaking Our Children* (Hagedorn 1995), was written to carry on the fight for reform through the printed word. I was happy to get back to gang research after serving a three year sentence in the welfare bureaucracy.

Perry Macon served a different and more traditional kind of sentence, and for more than three years. As cocaine became widely popular, Perry succumbed to it. By the time you read this, Perry will have spent most of the shelf-life of the book he contributed to in one correctional facility or another. His story, unfortunately, is one shared by too many of our respondents. In the America of the nineties, drug addiction and selling drugs are considered crimes, and politicians vie with one another to see who can can be "tougher." Come to think of it, isn't "toughness" one of those cultural traits usually attributed to lower class gang members (e.g., Miller 1958; Sanchez-Jankowski 1991)? But I'm getting ahead of myself.

With the expansion of cocaine sales, the gang scene was radically changing as *People and Folks* came out in 1988. I discussed the possibility of a follow-up study with many of the gang members I had interviewed. Along with Jerome Wonders, Clinton Holloway and some others, Joan Moore and I drafted a proposal to the National Institute on Drug Abuse to examine the "patterns of drug abuse and the structure of drug dealing among Milwaukee inner city gangs." In 1991, NIDA funded a three-year study of male gangs and later granted funding for a two-year study of female gangs.[1]

Our follow-up studies were collaborative, modeled after Joan Moore's earlier Los Angeles work (1978; 1991). Former gang members, including Lavell Cox, Amelia Holloway, Clinton Holloway, Rita Lewis, Dora Rodriguez, Frances Turloch, Jorge Silva, Angelo Vega, and Jerome Wonders worked together with Joan Moore, Mary Devitt, and me in developing the three-hour interview questionnaire. After being trained in interview techniques, these former gang members did most of the interviewing. They coded data in FolioViews™, entered it into SPSS™, reviewed drafts of all the articles, and assisted in presenting our findings at professional conferences. Our staff was the linchpin of the entire study.[2]

In 1991–1992, we interviewed 90 males who were on the rosters of 14 male gangs. We also interviewed 11 females, and we used those interviews to set up a second set of interviews in 1994 with 73 female gang members from 8 female gangs. Twenty-three of those we interviewed in these two studies had also been interviewed for *People and Folks*. Most of those interviewed for the follow-up studies were in their late twenties. Our questions asked them to look back over their lives in the gang, their family history, educational and employment history, future plans, and experience with drugs and drug dealing. We specifically focused on interviewing gang members from three different kinds of neighborhoods: one poor central city African American neighborhood, surrounded by other poor black neighborhoods (our staff named it "Hustletown"); one poor African American neighborhood undergoing gentrification ("Posse Park"); and a third Latino neighborhood of first settlement for immigrants ("La Parcela"). We also went over with each gang member what had happened to all of their homeboys and homegirls who were listed on our rosters. Finally, we surveyed non-gang residents in those three neighborhoods about their attitudes towards gangs and drugs.

Our method included three unusual features for gang research. First, unlike some other studies, we did not interview only those whom we could easily find, or those gang members who eagerly wanted to be interviewed. Would you go into a factory, police department, or hospital and interview only someone who jumped up and down and said "Interview me! Interview me!"? While you might get some "inside" information, wouldn't you want to interview others, to see if they were alike or different from the person who so eagerly wanted to "tell all"? Might there be different types of gang members (Hagedorn 1994b) and might interviews with only one or two similar members be misleading? In social science lingo, gangs are not "unknown populations" (Biernacki and Waldorf 1981) and they therefore can be sampled. One component of our collaborative method was to interview entire rosters of gangs, or, failing that, to interview a representative sample from a roster (see Moore 1991; Joe 1993).[3]

Second, even if you get a "representative" gang member, how can you tell if what he or she is saying is no more than a "show" to impress the interviewer? The trick of gang research is *not* to get gang members to say something outrageous. That's easy. Social science, in Goffman's (1959) words, needs to report conversations that take place "backstage," where more inside information is shared. We addressed the problem of "hype" by having lifetime friends of the respondents do the interviewing. How can someone lie about drug dealing when the interviewer sold drugs with him? We also could check wild or deceitful claims since we generally had interviewed most or all of the members of a gang.

Third, our interviews were not "one-shot" deals, where the respondents' only contact with the researchers was during the interview. Wild stories or lies were minimized in part because later in the day the respondent would have to face his/her interviewer back in the "hood." We spent many hours helping our respondents solve employment, housing, educational, and court-related problems. Our interviews most often "worked" because they were seen as legitimate by both our peer interviewers and most respondents.

Collaborative research has its problems (see Hagedorn 1996), but it netted us more than 3,000 pages of remarkable transcripts of interviews as well as vast amounts of quantitative data. But before I display for you some of the data, I need to spend a few pages streamlining the eclectic theoretical framework I used in *People and Folks*.

Social Science and the Impact of Economic Restructuring

The central issue in gang research in the last ten years has been a debate on the impact of economic restructuring on gangs. One contribution of *People and Folks* has been its reframing the gang problem in a manner which was compatible with William Julius Wilson's social disorganization theory. Others have also seen recent economic changes as having had a large impact on gang behavior (Taylor 1989, 1991; Bursik and Grasmick 1993; Fagan 1996) or have interpreted the impact in more nuanced ways (e.g., Moore 1991; Klein 1995; Spergel 1995). A handful of academics, however, have embraced some brand of cultural deviance theory (Miller 1990; Katz 1988; Sanchez-Jankowski 1991). These men have seen less change, and found the source of gang behavior in relatively stable character or lower-class subcultural traits.[4]

In reviewing this vast body of contemporary academic research, our earlier statement (p. 26) of "too much theory, too few facts" must be revised. We now have lots of studies, of uneven quality, but theoretical development has been almost completely stalled. While good research is still vital, an equally important task is to develop theoretical frameworks to understand the data, and to render it useful to those suffering most from economic restructuring. In my view, in order to develop new theory, we need (1) to pay more attention to the influence of gender in male and female gang behavior (Daly and Chesney-Lind 1988), (2) to explore what kind of values are held by underclass gang members (Miller 1969; Wilson and Sampson 1995), and (3) to revisit the debate of whether poor gang-ridden communities are "disorganized" or organized differently (Shaw and McKay 1942; Sutherland 1934; Whyte 1943). Exploring these three issues reveal some limitations of social disorganization theory. Let's spend a few pages looking at how contemporary gang research has treated these issues and then use our data to break ground for a somewhat different approach.

Female Gangs and the Stability of Gender Roles

First, there has not been much attention paid to the impact of economic restructuring on female gang members. Like water for fish, gender is still almost invisible in gang research. While social disorganization theory examines the influence of neighborhood on gang behavior, its proponents often forget that the same neighborhood conditions impact male and female gang members quite differently. To take an obvious example, male gang members are much more violent than female gang members. Thus it is something about *gender* that interacts with neighborhood conditions to produce different behaviors. Most male gang researchers have ignored the growing literature that sees men and women as "doing gender" and looks at variation in how different "masculinities" and "femininities" are constructed (e.g., West and Zimmerman 1981; Connell 1987, 1995; Messerschmidt 1993, 1995; Hagedorn 1997).

This benign neglect of gender in gang research has also contributed to the dearth of studies of female gangs (Daly and Chesney-Lind 1988; Naffine 1996). Most current studies still focus mainly on male gangs and treat female gangs as less important (e.g., Decker and Van Winkle 1996; Spergel 1995). One reason often cited for the lack of attention to female gangs is that they are less violent than male gangs. Law enforcement interests drive most gang research, and police are simply less interested in female gangs because they are less of a crime problem. This may be a good excuse for law enforcement, but it is no excuse for social scientists. The previous chapters of *People and Folk*s also failed to present an adequate analysis of the female gang experience, and I'd like to remedy my own one-sidedness here (see Hagedorn and Devitt 1996).

On the surface, it would seem that changed economic conditions and more "liberated" attitudes among women may have contributed to an increased number of female gangs and influenced them to become more violent (see Adler 1975). This viewpoint has been argued by Carl Taylor (1993), who has published the only book-length treatment of female gangs in the nineties. He found that while female gangs had been male auxiliaries in the past, the economic and social changes in Detroit's poor African American community led to new more independent attitudes among female gang members. Women, according to Taylor, have joined in the corporate gang life of drug dealing apparently as equals (see also Lauderback et al. 1992; and Bjerregaard and Smith 1995).

For others, changed economic conditions have not necessarily led most gang women to become "more like men." Meda Chesney-Lind (1993, 340), for one, argues forcefully that the media and academics like Taylor sensationalize female participation in gangs:

> As young women are demonized by the media, their
> genuine problems can be marginalized and then ignored.

Statistically, there does not seem to be much proof that women are becoming significantly more violent or involved with serious criminal activities (Steffensmeier and Steffensmeier 1980; Chesney-Lind and Sheldon 1992; Block et al. 1996). While there probably are more female gangs today than ever before, those gangs are apparently much less violent than male gangs and are less involved with drug dealing, especially at the upper levels (Maher and Daly 1996). Some recent research has concluded that the gang is a more harmful experience for women than for men.

For example, Joan Moore (1991) looks carefully at the impact of the gang on East Los Angeles women, and finds that Mexican gang women come from more troubled families than the men and are more stigmatized by the gang experience. Comparing adult women who had been gang members in Los Angeles to those in Milwaukee, Moore and Hagedorn (1996) found many differences, but similarities in the difficulties both groups of women had in their adult lives, particularly with respect to drug use. Curry's (1995) balanced review of the literature argues that while gender norms are changing for women, it is also likely that women may be more disadvantaged by gang membership than men.

The underlying issue to be explored, I believe, is the stability of traditional gender roles in an era of economic and social change. Are female gangs the lower class version of the modern "liberated" working women—tough and violent as men? Or might economic changes have reinforced traditional and oppressive gender roles—even for female gang members (see Chodorow 1978; hooks 1981; Bourgeois 1995; Hagedorn in press-b)?

Why women do or don't join gangs and their degree of involvement with violence—as either perpetrator or victim—should be just as important to social science as the behavior of gang men. We need to do more social science studies of the reality of female gang members' lives.

The Influence of Mainstream American Culture

A second issue for contemporary gang research is the rerun of an old controversy: whether gang members adhere to middle class values, or whether they have a separate, lower class value system. Walter Miller is the foremost representative of the culture of poverty school (1969, 1990), which sees lower class men internalizing norms which differ from those of middle class society. For Miller, male gangs are a predictable result of lower class culture, which is characterized by six "focal concerns," such as "toughness" and "autonomy." Therefore, changes in social structure, even those sweeping changes of the last decades, would not alter the basic nature and deviant values of gangs. Martin Sanchez-Jankowski (1991), William Sanders (1994), Jack Katz (1988), and Lewis Yablonsky (1997) are the main proponents of this cultural deviance perspective in modern gang research.

For culture of poverty theorists, violent behavior is not caused by changes in economic conditions, but is an age-old lower class cultural product—i.e., violence is caused by men acting out internalized norms of their violent "subculture." Katz (129) takes this position to an extreme and asserts that gang violence

> does not necessarily follow from the nature of the ghetto as
> an oppressive social background, rather groups must use
> violence to create an oppressive background if they are to
> bring into relief their effective presence as an elite.

William Julius Wilson (1996) disagrees with Katz's understanding of the source of deviant values. Following Ulf Hannerz (1969), he argues that lower class culture is more pliable and more responsive to the environment than cultural deviance theorists believe. For Wilson, writing with Robert Sampson (1995), mainstream values may have become "existentially irrelevant" for socially isolated gang members and many other underclass residents. Elijah Anderson (1994) argues that a "code of the streets" endorsing violence as a way of life arises as a response to social isolation and lack of jobs. Violence becomes valued and prized in itself and is transmitted to younger males as part of a violent gang subculture.

It is important to note, at this point, that the notion of the subcultural transmission of criminal and violent values has been historically controversial in both sociology and anthropology (see Kornhauser 1978).[5] For example, Charles Valentine (1968, 113) stressed that poor people do not form oppositional cultures but firmly hold "middle class values." He argued that

> whatever is distinctive about lower-class life may be no
> more than a situational adaptation to the structural position
> of the bottom stratum in a highly stratified society.

At issue, first, is whether gang youth hold deviant or mainstream values. Culture of poverty theorists have long been unable to rally many social scientists to their case (e.g., Braithwaite 1989; p. 113 of this volume). But, second, we need to assess how great an impact recent ghetto joblessness and social isolation have had on the culture and values of inner city youth. Have social isolation and depressed economic conditions led gang members to adhere to oppositional *values* which explain their violent and anti-social *behavior*? Is American mainstream culture really so weak and pliable that two decades of deindustrialization have given birth to a new set of destructive, violent values among the truly disadvantaged?

These questions prompt us to look more closely at key variables in Wilson's social disorganization theory. Is "social isolation" the main cultural problem for underclass gang members? Or might the internalization of some aspects of American culture by lower class gang members have particularly destructive consequences? This latter view would be more consistent with the views of Robert Merton (1938), who argued that much crime and violence arose from lack of opportunity plus the money-focused nature of a strong American culture (see also Lipset 1996).

How would we find out if gang violence and drug dealing represent mainstream or deviant values? By now, you should know how I would answer that question. We have to do the research and go to the source: gang members themselves.

Are Underclass Neighborhoods Disorganized?

In 1943, the dominant Chicago School social disorganization perspective came under sharp attack with the publication of William F. Whyte's *Street Corner Society*. Whyte argued that poor, gang-ridden communities, like the one he studied in Boston, were not disorganized, but had a discernable organization of their own.

> Cornerville's problem is not lack of organization but failure
> of its own social organization to mesh with the structure of
> the society around it.

Whyte carefully described the humanity of both the college boys and street corner boys of that poor neighborhood, and how the street corner boys organized to meet their economic and social needs. He pointed out that the principal issue for corner boys—actually unemployed young Italian males—was the question of mobility. If opportunity in the world of business was blocked, corner boys were stuck in the world of the rackets which allowed little mobility "up" into the respectable world.

For social disorganization theory, crime, whether the numbers game in Whyte's time or drug sales today, is seen as evidence of *disorganization*. But crime can also be conceptualized, in a manner similar to Whyte, as evidence of extensive illicit *organization*. Most contemporary gang researchers have seen crime as disorganization, but some have dissented.

Martin Sanchez-Jankowski (1991) has described gangs in poor communities as formal organizations, linked to organized crime, and enjoying the support of the community. Sanchez-Jankowski has criticized the social disorganization paradigm, but replaced it with a type of cultural deviance theory. Instead of Miller's "focal concerns" as stable cultural characteristics of lower class males, Sanchez-Jankowski claims that gang members exhibit "defiant individualist" character traits. Rather than humanize male gang members, Sanchez-Jankowski adds to existing stereotypes. Neither does Sanchez-Jankowski apply these "character traits" to women, who appear in his book only as sexual chattel or by-standers (Chesney-Lind 1993).

Others (e.g., Venkatesh 1996), however, have concluded that gang drug organization has a more nuanced role, with the community opposed to violence and the selling of drugs, yet welcoming desperately needed economic benefits. Venkatesh's analysis, and that of some others (Moore 1991; Fagan 1996) is reminiscent of the views of Betty Lou Valentine (1978), who argued long ago that drug selling and other illegal and informal "hustles" should be seen as "hard work."

"Hard work," however, has a different character in our post-industrial world than it did in the industrial era. Wilson (1996, 75) argues that drug dealing, off-the-books hairstyling and car repair, and other jobs in the informal economy are "disorganized" because they do not manifest "regularity of schedules and hours." However, low wage jobs, like those at McDonalds, and even many high wage service jobs, no longer provide—and some do not even require—such regularity (e.g., Toffler 1980, 261–281). "Women's work" has always been more interrupted and less conforming to 9 to 5 routines (e.g., Lorber 1994, 211; Gerson 1985). Knowing how to punch a time clock is less important today than it was when our educational system was training men to be "robots" in a factory (Katznelson and Weir 1985; Edwards 1979; Drucker 1986; Toffler 1990, 71–74).

Conditions in post-industrial poor minority communities, where most people rely on low wage labor, welfare, or illicit and informal "hustles," are unique (Moore in press). But the on-again off-again nature of work in those communties may not be so different than work in many low and high wage jobs in the information economy. Understanding the development of the male gang as an economic force within poor communities may require a more sweeping theoretical reconsideration (Hagedorn in press-c; in press-d).

Bursik and Grasmick (1991) have been among the first to attempt this challenge. They amended social disorganization theory and agreed with Whyte that the main problem for poor communities is their lack of integration with political and economic forces outside the neighborhood (see also Wilson and Sampson 1995). Social disorganization theory in the past has paid too much attention to the private level, or small groups, and not as much attention to the "public" level, or the capacity of a neighborhood to command outside resources. In their policy recommendations, Bursik and Grasmick advocate the inclusion of gangs in community control strategies (176), similar to Shaw and McKay (1969) and others (Moore 1978; Hagedorn 1988). On the other hand, Bursik and Grasmick agree with older versions of social disorganization theory by insisting that serious crime is a prime indicator of social disorganization (21) and, like most criminologists, they neglect gender.[6] Their work, though, coupled with Hunter's (1985), is an important contribution to our understanding.

At issue here is whether we should consider communities "disorganized" because informal and illegal economic organizations are now as prevalent as industrial jobs. Or should we see the problem mainly as a lack of integration of the newly created informal and illegal economic organizations within the formal post-industrial economy? Can we simply amend old theory, or does the post-industrial revolution require some new, and perhaps quite different formulations?

Its time to look at our data to help us shed some light on these theoretical and practical concerns.

The Impact of Economic Restructuring on Milwaukee Gang Members

1. What Happened to the People and Folks?

William Julius Wilson (1996) was only partially right when he argued that a principal characteristic of poor urban neighborhoods was the "disappearance of work." What mainly disappeared, our data show, was work in the industrial and other sectors of the formal economy. For the men especially, what replaced those licit jobs were low-wage, entry-level positions in the informal and illicit economy, particularly selling drugs. Here's a typical story:

> I got out of high school and I didn't have a diploma, wasn't no jobs, wasn't no source of income, no nothing. That's basically the easy way for a black young man to be—selling some dope—you can get yourself some money real quick, you really don't have nothing to worry about, nothing but the feds.

WHAT HAPPENED TO THE GUYS IN THE GANG?
228 founding gang members of 14 male gangs.

	African-Am.	White	Latino	Row Totals	SIG
WORK STATUS					.0001
Working	23.9% (26)	68.8% (22)	27.6% (24)	31.6% (72)	
"Hustling"	55.5% (60)	21.9% (7)	62.1% (54)	53.1% (121)	
Other #	21.1% (23)	9.4% (3)	10.3% (9)	15.4% (35)	
EDUCATION					ns
Graduate or GED	38.3% (31)	28% (7)	31.1% (23)	33.9% (61)	
Not Graduate	61.7% (50)	72% (18)	68.9% (51)	66.1% (119)	
DECEASED	6.4% (7)	6.3% (2)	5.7% (5)	6.1% (14)	ns
STILL LIVE IN HOOD					.01
Yes	50.6% (45)	41.4% (12)	68.1% (47)	55.6% (104)	
No ##	49.4% (44)	58.6% (17)	31.9% (22)	44.4% (83)	
BEEN TO JAIL					
Yes	67.0% (73)	34.5% (11)	69,0% (60)	63.2% (144)	.0001
No	13.8% (15)	46.9% (15)	18.4% (16)	20.2% (46)	
Unknown	19.3% (21)	18.8% (6)	12.6% (11)	16.7% (38)	
GANG INVOLVEMENT					
Some as adult	69.6% (71)	3.1% (1)	80.5% (66)	64.5% (138)	.0001
Same or more than as teen	33.0% (36)	3.1% (1)	54.0% (47)	36.9% (84)	
EVER SOLD COCAINE					.001
Ever sold	69.7% (76)	56.2% (18)	81.6% (71)	72.4% (165)	
Never sold	5.5% (6)	28.1% (12)	4. 6% (4)	8.3% (19)	
Unknown or deceased	24.7% (27)	15.7% (12)	13.7% (12)	19.3% (44)	
COCAINE USE ###					ns
Ever used	39.4% (43)	53.1% (17)	55.2% (48)	47.8% (108)	
Never used	24.8% (27)	21.9% (7)	13.8% (12)	20.2% (46)	
Used Daily	17.4% (19)	15.6% (5)	18.4% (16)	17.5% (40)	
Column Totals	109	32	87	N= 228	

\# in school, unknown, on welfare, or deceased.
\## does not include locked up and deceased
\### does not include locked up, deceased, and unknown

The fantastic promise of money from the dope game was a tremendous pull for unemployed and uneducated gang members. As young men, they had dollar signs in their eyes:

Q. Why did you start selling dope?

A. Shit, fast money, man. Don't you want a big car too? Don't you want cash? Don't you want a house on Lake Drive?

....

A. Why? For the money. For the profits, you know, make money, have everything that I can get. 'Cause the more I got the more I want, know what I'm saying?

Our rosters of the 228 founding members of 14 male gangs shows the avid participation of gang men in drug selling. Since the 1988 publication of *People and Folks*, almost three quarters of the gang men were reported as having been involved with the sale of cocaine. Of the African American men, most *reduced* their gang involvement and *replaced* it with drug selling. A majority of Latinos, on the other hand, actually *stepped up* their gang involvement as adults, while also selling drugs. Nearly all whites stopped their gang involvement, but most had sold drugs. Note that while white male gang members used cocaine at roughly the same levels as minority gang members, more than two thirds were working legitimate jobs, while only about a quarter of African Americans and Latinos held such jobs. Licit jobs hadn't disappeared for these working class whites. Almost all told us they found jobs by utilizing relatives to get them into jobs in remaining area factories.

While our data need more elaboration, it appears that those men who went to prison and returned to live in their old neighborhood were more likely to use drugs and to hustle for a living than those who moved out of their old neighborhood. Cocaine use for adults appeared to be more related to adult experiences of joblessness, prison, and loss of steady relationships, than simply the consequence of earlier family problems (Torres et al. 1996).

The male gang has undergone a fundamental shift in this post-industrial era. The color of money has replaced gang colors as the underlying rationale for the behavior of adult gang members and the structure of their gangs. While not all gangs in other cities have embraced this ethic of hustling, male gangs in Milwaukee, which are almost all involved with the sales of drugs, are quite different than the fighting or petty-criminal delinquent peer groups of past eras. For teenagers as well as their older brothers, the gang now is mainly a way to "make your money" (see Hagedorn, in press-c).

Women Take a Different Path

The situation was very different for the female gang members we studied. Unlike the men, nearly all the women left the gang by the time they turned twenty. In Milwaukee, there is no such thing as an adult female gang and there were few adult female gang members. While drug selling involves women as well as men, most women who did sell drugs were involved with men's drug selling operations, not their own. While almost all Latinas as well as African American women had left the gang by the end of their teenage years, a quarter (26.4%) of Latinas still lived in the old neighborhood, compared to less than ten percent (8.3%) of African Americans. For the women, as for the men, staying in the old neighborhood increased the risk of heavy drug use. The female gang itself has remained primarily an adolescent experience.

The female ex-gang members we interviewed had high hopes for their lives. While male gang members gave generally optimistic answers to our question about what they expect to be doing in five years—like working a full-time job, or owning an undefined business—female ex-gang members gave very specific responses. More than half (57.6%) had professional or para-professional career goals, most of them in traditionally female professions, like nursing, nurses aid, or teaching, but quite a few had non-gendered career choices. Another ten percent mentioned family-related goals, and ten percent mentioned both family and career goals. Many saw the gang experience as having severely harmed their futures, like this woman:

> **Q:**   All in all, looking back, do you think the gang was more of a positive experience for you or more of a negative experience?
>
> **A:**   Negative. Because I think I would have gone on to college had I not been in a gang. My life would have been different, even now.

The lofty plans of ex-gang women contrasted with a more sober reality, consistent with Joe and Chesney-Lind's (1995, 413) view that gang girls' "future aspirations are both gendered and unrealistic." Half of our sample were on AFDC and nearly three quarters had not completed high school. About a third reported that they had wanted to go to college when they were teenagers, but less than a fifth had any vocational or post-high school training.

While women may have been as carefree and aggressive as the boys while teenagers, their behavior changed as they became mothers. Most women considered the needs of their family far more than did the men. Some women, however, became depressed with family responsibilities, which they often faced alone, and lapsed into cocaine use. Nearly a quarter of the females were using at age 19, after they had left the gang. Half of the women who had children admitted to some cocaine use as mothers. Women who were more traditional, particularly Puerto Ricans, tended to be users of cocaine as adults. The frustration of high expectations of career goals may also contribute to adult strain and drug use. Those gang women who did use cocaine, as well as gang men, experienced a sharp rise in cocaine use in adulthood.

Nearly all the women we interviewed (88.7%) were mothers, with about half either married (5.6%) or with plans to marry (38.9%) the man they were with. More than half had been teen mothers. How to care for their children was a central question for these women, and many had repeated problems with the irresponsible behavior of men. Ten percent were uncertain about whether they would marry their partner and a sixth (16.7%) had no plans to marry the man they were with. More than a quarter (27.8%) had no steady man at the present time. Some, but not most of the women, were seriously harmed by the gang experience. A small number were sexually exploited by gang men. Those who viewed their gang experience negatively were significantly less likely to have ever held a good job.

This not-so-rosy picture is underscored when we look at what happened not only to our respondents, but to all the girls who were found on our rosters of eight female gangs. Since most of the women were young mothers and low-income, its not surprising that most (58.4%) were supported by AFDC and about a quarter (28.6%) were working. Two thirds (68.6%) did not graduate from high school. Nearly half (42%) had done some time in jail. Half had used cocaine to some degree. Almost all (95.4%) were reported as no longer being involved

WHAT HAPPENED TO FEMALE GANG MEMBERS? 176 Founding Gang members from Five African American and Four Latina Gangs*

	African Americans N= 84	Latinas N= 92	Significance
Working	36.3%	20.3%	p< .0001
On AFDC	43.8%	74.3%	p< .0001
No longer in Gang	98.8%	92.3%	N.S.
Completed High School	46.6%	21.9%	p< .0001
Completed less than 10th Grade	13.3%	35.6%	p< .0001
Ever Used Cocaine	12.7%	69.5%	p<.0001
Used Cocaine Daily	8.5%	45.8%	p<.0001
Still Lived in Gang Neighborhood	8.3%	26.4%	p< .001
Been to Jail	44.0%	40.2%	N.S

* There were no neighborhood-based white female gangs in Milwaukee when we did our interviews.

with the gang, and a large majority (82.2%) had moved out of the old neighborhood.

Latinas may have been more disadvantaged by their gang experience than African American women. Latinas were significantly more likely to be on AFDC, to have completed less education, and were more likely to still be living in their old neighborhood. While our data are not conclusive, it appears that those Latinas who were more traditional in their attitudes toward men and their role as mothers were the most disadvantaged by the gang experience (Hagedorn and Devitt 1996).

How did the men and women of our study interpret the impact of deindustrialization on their lives? Read on.

2. The Dark Side of the American Dream

Gang members have always been more like typical kids in poor neighborhoods than some crazed, far-out, deviant breed (see Short 1997). Neither male nor female Milwaukee gang members were homogeneously poor, and most did not come from dysfunctional families. A third of the male and female respondents in our 1990s study came from families who at one time owned their own home. Only a quarter of our respondents came from families with a significant history of drugs, gangs, or crime, while another quarter came from families with no history at all of criminality, drug use, gang involvement, or alcoholism. Half of the respondents were from families who came to Milwaukee fleeing problems in Chicago or another big city (Hagedorn in press-a). These families moved to Milwaukee looking for hope. But as their sons and daughters reached their teenage years, full-time, high-paying legal jobs had all but disappeared, clouding their future.

Gang women, as they became adults, had settled into traditional roles of motherhood, downgraded their expectations, and courageously tried to balance their mothers' duties with a modest career. Most of the gang men, however, fearing that the loss of good jobs meant they would have no future, acted more brashly. Seeing the money to be made selling drugs, as a group they swallowed the lure of the dope game, hook, line, and sinker. If the fetishism of money is an essential characteristic of the American Dream, the modal answer to the question "Why did you start selling dope?" went something like this:

> My main reason was for the money. I'm in love with the
> money!

Since conventional ways to make their money were blocked, a portion of poor males found other paths. In America, wanting more material goods is hardly a deviant goal, but the product of heavy advertising in a consumer culture (Nightengale 1993; see also Leach 1993). For gang members and other poor youth, the pursuit of money and success by innovative, illegal means is a close fit to both Durkheim's (1951) and Merton's (1938) concepts of anomie (see Hagedorn 1997; in press-a). People with this anomic mentality are clearly described by one writer as tending

> to be crass, excitable, street-smart, aggressive, and driven
> almost solely by the pursuit of quick profits.

You may be surprised to learn that those words are not a description of gang culture, but were written by James Stewart (1991, 36) describing the *culture of arbitrageurs* on Wall Street in the 1980s. Have I made my point? The cultural emphasis on making money "by any means necessary" is a general American malaise, *not* an example of deviant ghetto values (see Agnew et al. 1996; Lipset 1996).[7]

Wilson argues that violence, gangs, and other deviance is the result of "social isolation" (1987, 1996). Milwaukee gang members, however, while they may have been isolated from licit job networks, grew up totally immersed in American culture, just like you and I. In their homes too, the TV set was always on, showcasing media stars like Michael Jordan shilling expensive Nike shoes. Cop shows and violent movies were the nightly prime time "entertainment." Young gang members' daily lives were not only spent learning from an unemployed older brother, but being constantly tantalized by TV images of the lives of the rich and famous and seeing movie stars flaunt their flashy jewelry and fashionable clothes. Debra Prothrow-Stith (1991, 37) pointed out that the white and black consumers of heavy metal and rap music are the first generation of people "nurtured on television's steady diet of fictional and nonfictional mayhem."

For the men, music videos, among other media, portrayed women as little more than sexual objects for casual use by "macho" he-men. For male gang members, who had seen the American Dream fade as globalization snatched their jobs away, the media images of affluence created severe strains. What is the measure of manhood and the pre-eminent cultural goal for all red-blooded American men? Isn't it to have plenty of money...and foxy women too? The rap group N.W.A. translated these most American of values into street talk when they sang: "Life ain't nothin' but bitches and money." Milwaukee male gang members tried to live the way N.W.A. rapped. These dark elements of American culture exercise a strong influence on lower class men and women (for a contrary view see Kornhauser 1978).

But for Milwaukee gang members, the fast life burned out quickly. While male gang members made on the average about $2400 per month selling drugs, they made less than $700 monthly in legitimate jobs. So which do you think they did more?... No, you probably chose wrong. Despite the fact that they could earn four times as much by dealing, *most of these young adult gang drug dealers worked more months in low-wage legitimate jobs than they did selling drugs* (Hagedorn 1994b). The desire to settle down with a family has proved, over the long haul, to be more powerful for most gang members than the worship of fast money.

MEAN MONTHLY INCOME FROM DRUG DEALING: 1989–1991
87 African American and Latino Respondents[9]

Average Monthly Income From Drug Sales	African American	Latino	Totals
Never sold	15.8%	23.3%	18.4%
Less than $1000 monthly (Equivalent to less than $6/hour)	28.1	30.0	28.7
Between $1000 and $2000 monthly (Equivalent to $7–$12/hour)	28.1	6.7	20.7
Between $2000 and $4000 monthly (Equivalent to $13–$25/hour)	25.3	33.3	28.7
More than $10,000 monthly	1.8	6.7	3.4
Total N=100%	57	30	87

This young man realistically sums up the sober motivation for most gang members selling drugs.

Everybody needed money, and I think when we was growing up we needed money but we didn't know we needed money as badly as we do. So we was doing other things to try keep ourselves busy and happy cause we didn't have any money. And nobody was trying to help us to get jobs or trying to, you know, talk to us about what we were going to do in the future…but it seems like we weren't going to have a future. Seems like we weren't going to make it.

As far as economic-wise, everybody knew you have to survive. And that looks right now not trying to be a Donald Trump, but just thinking about trying to survive, keep a place, a roof over your head, food in your stomach. That's what people like us are trying to do right now, a hustle, yeah. Whether it's going to school or working or street hustling, which most of us do when we can't get a job. Because we have obligations, you know…our families and to ourselves. Okay?

This man ended his interview with this clear and human plea:

Q. The interview is over. Do you have anything to add?
A. Yes. I would like to say, uh, all blacks are not bad
people and all dope dealers are not bad people either.
But a person must do what they have to do to survive
in this world. And if it's giving drugs, then let it be....
They wanted work, can't get no work. So they got to
do what they got to do to take care of their families.

A minority of gang members—we call them "new jacks"—had given up any hope of settling down and recklessly committed themselves to the drug economy, at least for a time. But for most male gang members, the age-crime curve still held, and adult gang members were looking for steady "legit" jobs by the end of their twenties. Participation in the post-industrial male gang had been extended from the juvenile to the young adult years, but sharply tailed off by the time most gang members turned thirty. Significantly, most of these men settled down *whether or not they had been to prison.*

I have found that anomie theory, rather than a social disorganization perspective, is a better way to understand gang participation in the drug economy. In Merton's (1968) conception, *innovation* (that is, *crime)* is one response of poor people who are not able to conform to conventional success goals by legitimate means. Instead of being arenas for conflicting value systems, poor communities would be seen by anomie theory as places where residents embrace mainstream values but react in patterned ways to difficulties in attaining success.

An updated anomie theory would logically understand drug dealing today as the innovative response of young minority males to blocked opportunity resulting from economic restructuring (see Fagan 1996). In that sense, the *cultural* understanding of making money "by any means necessary" is no different for gang members on First Street than for arbitrageurs on Wall Street. And rather than seeing male behavior as some "hyper-masculine" response of emasculated ghetto males, anomie theory would look at gang men acting out mainstream "masculinities" under more severe economic conditions (see Connell 1987, 1995; Messerschmidt 1993; Hagedorn 1997, in press-b).

Women Talk About Their Lives

Anomie theory has been long criticized for ignoring women, but it is not hard to see how traditional gendered roles—for example, the "good mother," or the sexily coiffured Barbie doll—influence how female gang members, like other women, see themselves (Campbell 1991, 1993; Douglas 1994). For most gang women, like their white middle class counterparts, "relational" goals of motherhood and family have overall proved to be more important than male goals of success and money (Gilligan 1982; Leonard 1983). Our interviews were filled with frank accounts of gang women discussing how they and their families could make it.

Most women accepted the fact that the men were not able to support their families.

> **Q.** Has the father of your child met all his responsibilities?
> **A.** I mean the situation he's in...yes and no, but when things get better, he will do what he is supposed to do.

> **Q.** How does your daughter feel about that?
> **A.** She's a very understanding child and she loves her father, she loves her father very much.

> **Q.** How do you feel about him not meeting his responsibilities?
> **A.** Well I understand, you know, the situation at hand, so...I can deal with it until he can do better.

Most of our respondents, particularly the Latinas, wanted a traditional relationship, but were realistic:

> **Q.** The man should be the sole bread winner in the family.
> **A.** It would be nice, but you know, you know....

> **Q.** So you agree?
> **A.** Should. 'Cause a woman should do what she want to do...she shouldn't be working, if she don't have to.

Others, including most African American women, were more emphatic about the problems men caused them and the children, often based on hard experience. They were determined to properly support their kids, regardless of what the men did.

Q.   There aren't many men around today who would make good husbands.
A.   I agree.

Q.   You don't think there's no good men around?
A.   Nope. So don't put no trust or belief in nothing, never not again.

....

Q.   Have the father or fathers of all your kids met all their responsibilities?
A.   I guess you'd say no.

Q.   What do you mean by that?
A.   I can name a lot of shit that they ain't met. Met with shit financially. They don't spend no time, the right type of time with them, they don't try to nurture and teach them something when they are with them.

Q.   How do your kids feel about that?
A.   They don't like it.

Q.   How do you feel about that?
A.   I hate it too. But I don't care. They [the kids] goin' to have everything they need anyway, by *my* doing.

Despite few job opportunities and strained relationships with men, most women in our study looked bravely and confidently toward a conventional future:

Q.   Five years from now what would you want to be doing?
A.   Well, I would like to own my home or in the process of trying to buy me a home. All my kids be at school all day, you know.

Q. Five years from now, what would you *realistically* expect to be doing?

A. Realistically? I feel that that in five years I'm still going to [be doing okay] and I ain't going to stop at all. I'm on the right track and I'm going to stay on it. And nobody gettin' on my nerves!

Why didn't the women, like the men, get involved with the drug economy in large numbers? Men saw not being able to be the "breadwinner" as a blow to their masculinity (Cazenave 1981; Staples 1982) and risked all, including their families, to make money selling dope. While economic restructuring may have reduced the pool of "marriageable males" in the legal economy, the traditional ways these men related to women did not change. In fact, the "sex for drugs" nature of the drug economy reinforced wild, sexist, and misogynist attitudes among the men. It also surely discouraged women from participating in a "man's world" drug game (Bourgois 1995; Hagedorn in press-b).

In order to guarantee their continued availability to their children, women were more likely than men to settle into low paying jobs or accept AFDC than sell drugs. The main problems gang women had as adults were the same as other poor women in neighborhoods where legal jobs were disappearing: how to make ends meet and still raise a family, get adequate childcare and job training, and how to deal with lousy schools and gang and drug violence. While the men also eventually settled down, the women settled down much earlier.

Women chose to avoid the risk inherent in selling drugs, but they were still faced with forming relationships with men who had not changed their traditional attitudes toward women. While most African American women told us "the way men are today, I'd rather raise my kids myself," most Latinas and many African American women eventually settled into traditional, and sometimes violent relationships with men. In a country where one in every six wives are struck by their husbands at some time in their marriage (Gelles and Strauss 1988), the problem of domestic violence is a nationwide problem.

New Jacks and Violence

While the gang women in our study largely conformed to conventional behavior as young adults, some of the men not only embraced violations of the rules, but rejoiced in it.

> I love selling dope! I know there's other niggers out here
> love the money just like I do.... I'd sell to my own mother if
> she had the money.

Such new jack behavior is often used as evidence of deviant norms. But it can alternatively be conceptualized as *overconformity* to the all-American goals of success, individualism, and making money. In fact, as Messner and Rosenthal (1994) argued, instrumental violence is closely related to anomic attitudes of men who want to make money or achieve other success goals "by any means necessary." Our data, measuring new jack attitudes as amorality in means explicitly in this Mertonian sense, show statistically significant support for the relationship of new jack attitudes and intentional violence (Hagedorn, in press-a).

In other words, gang men who take part in drive-by shootings and violence related to drug sales are more likely than others to exhibit amoral "don't give a damn" attitudes. The drug economy has not created new values, rather it has created acute "anomie" or a state of normlessness in some of those who sell drugs. This means that for "anomic" gang members, anything goes in order to make money or to prove their manhood (Merton 1968, 217). Sixty years ago, Merton (1938, 679–80) saw the same process at work with Al Capone:

> Within this context, Capone represents the triumph of
> amoral intelligence over morally prescribed 'failure,' when
> the channels of vertical mobility are closed or narrowed in a
> society which places a high premium on economic affluence
> and social ascent for all its members

In our data, consider this young man, who vividly explained what selling drugs meant to him:

> **Q:**   How much power does selling drugs give you?
> **A:**   Oh it's given me a lot of power. You know, it's just a

> sensation of you can do anything you want. When you got money in your pocket, you can do anything you want. You can go out there and slap these bitches. You can go out here and shoot this nigger, you just get a power, you just think you are God because you have so much money you think you can do whatever you want to do and everybody knowed what you about.... They will not mess with you, they will respect you, they'll like you, because you make your money.

Note that the power of drugs is not only the power of money, but also power over women. New jack violence is as much related to men "doing gender" as it is to the amoral desire for money.

High rates of male inner-city violence appear to be basically the product of the intersection of poverty with masculinity: boys and men fighting over colors, turf, and respect, the universal possession of guns to settle disputes in the drug economy (Laub and Cook, in press), and the new jack fascination with violence I've just described.[9] An indication of the essentially "masculine" nature of violence can be found by looking at gender differences in exposure to violence.

LIFETIME EXPOSURE TO VIOLENCE BY GENDER

	Total Number of times Respondent was Shot at:	Mean per Gang Member	Total Number of People Respondent has Seen Killed	Mean per Gang Member
Male N=68	617	9.1	143	2.1
Female N=68	23	.33	21	.31

The N=68 of the males represents the fact that many Latinos refused to answer these questions, probably because of their continued involvement with drive-by shootings and other unsolved crimes. Thus our male data probably significantly underestimates male violence and underestimates the gulf between male and female exposure to violence.

Women participate in significantly less violence even though guns are available to everyone and having a gun "equalizes" women's generally smaller size. What accounts for these differences? For most adult men, doing gender still means doing violence. But for most adult women, doing gender means holding in and internalizing their rage and/or considering the needs of their family first (Campbell 1993; Cloward and Piven 1979). Many ex-gang members who were mothers told us that they would not have a gun around the house because of their children. On the contrary, today, for gang men, "doing gender" necessarily means having a gun. As Ronmin Ro (1996, 7) put it, street culture has "equated guns with masculinity."

3. The Drug Business and Social Disorganization

Like Whyte's study of young Italian men during the Great Depression, our study finds that economic restructuring has made neighborhood-based economic functions more important for lower class male peer groups. The drug economy is the most profitable kind of informal economic organization which rose to meet the needs of those victimized by deindustrialization. *One major impact of economic restructuring for poor communities has been a sharp reduction in the extent of the licit economy and the vast expansion of an illicit economy, especially the business of selling drugs.*

In order to determine how extensive drug selling was in Milwaukee, I traveled the streets of three different neighborhoods with staff and active drug sellers and mapped cocaine selling spots. The data below reflect only cocaine selling spots that were known to our informants. They exclude heroin sales which were widespread in La Parcela, one of our three study neighborhoods, and other places where different types of drugs were sold. As such they underestimate the true extent of drug dealing in those neighborhoods (Hagedorn 1994a).

These data show that, in at least three gang neighborhoods, there is a drug house or corner where cocaine is sold on roughly every other block. We estimated that each drug selling locale employed or provided work for an average of about seven persons. This meant that the cocaine economy in these selected parts of three neighborhoods, at any one

"DOPE HOUSE" SURVEY

Neighborhood	Blocks surveyed	Number of Drug Houses	All Places where Cocaine was sold	Percent of Drug Selling Places run by Gangs
Hustletown	30	16	23	61%
Posse Park	36	15	19	74%
La Parcela	50	30	43	49%
Totals	116	61	85	58%

time, employed at least 600 people, most of them young male gang members. *These young men grossed over $17 million dollars annually*, if they individually made our mean of $2400 per month. We identified at least 10 other similar high-drug sales gang neighborhoods in Milwaukee. We estimate more than 1500 young men were employed *in those neighborhoods alone* selling drugs in Milwaukee at some time in the early 1990s. It is likely today that drug sales is the largest single employer of young African American and Latino males in Milwaukee.[10]

Tragically the extent of minority participation in the drug economy is the latest twist in a long American saga of racism and discrimination. In what Spear (1967) called an "institutional ghetto," discrimination kept minorities out of the factories and led to many African American men to rely on the numbers game. In fact, Drake and Cayton (1970) found that the numbers game employed more African American males than any other sector of the 1940s Chicago economy. As the formal chains of *de jure* segregation were broken after World War II, industrial jobs opened up for African Americans. But those were the twilight years of the industrial economy. As the industrial jobs disappeared, states like Illinois and Wisconsin began to be ravenous for revenue. State-sponsored lotteries caused the illicit numbers game to wither away and with it jobs as "runners" and other positions which had been mainly held by poor minority males. The hated-by-almost-everyone drug economy became the only viable alternative for economic survival for many African American and Latino males. And like all capitalist concerns, while the drug business provides work, it is mainly profitable for outsiders, not locals.

Gang Drug Selling Organization and Poor Neighborhoods

Cloward and Ohlin (1960) speculated that different neighborhood opportunity structures would produce different kinds of gangs. Today, gang drug selling organizations, like legal businesses, vary by the nature of the opportunity structure or market (Hagedorn 1994a). Where most drug sales were to poor residents, gang drug organization typically dissipated, with individuals competing with one another in "dog-eat-dog" fashion. In neighborhoods adjacent to white or middle class areas, where profits were higher, gang men built small businesses from the ground up. This story may be familiar to anyone who has tried to start any type of small business.

> **Q:** You said before that you sort of tried it, failed, and that the business sort of stopped and started through the years. What do you mean by that?
>
> **A:** It's like, you know, when we first started we didn't know nothing about how to sell it. We just seen everybody else doing it and we just tried to do it, you know. We were seeing everybody else, and it just wasn't working.
>
> **Q:** Like what do you mean? Explain that to me.
>
> **A:** For one, we was giving away too much dope for the price, for the money that we was taking in. And then, for the second part, we was sitting back smoking too much dope. And I think like the worst part of it all was we were going to buy dope and everything, and it'd be so mixed up [not pure cocaine], don't be worth selling. We bought it, we got stuck with it, and it don't be nothing but a loss, and at the time it'd be all our money tied up into it.

Q: So it took a while before you figured out the mechanics of this, how to do it right?

A: Um-hum. It takes time, I say for a person just to jump off into it, if you don't know nothing about it like we did. You gonna end up wondering why in the hell did everybody else make money off it and we can't. And you sit there...you see the dope, you buy the dope, and then you're selling the dope. But then you see you ain't making nothing but what you paid for it, and then after a while, you know, like we started asking questions, figuring out what are you going wrong at....You learn how to go about it without getting beat.

Like gambling before it, the drug economy is looked down on by most respectable citizens. Along with our interviews of gang members, we surveyed their non-gang neighbors and found hostility to youth gangs varied by stake in the neighborhood: i.e., the more committed to the communities adult residents were, the more they thought there might be "some good" in gangs (Moore and Hagedorn 1995). However, there was nearly unanimous condemnation of drug dealing.

This hostility of neighbors toward drugs and gangs was inconsistent, however, with the perceptions of gang drug sellers. Local gang dealers estimated that between a third and half of their neighbors were not only drug users, but their *customers*.[11] This may be an over-estimate and differed from the view of most residents surveyed. Nonetheless, a substantial *minority* of residents we surveyed gave similar estimates of how many of their neighbors used drugs. Gang estimates also corresponded to our data on the extent of drug dealing in those neighborhoods.

Regardless of the true number of area drug users, it is clear that drug selling organizations are deeply rooted in the economic needs of poor young African American and Latino males. The web of relatives and friends who surround these young men have strongly ambivalent feelings about selling drugs. As Venkatesh (1996, 254) points out in Chicago:

In communities such as Robert Taylor Homes, the gang has an economic dimension that is historically unprecedented. With this role, there emerge contradictions and conflicts... in which residents simultaneously support, yet loathe, their local gang.

NEIGHBORHOOD SURVEY

Characteristics of respondents	Hustletown	Neighborhood Posse Park	La Parcela	Total
Ethnicity:				
African American	98.0%	96.0%	8.0%	67.3%
Latino	0	2.0	72.0	24.7
Anglo American	2.0	2.0	20.0	8.0
Respondents who were working	32.7%	40.0%	36.0%	36.2%
Households receiving AFDC	40.0%	48.8%	50.0%	46.2%
Length of residence:				
Less than 6 months	10.0%	8.2%	18.0%	12.1%
6 months to 1 year	12.0	30.6	20.0	20.8
1 to 5 years	22.0	24.5	36.7	26.2
More than 5 years	56.0	36.7	30.0	40.9
Owns his/her own home	32.7	14.3	32.0	26.4
Visits neighbors	54.2	63.2	64.7	60.7
Is a member of some organization	24.5	24.3	13.0	17.4
Feels neighborhood is a good place to live	6.1	24.0	18.0	16.1
If possible, respondent would				
Stay in neighborhood	47.9	71.4	36.7	52.1[†]
Move	52.1	28.6	63.3	47.9
Feels unsafe in street after dark	75.0%	68.8%	72.0%	71.9%
Looks the other way with problems	39.1	31.9	59.6	43.6*
Sees gangs as one of 3 major problems	2.5	36.1	80.9	35.4[†]
Agrees that "gangs are not all bad"	18.4	28.0	18.0	21.4
Would join an anti-gang organization	91.3	83.3	69.4	81.0[‡]
Total N (= 100%)	(50)	(50)	(50)	(150)

[†] Differences between neighborhoods significant past .001.
* Differences between neighborhoods significant past .01.
[‡] Differences between neighborhoods significant past .05.

These deeply ambivalent feelings are mirrored by drug-selling gang members, most of whom saw selling drugs as "unmoral," as one gang member called it, wrong *but* necessary for survival. Here are a few typical views:

Q. Do you consider it wrong or immoral to sell dope?
A. I consider it wrong. But ain't got no jobs out there, they're going to do something to make the money.

. . . .

Q. Do you consider it wrong or immoral to sell dope?
A. Yes and no. Yes, because you know it's wrong. And you consider—really you put poison in the street and you're selling it to your own people. And you selling it to the people that you be around. Even if you ain't cool, there's people in your neighborhood. They ain't going to say no, because if you ain't got no job or no other source of income, what else is there left?

. . . .

Q. Why do you keep selling dope? Why not just get any kind of straight job and work your way up the ladder?
A. Because it's not enough money to pay bills, to pay rent, to buy food, and all that 'cause they just give you minimum wage you know. Yeah, money was too good and good jobs is hard to find, man. 'Cause you go to apply, they think because you're young, they want to try you out and you being in the gang, and they see you young and wear funny haircuts and earrings and all that, people just don't want to try you out.

In other words, gang men sell drugs in order to survive, but they don't like it any more than their neighbors. And like Whyte found a half century ago, the forms of illicit economic and social organization open to young men do not easily translate into finding a "good" licit job. The desire of about a quarter of the men we interviewed was to amass enough money selling drugs to set up their own businesses. I don't think any succeeded. Our data agree with Whyte's argument that poor

communities are not disorganized, but contain a vast array of different
kinds of illegal and informal kinds of economic and social organization.

Violence and the Rise of the Illicit Economy

One compelling argument advanced by those who see poor neighborhoods today as "disorganized" are high levels of underclass violence. Violence is seen by some as one result of the decline of intimate "primary"
relationships (Bursik and Grasmick 1993, 35). For Elijah Anderson,
such violence is the result of a "code of the streets," new norms which
sanction the use of violence. For Wilson, such violence is "less than fer-
vently condemned" by residents who are "collectively different" (1987)
than the poor of the past.

What are the sources of violence in poor communities? Poor
neighborhoods, particularly African American areas, have always had
higher rates of violence than more affluent white neighborhoods (see
Short 1997 for a thorough review). Sampson (1987) has looked at these
racial differences and found that they could be largely explained by differences in family disruption. In other words, children from families that
experience intense strains, such as break-up, tend to express those
strains in a violent manner. The culture of masculinity also promotes violence, especially accompanied by alcohol and substance use (Majors
and Billson 1992). Gang men construct their masculinities as "tough
guys," "reluctant warriors," and "new jacks" (Hagedorn in press-d) all
conceptions of "being a man" that are inclined to violence (see also
Horowitz 1983). In poor minority areas there are simply more opportunities for unemployed, frustrated, young men who are hanging out and
drinking to get in trouble (Oliver 1994),

This helps explains class differences in the use of violence by men;
it does not explain why rates of homicide skyrocketed in the 1980s in
poor communities across the U.S., including Milwaukee. Alfred Blumstein (1993) has argued that increased rates of homicide are tied to the
establishment of new cocaine markets in urban areas and a flood of
handguns on our streets (see also Hamid 1990). The epidemic of violence, in other words, was tied to the regulation of the drug industry, including establishing new markets, reducing or eliminating competition,

disciplining employees, and handling dissatisfied customers (see Black 1981).

Some researchers have disputed the extent of gang involvement in drug-related violence (Block and Block 1991; Howell 1996; Maxson and Klein 1996). However, our respondents made it perfectly clear that money, drugs, and guns are at the root of most gang violence, especially among adults.

> **Q.** Our last study was done in 1986. What has happened to the gang these last five years? What's changed the most?
>
> **A:** The money.
>
> **Q:** What do you mean by that?
>
> **A:** It's so much of it available. I'm talking about hundreds of thousands, millions. That's how America was founded, you know what I'm saying, by corrupt crime, and money period. That's what changed everything. And the ready access to guns.

Another young man adds:

> Since the dope came about, it seems like everybody's just killing. Really it's a whole lot of senseless killing that's going on. When back then, you know, you made different type of hustles. You had your car thieves, purse snatchers, your robbers, your burglars. But there wasn't as many guns around. Everybody you see now got guns.

We also asked our respondents to describe the last three fights they were involved in, the last three times they were shot at, and the last three people they personally had seen killed. Most male gang violence is still tied to men "doing gender" in bars and on corners, and women are more victims than perpetrators. However, we have concluded that nearly half of all violence by gang men in our study is related in some way to the cocaine trade.

Homicide rates soared in Milwaukee and other cities as cocaine markets were being established and fell in some cities (not yet in

GANG DRUG RELATED VIOLENCE IN MILWAUKEE

Type of Incident	While Ripping off to get Drugs	Happened after the drugs were all gone	Related to a dope deal gone bad
Last three fights N= 129	4.70% (11)	12.00% (28)	6.00% (6)
Last three times R was shot at N= 115	5.80% (10)	13.30% (22)	11.20% (19)
Last three persons R has seen killed N= 77	19.60% (19)	18.80% (13)	23.20% (23)

Milwaukee) after drug markets stabilized. Here is a description by one gang member of the violence his gang instigated as they tried to set up drug markets in neighborhoods where other gangs were already selling drugs.

Q: Can you talk a little bit about what happened when the Citywide Drug Gang started out?

A: Well, when they first started it, for one thing they had the guns, the dope, and the money, so they had the foundation.... They recruited so many people and put them up on this thing. As far as the business aspect they already said, well, hey, we already got the work, we got the know-how, all we need is you to help us get it done.... They wasn't scared, wasn't scared of nobody.

Q: Yeah, but here in Milwaukee it wasn't a neighborhood that you went to....

A: No, no. Any neighborhood was ours.... Just move in that neighborhood and let everybody know we here.

Q: Don't the people that were there that were selling, or it was their neighborhood, didn't they get a little upset about that?

A: What could they do? We was fully equipped. Any

situation we could handle it. We would outnumber them, so what could they do.... Like we went into one neighborhood and there was some peoples.... We just told them, fuck 'em, they want a war, we took 'em to war, we smoked 'em out of it. Where ever they staying, we shoot their house down. They ain't gonna stick around if they ain't got no house to sit in. 'Cause, you know, we all have different ways of going about it. You scare the shit out of them, they ain't gonna do nothing but just hit it.

Q: How did you get their share of the market? How did you get their customers?

A: Easy. You give them a better product. You know, give 'em quality. I mean, first of all, when you set up in any type of business like that, you try to do something that the other person don't do, you know. And then we draw their confidence that way and then we got 'em.... Or even maybe, they might want one until tomorrow [pay the next day]. That's something the person across the street wouldn't do, and that's what we'd do. Their confidence go to you. Simple as that.

Q: So it's just basic business tactics is what you're doing, backed up with some muscle, right?

A: Right. That's the whole key thing, backed up with muscle.

Rather than seeing violence as adherence to new norms and values by deviant underclass males, gang violence increasingly is a mechanism to regulate the illegal drug industry. The norms involved here are not deviant, but old familiar ones like making money and success. Those dealers who told us they sold dope "24-7," or around the clock, are prime examples of the Protestant work ethic. As Durkheim (1951, 256–7) pointed out, in a capitalist society, especially during crises (like economic restructuring), anomic actions by those few who want to "make their money" by any means necessary are *inevitable*.

In poor neighborhoods today, an uneasy truce reigns between respectable citizens in community agencies and disreputable groups like gangs and other drug selling cliques (Hunter 1985; Hagedorn 1991).

Community policing and various law enforcement strategies often aim to unite the "respectable elements" against "criminal elements," like drug selling gangs (Davis and Lurigio 1996). This strategy often splits job-forsaken communities that desperately depend upon the informal economy in order to survive. Violent police tactics often exacerbate the problem (Hamid and Curtis 1996).

Violence and the Status of New Organizations

As a final word on this subject, we should look at violence through the lens of what we know about the relationship between violence and new organizations of less powerful classes. Arthur Stinchcombe (1965), reviewing the history of organizations, pointed out that rapid structural change introduces uncertainty into the ranking of organizations. Stinchcombe was referring to capitalist enterprises in feudal Europe and worker unions in the industrial era. The conditions for violence exist, according to Stinchcombe, when the leaders of new organizations, who have rapidly risen to power, are not socialized to the norms of conventional society nor accepted into respectable society. The new young leaders become "anomic" or lack commitment to basic norms and are willing to do "anything" to succeed. In our parlance, they become "new jacks" who are acutely anomic (see Merton 1968, 217). When the government attempts to incarcerate these leaders and destroy their organizations by the use of the police or military, violence results. Failure to accommodate the leaders of new organizations, Stinchcombe concluded, has led in the past to "revolutionary situations."

In post-industrial America, the war on drugs has aimed to suppress the new underclass drug-selling organizations and imprison their young leaders. Make no mistake, gang drug dealers are not revolutionaries. However, contemporary gangs across the United States have increasingly become active in the political arena, just as they have in the past (e.g., Whyte 1943; Royko 1971; Hamid and Curtis 1996; diChiaria 1997). The hope of most adult gang members in the drug business is to be accepted in respectable society, just as movies like *Scarface* and the *Godfather* claim. But with Democratic and Republican politics targeting the "underclass" for repression and cutbacks, these disenfranchised men and women of these poor neighborhoods often have nowhere else to turn except to ever-present gangs and drug organizations. *Post-indus-trial gang violence, in other words, is not so much a property of individual deviance, but the historically predictable response of underclass men blocked from attaining legitimate economic and social goals.*

The Path Ahead

The story of the people and folks in Milwaukee is a story of contemporary urban America. The male and female gang members we studied have struggled to become productive and happy adults, only to watch their economic security snatched away by forces over which they had no control. Young women mainly held on to traditional gender roles and tried to raise their families under more trying conditions. What the future holds for them is uncertain. The cuts in welfare are sure to add to the difficulties of their lives and make despair, prostitution, and the use of cocaine a more likely temptation. Some will rebel, but many more will probably "endure" the new, greater indignities of life, as women always have (Cloward and Piven 1979).

The more reckless men, on the other hand, predictably responded to the loss of legitimate jobs by "going for the gold" in the drug economy. Their response was predictable because the values they held and their cultural understanding of them is familiar to us all—they wanted their piece of the pie. The fundamental tenets of the American Dream are alive and well on the corners of our central cities. The gang men and women we studied are more like you and me than they are the deviant creatures with "alien" values that some claim (e.g., Katz 1988).

The fate of the men and women who formed gangs in Milwaukee has convinced me of the strength and stability of American culture, of racism, and traditional gender roles. William Julius Wilson's social disorganization theory remains a powerful description of the dynamics of economic restructuring, but it lacks a convincing analysis of the informal economy and underestimates the impact of mainstream culture on the "ghetto poor."

Try as I might, I just can't locate deviant subcultures or "cognitive landscapes" where new values light up a violent "code of the streets." What I see are underclass men violently "doing gender" and chasing after the almighty dollar, while poor women try to be good mothers, make a living, and raise a family in dangerous neighborhoods. Some-times these women succeed, sometimes they are overwhelmed. Rather than "disorganized" ghettoes, what I have found are communities with few licit jobs, but teeming with illicit organizations, where people are doing their best to find innovative ways to make ends meet. Sometimes they become their own worst enemies.

The drug economy is violent not because it is inhabited by crea-tures living in a subculture of violence, but because (1) economic re-structuring has made legal opportunities scarce; (2) the government has decided to regulate the drug economy by suppression; and (3) America promotes a culture that prizes money and success as the true definition of masculinity and glamorizes those who break the rules to get what they want. Economic restructuring has not changed the cul-ture or character of those in the underclass, but pushed them into illicit, stressful, and dangerous ways of making a living. What would you do under such circumstances?

What we need are some new ways to look at gangs in post-indus-trial conditions. Research studies like ours, which collaborate with gang members or others from poor communities, are the best means to develop a much needed "emic" or insider's understanding, of the truly disadvantaged (Vigil 1990). This is a first step toward building new theory.

My picture of post-industrial Milwaukee gangs, however, is incom-plete without a short glimpse at the public policy response since *People and Folks* first appeared. It is to that sad story that I must turn as I end this final chapter.

Public Policy as Warfare

In Chapter Seven of *People and Folks*, I argued that gangs had been de-fined as a crime problem rather than being seen more broadly as a con-sequence of the post-industrial revolution. Indeed, gangs today, I've tried to show, are as much a by-product of post-industrial economic re-lations as the gangs of yesteryear were a by-product of the industrial era (Hagedorn, in press-c). Public policy almost everywhere continues to treat gangs not only as a crime problem, but as the enemy, the targets of the war on crime and, more specifically, the war on drugs.

The war terminology, I think, is quite instructive and deeply tied to our cultural beliefs in money and success. For if most of us are unable to realize the riches of the American Dream, whom are we to blame for our failing? We could blame ourselves, but none of us one wants to do that. We could blame capitalism and the structure of the American economy, but that would be subversive. We could blame the materialist and sexist culture of a consumer society, but that would make us too uneasy as we flip channels on our big screen TV or sip our cup of Starbucks coffee. No, the American Dream, if it is to "get over" on us, needs a scapegoat at all times. With the fall of communism, it has been vital to find someone on whom to vent our fury, someone on whom we can displace our feelings of insecurity. Dark-skinned gang drug dealers are as good an enemy as any we could find. So we have allowed the government to wage a war on our own youth.

Since *People and Folks* was released, this country has witnessed the largest prison-building movement in our history, surpassing even the Jacksonian era. Most of the men and half of the women in our study have spent some time behind bars. In 1990, expenditures on the criminal justice system as a whole exceeded $74 billion, about half for salaries of 1.7 million employees. Expenditures on the criminal justice system increased over 600% over the past twenty years (Martin and Jurik 1996). In 1991, more money was spent on the war on drugs ($31 billion) than on AFDC ($25 billion), and this was *before* Clinton's welfare cuts (J. Miller 1996, 1).

I am still opposed to developing new diversion or other criminal justice programs as a response to gangs. The criminal justice system needs to be vastly reduced, not to be fed and have its net widened. One response for those working within welfare and educational bureaucracies has been local reforms aimed at making them more neighborhood-based and family-focused, and less entwined with the criminal justice system (Hagedorn 1991, 1995). These changes, however, are slow and uncertain and bring heartfelt but limited results. I believe those of us wanting fundamental changes in public policy need to forthrightly argue for more drastic changes, know that our counsel will be rejected, and wait for the inevitable crisis. Then frightened policy makers might look for solutions they may have earlier thrown into the "garbage can" (Cohen 1972). Maybe they'll pick out ours.

Unfortunately, with Piven and Cloward (1980), I believe it will not be rational counsel, but riots and violence, perhaps by male prisoners, or

even by mothers protesting reduced welfare benefits, which will ulti-
mately force a broader debate. In many ways, today's depoliticized, post-
industrial underclass may resemble the pre-modern, primitive "city
mobs" of Hobsbawm (1959, 111) who rioted simply because they wanted
better economic conditions. Sadly, in the absence of a sustained mass
movement of the poor, we have no assurance that the reaction of the
powerful to the inevitable "fire next time" will be progressive. Does that
sound too cynical? Think about the last thirty years of public policy and
the current policy positions of both political parties and tell me where
there are grounds for optimism.

But such realism does not mean that we can do nothing. There are
three areas I think we should work on in the interim: jobs, violence-re-
duction, and education on cultural values. Let me sketch an outline of
my thinking as the concluding thoughts of this book.

**First, we need to support any and all public and private job
programs, for both men and women.** I agree with Wilson (1996) that
we need to support programs to get the poor from the central city to
outlying areas were the jobs are more plentiful. This should not be seen
in opposition to necessary efforts to invest in central cities. We should
support any policies of either Democrats or Republicans which produce
economic benefits for the very poor. We should also oppose "welfare reform" measures that push poor mothers away from their children just
when their "at-risk" children need them most and provide inadequate
childcare.

We need special job-creating efforts directed at gang members. In
Milwaukee, Jim Holub, S.J., has begun a business, Homeboyz Graphics,
which trains and employs rival gang members to design and sell web
sites to business and government (http://www. homeboyz. com). Gang
members, like others in poor communties, are talented and industrious,
and can do more than sweep floors or flip burgers. Jobs like those at
Homeboyz Graphics rely on talent and creativity, have flexible hours,
and maximize the potential of those used to the rhythms of the street.
Such programs targeting gang members need to be replicated.

Creating jobs also means a strategy of sending fewer people to
prison. In our study, most gang members possessed less than five grams
of cocaine at any one time while they were selling. In Milwaukee, 80% of
all those sentenced to prison for cocaine-related charges had less than
five grams of cocaine on them. Five grams, for those of you not up on
your weights and measures, is the weight of a nickel. In other words,

our prisons are filling up with penny-ante, or more precisely, nickel-ante drug offenders like our "homeboys" who are not drug lords, but are either users or just struggling to survive.

We proposed alternative sentencing options of jobs and drug treatment for drug offenders who possessed, for any reason, less than five grams of cocaine. The proposal was made by the Drug Posse and Homegirl Study staff and we brought it to state legislators and published it as an opinion piece in the Milwaukee Journal Sentinel (September 10, 1995). But legislators threw the proposal in their garbage cans. For the big dealers and corrupt public officials who conspire to poison our streets with dope, I don't really care what happens. It's those 80% on the bottom rungs of the drug game, like our homeboys, that matter to me. In the absence of policies like those we proposed, new prisons will continue to be built, threatening public funding for education and other social welfare programs. Unfortunately, one of the most important agenda items for research in the immediate future is understanding the impact of prison on poor communities (see Fulbright 1996).

Second, the reduction of violence is a high priority for us all. Homeboyz Graphics has as part of its unspoken agenda the creation of a core of rival Latino gang members who can intervene with younger people to restrain the violence. While politicians and police claim that prison-building and more police are responsible for the decline in homicide rates, might one main reason for the decline in violence be the changed outlook of those who have been committing the violence? We blamed them for starting it, why not give them some credit for curtailing it? The stabilization of drug markets has brought declines in violence in many cities, but that stabilization means that people, like those in our study, who are selling drugs, are pulling the trigger less. Why? We don't know. This is one of the areas of my current research.

I believe gang truces and gang political organization need to be supported in so far as they reduce violence and advance a progressive agenda for the underclass. Most of our respondents, like some gang members in Hartford and New York (DiChiaria 1997; Hamid and Curtis 1996) are openly rejecting violence and looking for less deadly ways to resolve conflicts. Gang drug dealers organizing political movements is the price we are paying for the failure of mainstream politicians to seriously advocate the interests of the very poor.[12]

We also need to develop more community-based programs which employ older gang members to work with youth to help restrain the

violence. But we must be realistic. The vast amount of guns on our
streets all but doom us to higher levels of violence than in the past. Half
measures of gun buy-backs or gun control laws will not work. Elimina-
tion of hand guns for everyone is the only effective policy direction
(Hagedorn, in press-c). Conflict mediation programs, which teach skills,
redefine masculinity, and utilize gang members, can be especially helpful in schools and in poor neighborhoods (Prothrow-Stith 1991).

Violence against gang women is also a serious problem, and some
data suggest it is getting worse (Block et al. 1996). Our data found that
not all women were harmed by the gang experience, but there was a set
of women who were sexually exploited and abused by men in the gang.
These women, mostly young teenagers, need a refuge to escape male violence. Women's groups of all classes and races need to be mobilized to
assist in an effort to set up "safe houses" for female gang members in
distress. We also need to point out to these groups that funding for programs for women is not available because so much money goes into
building prisons, not just for men, but increasingly for female victims of
the war on drugs.

**Finally, we need to be critical of core elements of American
culture.** Gangs are a problem of social structure, but they are also a
problem of values. As I have pointed out, there is a dark side to the
American Dream, one that emphasizes money and material success, and
defines masculinity as the domination of women. These dark elements
have been deeply internalized by all segments of American society. I
have concluded that it is the intersection of these dark elements of our
culture with lack of opportunity that is mainly responsible for the high
levels of violence in the United States (see Lipset 1996).

To argue, as I have, that the problem is mainstream, not ghetto
values, makes our job more difficult. What we need is not so much to
embrace "traditional" values, as conservatives claim, but rather to advocate values of cooperation and non-violence—and not just in ghetto
schools, but everywhere. Educational reform of our schools needs to
emphasize teaching of these cooperative, non-violent values along with
basic academics.

This new "values agenda" will not be welcomed with open arms
by proponents of a competitive capitalist culture. I believe there is
much common ground which can be found between those advocating
communal and cooperative values among African Americans and other

minorities and a feminist ethic. This possibility offers some political hope for the future.

Concluding Note

Why did I add a new chapter to this book? First, many people asked me what had happened to the people and folks, and I thought I ought to tell them. Second, I've learned a few things since this book first came out, and I believe I have a responsibility to share what I've learned. I wanted to reinforce the message that gang members are people, like you and me, trying to figure out how to survive in these new, uncertain, post-industrial times. Still, it is clear that I am quite pessimistic about any immediate possibilities for fundamental change. So why should I waste your time and mine writing about it? I've thought long and hard about that.

I think that history will judge current American public policy harshly. The consequences of economic restructuring have left millions with few hopes. At the same time "tough guy" politicians vie with one another to see who can cut welfare the most and who can spend the most money on prisons and police, while obscenely increasing "defense" spending above cold war levels. Nero may have fiddled as Rome burned, but at least he didn't light the match. Politicians today are playing with fire while allowing no room for substantive debate. Unfortunately, neither are our streets echoing with demands for reform by today's "sans culottes," the urban propertyless classes. Left to our current course, we are sure to witness many desperate acts of violence and rebellion. These rebellions may not change policy for the better, but they will point out to those paying attention that all is not well in the U.S.A.

Given those realities, books like this serve to remind us that current paradigms are not the only ones. Books like *People and Folks* are not written to help rationalize mainstream public policy. No, I've added this final chapter to *People and Folks* mainly to make my readers uncomfortable. Being uncomfortable with the status quo is the first step toward change, getting us prepared for future startling and unexpected events. If what I've written has made you uneasy, nervous, or maybe uncertain about something you thought you knew—then perhaps I've done my job. I remain hopeful.

APPENDIX I

DECEMBER 1985
HISTORY OF GANG INVOLVEMENT: QUESTIONS

The following questionnaire was used in the Milwaukee Gang Research Project.

I. General Background

1. (a) Name of Gang   (b) Clique Name

2. How old were you when you first got involved with your gang clique?

3. Did you start the gang clique or was it already there?

4. How were you brought in to the gang? Were you recruited, jumped into the gang, or raised into the gang?

5. What other gangs did you belong to before you joined? In Milwaukee, in Chicago, or elsewhere?

6. (a) How many people were in the gang then?
   (b) How many were your age?

7. How many of the members then grew up in the same neighborhood?

8. Were there girls in the gang then?
   If yes, were they in a separate clique?

9. Who was the first leader?
   (b) How was he chosen?
   (c) What were the other ranks?

10. How many people were in the gang opposed to yours when you were heavy into gangbanging?

11. How did most of the people in the neighborhood act toward the gang?

12. Can you give me an example?

13. How did the police treat your gang?

14. How did the school administrative staff react to the gang?

14a. How should they react?

15. How did your parents react to the gang?

16. How important are Youth Agencies in your life? What should they be doing to better help kids in gangs?

17. Was your girlfriend involved with the gang too?

18. What did she think about the gang and your membership in it?

19. What do you do most of with the gang?

20. Do you have time to yourself while you were in the gang?

21. When did you begin to call your gang by its name (e.g., V-L, BGD, Cobra, King)?

22. Do you remember a "turning point," any event that marked when things got more serious, or the gang got a lot larger or smaller?

II. Territory

1. What was the original turf of the gang?
   a. Do you recruit at Milwaukee Public Schools?
   b. How important is the neighborhood a recruit comes from?

2. How many members live outside the neighborhood?

3. If someone from rival gang comes on your turf, what does the gang do?

4. How often in the last months is your neighborhood something you defend against outsiders?

5. What happens to someone who refuses to join your gang from your neighborhood?

6. What does the gang do if they see somebody rob or break into a car in your neighborhood?

7. How important was the gang to you during the time that you were heaviest into the gang?

8. Why was that? (Probe: What changes was respondent going through then?)

III. Organization and Leadership

1. How is the leader chosen?
   (a) What is his title?
   (b) How many ranks are there now?

2. How many members are now in the gang?
   (a) What is the initiation?
   (b) How does initiation differ with different people?

3. Are there different kinds of members? What is the difference between a real member and someone with you but not really in the gang?

4. Are there girls in the gang or do they have a separate gang?

5. What happens if a girl in the gang goes out with someone from another gang?

6. How well organized do you consider your gang?

7. How is your gang different from the other gangs?

8. Do you have dues?
   (a) Does everyone always pay?
   (b) What are they used for?
   (c) How much?
   (d) How do you make money?

9. What is the biggest cause of fights?

10. How has the gang changed since it started?

11. Tell me about the juniors. How many junior groups are there?
    (a) What are their names?
    (b) What ages are they?

12. Do you fight with the juniors?
    Do they do what they are told?

13. What do the juniors do different from the gang?

14. Do you party with the juniors?
    Do you party with other gangs?

15. What does being in a gang mean to you?

16. Many people say Milwaukee gangs take orders from Chicago. How true is that?
    How is your gang tied to a Chicago gang?

17. Do you have a gun? What kind?

18. How did you get it?

19. When do you carry it?

20. Have you ever used it?
    (a) When?
    (b) Did you hit anyone?

21. Now I'd like you to list for me that street names or initials of all the fellas that started the gang and what they are doing now. Are they employed? Have they graduated from high school? Have they been to prison? Are they still involved in the gang as adults?

IV. Family Life

Now, let me switch a little to what things were like in your family.

1. Where was your father born?

2. What was your father's occupation when you were growing up? (Probe for more than one occupation.)

3. How far in school did your father go?

4. Where was your mother born?

5. What was your mother's occupation when you were growing up? (Probe for more than one occupation.)

6. How far in school did your mother go?
   (If mother was not in the household when respondent was 15, ask for education and occupation of female head of family.)

7. When you were 15, did your family own a car?

8. Did your parents own their home when you were 15?

9. Compared with the other people in the neighborhood, was your family poorer, about the same, a little better off, or what?

10. Do you know who mostly took care of you when you were a baby?

11. When you were growing up, would you say your father was
    (1) a pretty happy person
    (2) grouchy a lot or how would you describe him?

12. When you were growing up, would you say your mother was a
    (1) pretty happy person
    (2) grouchy a lot
    (3) or how would you describe her?

13. How did your parents get along with one another?

14. Was your mother (or whoever cared for you) strict or easy? (Probe: Give me an example of why do you say that?)
    Was your father (1) strict (2) easy (3) other?

15. Did your mother really enforce the rules or just let things ride?
    Did your father enforce the rules or let things ride?
    b. Give me an example—tell me something that happened.

16. When you were 12, were you punished?
    (a) For lying?
    (b) For swearing?
    (c) For stealing?
    (d) What were you punished the worst for?
    (e) Did you get hit?

17. What would your parents do if you got good grades in school?

18. What about when you got into trouble in school? What did your father (stepfather) do?

19. Some parents get into the habit of putting their kids down. Did your parents ever put you down?

20. When you lived with your parents, was your birthday a special day or just another day?

21. Everybody feels proud about something in their family. When you were a teenager, what were you the most proud about in your family?

22. Everybody feels ashamed about some things in their family as well. What were you the most ashamed of?

23. Did you ever see your father beat up your mother?
    (If yes)
    a. How often did that happen?
    b. What did you do during these times?

24. Did you ever see your mother beat up your father?
    How often did that happen?

25. Did anybody in your family ever make any sexual advances to you when you were growing up? (Assure respondent that it happens a lot, that we are just trying to get to set the record straight.)
    Did anybody help you with that? (Probe for whom, how they found out, what happened as a result.)

26. Was anybody in your home sick a lot or handicapped when you were growing up?
    (If yes:) Who was that?

27. Did anybody in your home get busted when you were growing up? (excluding respondent)
    a. How did you feel about that?
    b. How old were you?

28. Did anybody in your home die when you were growing up?
    b. (If yes:) Who was that?
    c. How did you feel about that?
    d. How old were you?

29. Was anybody in your home an alcoholic when you were growing up?
    (If yes:) Who was that?

30. Was anybody in your home an addict when you were growing up?
    (If yes:) Who was that?

31. Who's the most successful person in your family?
    (Probe: How does respondent define success?)

32. What kind of job does he/she have?

33. Who's the biggest failure in your family?

34. Why?

35. Looking back over your life, who in your family would you say was the biggest influence on you?
    Why do you say that?

36. Did you ever run away?

37. (If yes:) How old were you the first time?

38. Did you ever run away again?

39. (If yes:) How many other times did you run away?

40. When did your family move to Milwaukee? (Give year.)

    a. Was your family involved with a gang before you moved to Milwaukee?

    b. What were the specific reasons your family moved to Milwaukee?

    c. Did you know anyone else from your old neighborhood in_____ _____who also moved to Milwaukee?

    d. Do you still visit relatives and friends in_____?

V. Education and Employment

1. What was the highest grade you completed in school?
2. What troubles did you have in school?
3. Why did you leave?
4. How many times were you suspended? Why?
5. Do you consider any gang members successes in their life? Give me some examples of each.
6. Do you encourage younger kids you know to stay in school or not? Do you have a family?
7. What kind of job would you want when you are thirty?
8. What kind of job do you expect to have when you are thirty?

VI. Drug Time Line

Now let's turn to this next time line and talk about the drugs you've been using.

1. Drug Time Line Table
   Age   Drug   Who With?   How Scored   Busted
2. When do you get high?
3. (a) How often do you sell drugs?
   (b) What kind?
4. How often does the gang sell?
   (a) Where do you get the drugs
   (b) Are the major dealers in gangs?
5. Is drug use increasing or decreasing in the gang?

People often take pills or medicine for physical problems and other things. Have you taken pills or medicine for any of the following purposes during the past 12 months?

	1. OFTEN	2. SOME-TIMES	3. RARELY	4. NEVER
6. To help you go to sleep	___	___	___	___
7. To relieve a headache	___	___	___	___
8. To help you stay awake	___	___	___	___
9. To calm down	___	___	___	___
10. To lift your spirits	___	___	___	___

	1. OFTEN	2. SOME-TIMES	3. RARELY	4. NEVER
11. For colds or coughs	___	___	___	___
12. To settle an upset stomach	___	___	___	___
13. For allergies	___	___	___	___
14. To lose weight/gain weight	___	___	___	___
15. To relieve other pains	___	___	___	___

VII. Being Black/Puerto Rican

On a scale of one to five:

1. Do you think blacks and Puerto Ricans are discriminated against in this society?

2. Are you proud to be (black/Puerto Rican)?

3. How much respect do you think black/Puerto Ricans have in Milwaukee?

4. How much power do you think black/Puerto Ricans have in Milwaukee?

5. How much respect does being in a gang give you?

6. How much power does being in a gang give you?

7. How much pride do you get by being in the gang?

8. Do you think things are getting better or worse for black/Puerto Ricans in Milwaukee?

9. How much do you see your gang as trying to help the black/Puerto Rican community?

VIII.

Now I have a couple of questions about your opinions of how things are run in this country. Do you agree or disagree with the following statements? (On a scale of one to five:)

1. Public officials care much what people like me think.

2. The way people vote is the main thing that decides how things are run in this country.

3. Voting is the only way that people like me can have any say about how the government runs things.

4. People like me don't have any say about how the government runs things.

5. Sometimes politics and government seem so complicated that a person like me can't really understand what's going on.

6. Are you registered to vote?

7. Did you vote in the last election?

IX. Police, Prison, Children's Court

1. How often have you been arrested?
   Describe the last time for me.

2. How good a job do you think the gang squad is doing?
   What should they be doing?

3. Have you ever been to prison or to Wales?
   (a) Do you expect to go to prison?
   (b) Did you join a gang in prison/Wales?
   (c) Tell me about gang life in prison.

4. How many times have you been taken to Children's Court?
   Describe what happened.

5. Are juveniles in the gang afraid to be taken to Children's Court?
   What about Wales?

6. What effect does going to Wales have on a member?

7. What effect does going to the House of Correction have on a member?
   What about prison?

Finally, I have a few questions about prison and narcotics and how they affect people. Please tell me if you agree or disagree with the following. (On a scale of one to five:)

8. Prison has a good effect because it punishes people who have done wrong.

9. Prison has a good effect because people can learn a trade for when they are released.

10. Prison has a bad effect because people learn how to become better criminals.

11. Prison has a bad effect because it dehumanizes people.

12. Using drugs is a sin.

13. Using drugs is a family problem.

14. Using drugs is an escape.

15. Using drugs is a psychological problem.

16. Using drugs is a gang related problem.

17. Ex-convicts' main problems are connected with their drug or crime problems.

18. Ex-convicts represent a problem to the community because they do not fit in once they are out of prison.

X. Conclusion

1. In the past five years, what do you think have been the biggest influences on you?

2. Is there anything that you think might help in the neighborhoods that we might add to our report?

3. If the governor gave you a million dollars to help solve Milwaukee's gang problem, what would you do with the money?

APPENDIX II

GANGS INTERVIEWED, ETHNICITY, AND YEAR GANG FORMED

Gangs	Ethnicity	Year Formed
Punk Alley	White	1973
Cobras	Hispanic	1975
Kings	Hispanic	1975
Sheiks	Black	1979
Hillside Boys	Black	1980
Time Boys	Mixed	1980
Cobra Stones	Black	1980
3–4 Mob	Black	1980
2–7 (Originals)	Black	1981
1–9	Black	1981
2–4	Black	1981
Cameo 2–7	Black	1982
Castle Folk	Black	1982
6–4's	Black	1982
V-L Queens	Black	1982
Vicelords	Black	1982
Four Corner Hustlers	Black	1982
7–11	Black	1983
2–7 Syndicates	Black	1983

APPENDIX III

BLACK UNEMPLOYMENT IN MILWAUKEE AND OTHER U.S. CITIES

City	Black %	White %	B/W Ratio
BOSTON	4.5%	3.4%	1.32
WASHINGTON	7.9%	3.9%	1.74
MIAMI	7.9%	2.1%	3.76
DENVER	9.1%	4.3%	2.12
ATLANTA	9.9%	3.1%	3.19
SAN FRANCISCO	10.5%	5.3%	1.98
DALLS/FT. W.	10.8%	4.0%	2.7
NEW YORK CITY	11.1%	6.6%	1.68
LOS ANGELES	12.3%	6.6%	1.68
PHILADELPHIA	13.8%	4.6%	3.0
INDIANAPOLIS	14.2%	6.6%	2.15
KANSAS CITY	14.4%	3.1%	4.65
CINCINNATI	15.8%	7.8%	2.02
ST. LOUIS	17.4%	4.9%	3.55
MINNEAPOLIS	19.9%	4.5%	4.4
CLEVELAND	21.5%	6.7%	3.21
PITTSBURGH	23.5%	9.6%	2.45
CHICAGO	24.5%	5.6%	4.38
BUFFALO	27.8%	7.5%	3.71
MILWAUKEE	**27.9%**	**6.0%**	**4.65**
DETROIT	29.9%	6.5%	4.6

SOURCE: National Urban League, 1987

APPENDIX IV

BLACK REPRESENTATION IN WISCONSIN: 1967–1987

Offices	# of blacks: 1967		# of blacks: 1987	
City of Milwaukee				
Executive Offices	0	0%	0	0%
Common Council	0	0%	3	19%
School Board	1	7%	3	22%
Milwaukee County				
Executive Offices	0	0%	1	14%
Board of Supervisors	0	0%	1	14%
State of Wisconsin				
Executive Offices	0	0%	0	0%
Senate	0	0%	1	14%
Assembly	1	1%	3	3%
Congress				
Senate	0	0%	0	0%
House	0	0%	0	0%
Judicial Offices				
All Milwaukee	0	0%	2	5%
State Supreme Court	0	0%	0	0%
Totals	**5**	**2%**	**14**	**5%**

Source: *Milwaukee Journal,* July 7, 1987.
(Note: Milwaukee was about 10% black in 1967 and 25% black in 1987).

APPENDIX V

NUMBER OF AGE-GRADED GROUPS IN 1985

Gangs	Number of Age Groups
Hillside Boys	Four
Punk Alley	Three
Cobras	Three
Kings	Three
Time Boys	Three
6–4	Three
Sheiks	Two
2–7 Syndicates	Two
2–7 (Originals)	Two
1–9	Two
Four Corner Hustlers	Two
2–4	Two
Castle Folk	Two
V-L Queens	One
Vicelords	One
Cameo 2–7	One
7–11	One

Introduction

1. Thus, in Phoenix, the police explicitly compare the Chicano gang structure to a "military pyramid" with *veteranos* called "chiefs of staff," *vatos locos* called "commissioned officers," and "TJs" called draftees (Phoenix Juvenile Gang Reduction Unit, n.d.). In a number of the gangs studied by Hagedorn and Macon, members talk as if they have clear-cut tables of organization. They thus conform to the notions of the police. But, even in such gangs, the reality generally falls far short of this image, and most such gangs are in fact much looser. In the Chicano gangs that we have studied in Los Angeles, there is definitely no such hierarchical organization, and even to talk about a "leader" in these gangs is to violate the egalitarian norms.

2. "Underclass" is used in this manner by some researchers (cf. Heer, 1986). But such an application is relatively rare in the United States.

3. These statements refer to data collected under NIDA grant number DA03114.

4. Both tactics—conspiracy charges and sweep arrests—proved later to be illegal. The convictions of the Sleepy Lagoon defendants were overturned in 1944 and the sweep arrests were outlawed.

Chapter One

1. Many social scientists seem to think so. For example, gang theorist Walter B. Miller has disputed the notion that the nature of gangs, at least in the sixties and seventies, has changed much since he studied Boston gangs in the fifties or the immigrant gangs of the twenties. In a polemic "Gangs in the Urban Crisis Era," Miller concludes: "Youth gangs in the urban crisis era show marked similarities to their predecessors in the earlier periods described by (University of Chicago sociologist Henry) McKay" (Miller 1976, 120).

2. There is a small, but growing literature on adult gang membership. Moore (1978) and Horowitz (1983) have examined the phenomenon in Chicano gangs and Spergel (1984) in black and Puerto Rican gangs. We will examine adult involvement in more detail in Chapter Five.

3. William Kornblum, "Ganging Together," *Social Issues and Health Review,* 1987.

4. *Milwaukee Journal,* July 11, 1984.

5. *Franklin County Community Profile,* Metropolitan Human Services Commission, Franklin County, Ohio. June 1986. Educationally, drop out rates are declining for the county as a whole and the percentage of high school and college graduates show large increases. But none of these impressive educational statistics are disaggregated by race or class.

6. See Wilson's argument in Chapter Five of *The Declining Significance of Race.*

7. *The Columbus Monthly,* March 1986.

8. *The Milwaukee Journal,* January 27, 1984.

9. *Twin Cities Task Force on Gangs,* p 6. While most of the task force reports claimed to interview one or two "gang members," none did so systematically or presented findings based on the gang interviews alone. None of the reports indicated how the "gang members" were identified, the name of the gangs they were from, why they agreed to be interviewed, whether they were in custody, or how their responses differed, if at all, from the responses of other people interviewed.

10. See, for example, Miller's surveys, which found that today's gangs are overwhelmingly of "African, Asian, and Hispanic" origins. "Today there is no "majority" ethnic category, but the bulk of gang members, about four fifths, are either black or Hispanic" (Miller 1975, 27). Miller points out that police can no longer locate a single Irish gang in New York. Campbell found it necessary to ask female New York gang members why there weren't any white gangs. One woman's retort was that the only white gangs today were the police and KKK (Campbell 1984, 249).

11. Wilson (1978) has been attacked for raising the problem of class within the perspective of "historical discrimination." Perkins (1987) criticizes gang theories for lacking a critique of "institutional racism." Bloch and Niederhoffer (1958) exemplify the tradition of seeing gangs as solely an "adolescent problem," as does Cohen (1955). Miller, in criticizing the belief that gangs in the "urban crisis era" are significantly different than the gangs of the past, fails to analyze structural factors or any of the economic changes which by the mid-seventies were quite apparent in large cities (Miller 1976, 95).

12. Ohio State criminologist Ron Huff is completing a comparative study of gangs in Columbus and Cleveland, Ohio, which includes taped gang interviews and should yield valuable data.

13. Klein's (1971) discussion is perhaps the best short overview of the literature. Short and Strodtbeck (1965) careful analysis of the major current gang theories is by far the best treatment of the era. For understanding theories of group delinquency, the best textbookish treatment is Empey (1978) and the most perceptive, Kornhauser (1978). Cohen, whose own theory has been roundly criticized, laments, "It is remarkable, however, how insufficient are these 'known facts' for

the conclusive validation or further modification of this (his) theory" (1955, 170). Interestingly, for Cohen "known facts" of ethnicity and race were insignificant, and he concentrated his theorizing solely on adolescent "working class" processes. We hardly concur with Hardman (1967, 27) in an essay, "The History of Gang Research": "In more than one area of research we have seen that attempts to force naturally occurring phenomena into prefabricated typologies have retarded rather than enhanced research. . . . The above research suggests that, whatever area of gang phenomena is explored, a widespread diversity rather than clear-cut typologies will likely be found."

14. In addition, white and minority liberal academics have been stung by the bitter criticisms surrounding the "Moynihan Report." As William Julius Wilson observed, "One of the consequences of the heated controversy over the Moynihan report on the Negro family is that liberal social scientists, social workers, journalists, and civil rights leaders have been, until very recently, reluctant to make any reference to race at all when discussing issues such as the increase of violent crime, teenage pregnancy, and out-of-wedlock births." (Wilson 1987, 6) For commentary on the Moynihan controversy, see Rainwater and Yancey (1967).

15. See the excerpt of John P. Dean and William Foote Whyte, "How do you know the informant is telling the truth?" (McCall-Simmons 1969, 105).

16. One method of solving this problem was attempted by Kleiner et al. in Philadelphia in the late 1960s. Due to hostility from the black community toward research, Kleiner hired black paraprofessionals to conduct all the gang interviews. Miller, and Short and Strodtbeck both make extensive use of reports by detached workers, accompanied by formal interviews with gang boys. See Moore (1978) and Blauner and Wellman (1973, 321-324).

17. One of these was the Coalition for Justice for Ernest Lacy. Lacy was a black youth whose unjustified killing set off demonstrations of up to ten thousand Milwaukeeans in 1981. Three officers were indicted for homicide by reckless conduct by a coroner's inquest on October 14, 1981. Legal maneuvering kept the officers from trial. None were ever convicted of a felony and only one was fired. While this drama was unfolding, Milwaukee's gangs were in the process of formation.

18. The Chicago Gangs Crimes Unit also alleged that Milwaukee gangs were manipulated by Chicago gangs or even had become a "branch of Chicago gangs." One article on a speech by Chicago police officials began: "Milwaukee youth gangs have links with a Chicago gang, a Chicago police official said Saturday." Interestingly, the gang the Chicago officer was referring to, the Vicelords, was the gang formed by Perry Macon. The nebulous relationship between Macon's gang and the Conservative Vice Lord Nation in Chicago will be discussed in Chapter Three. *Milwaukee Journal,* July 10, 1983.

19. Miller (1974) questions the reliability of gang interviews, pointing out that it is "folly to accept that testimony (of gang members) at face value." He goes on to say, "The capacity of the gang member to furnish accurate estimates, descriptions, or explanations is significantly affected by strong perceptual influences related to his age, his social status, his locality." But that is true of

interviews or ethnographic treatments of anyone: a policeman, social worker, or gang member. We agree with Miller's balanced approach: "any informed treatment of gangs must of course ascertain and take into account the testimony of gang members." (Miller 1974, 306) It is our point that such "testimony" has long been lacking in gang research, and the information we currently have is decidedly one-sided.

20. While UWM's Urban Research Center agreed to sponsor the study, UWM's Institutional Review Board, a body ostensibly concerned with protecting human subjects from misuses of research, held up the project for months. They insisted that Hagedorn inform those interviewed that transcripts of their interviews may have to be turned over to the District Attorney, if subpoenaed. Hagedorn, Macon, and Moore were outraged by the notion that their research might not be strictly confidential. We insisted on informing those interviewed that under no circumstances, including prosecution, would transcripts or names be turned over to authorities. The dilemma was finally resolved by the issuance of a Certificate of Confidentiality by the National Institute on Drug Abuse. This document permitted sources to be protected and prohibited the subpoena of tapes or transcripts. In the "Informed Consent" statement all respondents were required to read, they were assured that the researchers would not allow names, tapes, or transcripts to be scrutinized or seized by law enforcement. This solution is less than satisfactory, however. Will universities sponsor only "state-sanctioned" research? It seems the independent role of the university has seriously eroded.

21. The use of open-ended questions rather than questions with "multiple choice" or precoded answers allows maximum use of the relationships developed by the researcher and does not limit the response of the person interviewed. For a discussion of the methodological issues, see Zelditch, "Some Methodological Problems of Field Studies" (McCall-Simmons,1969, 5-19).

Those interviewed should be seen as "key informants," the best qualified to relate the history of their gang and the present circumstances of its founding members: but they are not representative of all gang members. This method, in which the respondents locate other key informants, is known as a "snowball sample."

Paying for interviews was an important part of the collaborative nature of our research. We had a principle of reciprocity: the gang founder had something of value for us and we insisted on giving back something of value. See Blauner and Wellman (1973, 316-318) for a discussion of reciprocity in interviews with ghetto residents. For gangs interviewed, see Appendix II.

22. Hagedorn conducted forty interviews and Macon seven. All interviews were taped and transcribed. Key questions were compared to look for variance between Hagedorn's and Macon's interviews. No patterns of differences could be located nor did significant differences appear in transcripts. In all but two gangs, more than one founding member was interviewed and answers compared. In all cases, members of rival gangs were interviewed and questioned about crucial events in gang formation. In this way we could construct a history of gang formation from several different points of view. Names have, of course, been changed to protect the identity of those interviewed. While about half of

the interviews were conducted with young men and women with whom we had previously built a comparatively high degree of trust, the other half were either "referrals" from those already interviewed or were recruited by Perry Macon right off the streets. Macon hung out and told "fellas" on corners and play-grounds that we wanted to interview "top dogs" about how the gang formed and we would pay $20.00. Usually we were looking for a specific person. Other times, we had to test the potential recruit to see if he knew key actors from gang origins. There was a great number of "fellas" willing to be interviewed for $20.00, but we were quite selective.

Chapter Two

1. Stories of Irish, Polish, and German youths "ganging" spice some histories of Milwaukee. Accounts of the "Bunker Boys" in 1861 who repeatedly escaped from reform school led to familiar citizen calls to end lenient treatment of such "hardened" youth.

2. Joe William Trotter, in an interesting account *Black Milwaukee,* looks at the black experience through a framework of black "proletarianization." The tradi-tional framework of spatial segregation and race relations, Trotter points out, has "misrepresented two essential features of black urban life: occupational sta-tus and class structure" (Trotter 1985, 275). Trotter, whose account unfortu-nately ends at the conclusion of World War II, shows the central importance of industry and the wages paid the new black migrants for all classes in the black community.

3. "Wisconsin Industry Projections to 1990," DILHR Labor Market Informa-tion, Madison, 1982.

4. This data supports Wilson's provocative thesis that the economic crisis has had a differential impact on various classes within the black community. Mil-waukee's black managers have increased nearly tenfold from 1970 to 1980, from less than 2% of the black workforce to about 10%. While no data is avail-able on the 1980s, it is clear that a black professional class emerged and pros-pered in Milwaukee in the 1970s. See Wilson's argument in Chapter Six of *The Declining Significance of Race.* All data listed in the text, unless otherwise noted, are from the U.S. Census Bureau, *Characteristics of the Population,* 1960, 1970, and 1980. These economic changes, of course, had been foreseen by black social scientists and others. One sociologist predicted that "the patterns of change within Milwaukee's economy are going to aggravate the economic plight of blacks and other minorities... blacks are going to be trapped in the more backward sectors" (Edari 1977, 31). See Appendix III.

5. There are many other statistical indicators of the slide of much of Milwau-kee's black and Hispanic communities into the underclass. AFDC cases have in-creased from under 5,000 in 1965 to over 35,000 cases by the mid-eighties. More than two thirds of all AFDC clients are black. General Assistance has

risen from an average of about 3,000 persons in 1965 to a high of 13,500 in 1986. Eighty percent of G.A. recipients are black. Most of the increase in General Assistance and fully a third of the increase in AFDC cases have come since 1980. UWM Urban Research Center Director Sammis White (1986) found that 55% of the 18 year old General Assistance enrollees were now from AFDC families. Milwaukee's highest in the nation teen pregnancy rate is a clear warning that Milwaukee's new poor underclass is beginning to reproduce itself.

There is one other place blacks are disproportionately concentrated: in Wisconsin's prisons. While record numbers jam prisons in almost every state, Wisconsin prisons are jammed with black males. One in every one thousand white males in Wisconsin is incarcerated in a state prison; but one in every 59 black males is currently behind state prison bars, one of the highest rates in the nation. If you add to that total the number of black males incarcerated in local jails, every block in Milwaukee's black community has at least one male representative behind bars.

6. See also Colin Greer's analysis in *The Great School Legend.* As Greer put it: "The problem today is that there is an increasing shortage of even low-level employment options for those on the lower levels of the public school totem pole. As a result, the schools now produce people who are a burden upon, rather than the mainstay of, the socio-economic order" (Greer 1972, 152).

7. The Wisconsin Department of Industry, Labor, and Human Relations predicts that "Wisconsin business and industry will face a severe labor shortage in most skill areas in the last decade of the 20th Century, unless young people are trained today to meet the job needs of the 1990s." (*Wisconsin Industry Projections to 1990,* 1). Recent research in New York City concludes: "Movement toward increasingly higher levels of educational attainment has been the main direction of the American labor force. This suggests that the shift to better paying, higher quality jobs is not problem free. It has serious implications for New York City where the high school drop out rate is running at 35%........." (Ehrenhalt 1986).

8. The Study Commission on the Quality of Education in the Metropolitan Milwaukee Schools, October 25, 1985.

9. U.S. Dept of Education quoted in the UWM Graduate School "Minority Newsletter," 1986-'87. For UWM statistics, *UWM Report,* 6:16, May 6, 1986.

10. The major academic exceptions are Moore (1978) and Vigil (1983). Perkins (1987) explicitly criticizes existing gang theory for ignoring "institutional racism." The major academic gang theorists have avoided the question of racism, sometimes treating it as merely an excuse, or rationalization, as affecting only a minority of the gangs. Short claims that racist violence and the civil rights movement in 1960s Chicago had "little impact" on black gangs (1976, 133). Cohen (1955) doesn't even mention ethnicity in his classic work. Spergel (1964) carefully examines three different communities, but analyzes them in terms of "neighborhood characteristics," despite the fact each "neighborhood" analyzed was composed of several different ethnic groups. In Spergel's attempt to validate Cloward's and Ohlin's typology, ecological variables, not ethnic variables, were considered. In another work, Short and Strodtbeck explore "racial differ-

entials" in gang behavior and find "Negro gang boys in our study are more firmly embedded in the lower regions of the lower class" (1965, 106). They conclude: "The nature of delinquency-supporting relations between adults and adolescents differs in lower class Negro and white communities . . . . social control is relative, and the institutions of lower class white communities . . . . are more capable of concerted effective action than is the case for Negroes" (114-15). However, while finding "community-level" differences that clearly account for differences among black and white gangs, the authors did not pursue the subject (see our Chapter Six).

On the other hand, Erlanger (1979) looks at Chicano gang violence in East Los Angeles as the result of "estrangement" of Chicano youth. He sees the violence of Chicano gangs as the result of blocked opportunities, not a "subculture of violence." Further, he finds a direct correlation between gang homicide rates and the declining political involvement of Chicano gangs in the 1970s. Suttles (1968, 216-17) found that four of the oldest black gangs in the Chicago Addams area were drawn into civil rights activity in 1964 and their gangs dissipated. However, other gangs quickly took their place.

11. Milwaukee' long socialist tradition (the city had a socialist mayor until 1960) has not exempted it from racism. Victor Berger, one of the most revered figures of Milwaukee German socialism, was an avowed racist, stating there was "no doubt that the Negroes and mulattoes constitute a lower race" (Allen 1975, 223).

12. The spring 1988 election has seated a new mayor and county executive. Change may finally be arriving.

Chapter Three

1. Cay Shea, Court Services Supervisor, Hennepin County (Minnesota) Home School. September 10, 1986, report to the Youth Coordinating Board.

2. The AIDS epidemic may be providing some lessons for those concerned with the spread of gangs. To facilitate computer tracking of gang members, some zealots are suggesting a form of mandatory testing for a gang history for all migrating blacks and Hispanics. Such screening was seriously suggested as a possible means to control the movement of gang members into Milwaukee's Housing Projects. The proposed legislation on organized crime is from Los Angeles (*Christian Science Monitor,* June 12, 1987). Many midwestern cities have seen their task forces propose a federal program, SHO/DI, which stands for "serious, habitual offenders, possibly drug involved." For a discussion of the problems of the law enforcement approach, see Chapters Four and Seven.

3. The Evanston and Ft. Wayne reports list Chicago gangs as among the gangs in their cities. Evanston reports five gangs: three indigenous and two "satellite" gangs. No supporting data is given for this assertion. Columbus, Ohio, reports that one gang, the "Crips," originated from a migrating Los Angeles black

youth who belonged to the L.A. Crips gang. Columbus police, however, take a more realistic view of the "satellite gang" hypothesis. The Racine report says "further research is required to examine whether gangs from Chicago and/or Milwaukee are highly organized to recruit or establish branch gangs."

4. Yablonsky, for example, who at least did research on 1950s gangs, relates the history of the "Balkans," but begins that history with a violent encounter between the "Balkans" and another gang (Yablonsky 1966, 28). In fact, the very existence of the "Balkans" came as a surprise to the neighborhood social agency where Yablonsky worked. Yablonsky was mainly concerned with proving the violent nature of "modern" gangs, and not with understanding the various ways they originated.

Spergel's gangs began generally with ethnic conflict in "interstitial" areas of his large eastern city. Other gangs were described as beginning in "playgroups" (Spergel 1964, 64-67). We'll say more on the role of conflict in gang formation later in this chapter.

5. Delinquency was a "normal" response among many poor youth. This insight was confirmed by Suttles in his Ph.D. dissertation and later classic study of a Chicago slum. For a fuller explanation, see Kornhauser (1978, 56-61). For Thrasher the gang is a form of social organization to be studied and crime/delinquency is only one aspect of their behavior. Gangs are "tropho-criminal," or permissive or nourishing of crime, not "crimogenic," or productive of crime, according to Moore and Vigil (1983, 2). For modern data in Phoenix, Arizona, see Zatz (1987).

6. Bordua 1961, 136. Bordua notes that the sociological discussion of gangs since Thrasher has changed. "In general, views of the nature of gang activity have shifted quite fundamentally toward a more irrationalist position. Thus, the gang's behavior seems to make no sense." Thus, studies "deal very little with the developmental processes involved in the formation of gangs . . . Current theory focuses so heavily on motive and culture to the exclusion of group process that some essential points are underemphasized" (1961, 122). Bordua's essay is the best short treatment of subculture theories.

7. Of course, the Vicelords have lasted at least thirty years, unlike any of Thrasher's "interstitial" groups. After his history of "Vice Lord Development," Keiser goes on to describe some rather fanciful organizational details and discusses what he calls "heart ideology," rapidly losing the serious reader.

8. The Youth Diversion Project, the gang intervention program in which the authors worked, organized a breakdance competition in spring of 1984 to attract youth involved with breakdancing. The contest attracted one thousand spectators and over thirty different breaking groups. By this time, however, the breakdance fad was ending and the gangs had largely moved on to other activities.

9. The Sheiks are the only example we found of a female gang that was not a male adjunct. In fact, Jeanetta's personality and fighting ability received so much acclaim that eventually a male auxiliary, the "Boy Sheiks" was formed.

10. We should explain our usage of the words "niggas" and "niggers." When some of the gang members we interviewed read the draft of the report on which this book is based, they differentiated between "niggas," which is a positive word for those who are with you, and "niggers," which is a derogatory word for enemies. We've followed their suggestions in the text.

11. The existence of city-wide gang coalitions was noted by Thrasher. "Like nations, gangs are prone to form federations for defensive and offensive purposes" (125). These coalitions were tied to cycles of war and peace between neighborhoods. Chicago's modern coalitions have assumed a kind of permanence, with accompanying ideologies.

12. One gang leader after such a trip to Chicago brought a copy of the laws and literature of the Chicago gang over to the principal author's home. Possession of the laws gave him added stature in the gang, and the leader wanted be helpful to our research as well as to show off a bit. Little did he know that copies of Vicelord and Gangster prayers and laws, obtained from law enforcement sources, were sitting in an upstairs file cabinet. A copy of Keiser's book on the Vicelords at one time was "borrowed" from the principal author's home and copied for distribution.

13. Spergel, analyzing gang homicide within the Chicago area, writes: "Use of the same name by different gang units does not necessarily indicate complex, well-organized, highly solidary gang structures, city wide"(1984, 225, n25). We will look at gang structure and allegations of "organized crime" in the next chapter.

14. "The scholarly literature on juvenile gangs in small-sized cities and towns is deficient" (Takata and Zevitz, 1987).

15. Kornblum (1987) writes without comment: "According to law enforcement officials, gangs in towns and smaller cities aren't involved in turf fights and other forms of inner-city, inter-gang violence. These small-town gangs tend to be more exclusively criminal—robbing citizens, stealing cars, or dealing drugs at street level." Kornblum's entire article is a good example of what results when research is lacking, law enforcement opinions are taken as fact, and analysis is based on dated theoretical suppositions. See also speculation that suburban gangs "are less violent than inner city gangs, have fewer wars over turf, and generate fewer gang-related killings" (Johnstone 1981, 372).

Chapter Four

1. Geis (1965, 1) even gives us a lesson in etymology. The word "gang" came from early English usage of a word for "journey," often a sea journey, thus the "gang" of a ship. It acquired a derogatory usage with Chaucer, using "gonge" as a synonym for "privy." He compared "fool women" with a "common gonge."

Shakespeare continued this usage, noting in "The Merry Wives of Windsor,"
"there's a knot, a gang, a pack, a conspiracy against me." See also Arnold
(1966) for an attempt to redefine "a gang," and Miller's rather lengthy discussion (1976).

2. For example, Short and Strodtbeck (1965), and Moore (1987). Only Spergel
(1964) has claimed to have found data confirming Cloward and Ohlin's types,
but he has been firmly rebutted by Kornhauser (1978, 177-78). Spergel's empirical study of three communities is hampered by his adherence to the Cloward
and Ohlin typologies. Instead of exploring obvious ethnic variables in gang behavior and structure, Spergel attributes gang characteristics fundamentally to
certain types of neighborhoods and their corresponding "subcultures."
Spergel's book is a good example of how theory can mislead research. Like
Short and Strodtbeck twenty years ago, in our research we hunted far and wide
for a "fighting gang," a "criminal gang," or a "drug-using gang" and we
couldn't find them either (Short and Strodtbeck 1965,12-13).

3. Zatz (1987), in a well-researched paper comparing characteristics of juvenile
gang members to non-gang members referred to the Arizona Division of Corrections, finds that juvenile gang members are not referred to juvenile authorities for violent crimes any more frequently than similar non-gang youth. Suttles
(1968, 205-20) and Spergel (1964) support Thrasher. See Kornhauser (1968, 59-
61) for a theoretical review of this point.

4. Perhaps some gangs have organized in the bureaucratic format. Campbell reports female New York gang members telling her that their gangs are organized
in a "pyramidal" fashion that is a reflection, according to Campbell, of "corporate America" (1984, 240).

5. Consider this description received from correctional sources in Beloit, Wisconsin (letter to author). "Criminal justice professionals have come to recognize
street gang activities as a never ending problem. Today's gangs are organized
along a military style, and are highly mobile. The gangs are highly successful in
their dealings of narcotics, trafficking, extortion, intimidation, assault, and
murder. Recruitment is in full force throughout the nation."

6. Five gangs reported the sole group either dissolved or merged with another
group. Two of these gangs, Cameo Boys and 7-11, merged into the 2-7s and Westlawn, respectively. Three gangs have pretty much discontinued operations.
The original Vicelords, though still hanging out on 3rd Street, ceased operations when the Youth Diversion Project referred most of their members all at
once into temporary jobs in 1984. The Vicelord Queens broke up at about the
same time. Other gangs named "Vicelords" exist today, but are not related to
the Vicelords in this study. (See Appendix V).

7. The size of the gangs has been another matter of controversy. Do we estimate
the "hard core" or the "fringe"? How many "card-carrying" members are
there? The estimates arrived at in this study will not help any numbers debate.
We asked how many people were in the "main group" of the age group at the
time (1983-'84) when this age group was most active. Some answers were
clearly exaggerated or at least took the question to mean "main group" plus
"Wanna bes." Some of those interviewed may have wanted their gang to appear

stronger, and some may have wanted it to appear weaker. But since we interviewed more than one person from each gang, we could compare answers and try to estimate the size of the main group of the age group in very rough terms. When we asked those interviewed to list just those who began the age group, the "originals," they listed 260 original members from all nineteen age groups. The "originals" founded the main group of the gang. When we asked for estimates of the size of the main group of each of the age groups, almost all estimated the main group to be "more than 20" and a much larger number of "Wanna bes" surrounding the main group at any given time. To clarify "membership," we asked the difference between a "real" member and a "Wanna be." Most answered a real member (often called "true blue") will "stay with you in a fight"(13) or "hangs out with you all the time" (6). Only one person answered a real member "knows his prayers and laws" (meaning memorization of "literature" from Chicago gangs).

There were several hundred teenagers who were the "real members" or were in the main groups of the first clique of these nineteen Milwaukee gangs and a considerably larger fluctuating group of "Wanna bes." There were at the time of our initial study (1985) two to four age groups within each of twenty or so gangs that had persisted since 1983. There were also dozens of smaller groups forming and dissolving or merging with other gangs at any time. There is no way to calculate the membership of a gang, as you might of the Republican Party or of a college fraternity. The number arrived at depends upon what you count. If you are looking for how many people founded the gangs, we have a pretty good estimate of 260 plus several dozen more from three or four gangs we did not interview. If you want to count how many were in the "main groups" of the gangs in 1983-'84 when the original age groups were most active, our respondents seemed to estimate more than four hundred and less than a thousand. If you want to total up the "main groups" and the "Wanna bes" of each age group of each gang, you will, of course, get a larger number.

8. Following Thrasher, Whyte (1943) looked at corner group activities from the point of view of understanding its routines, which were far from habitual criminality. Short and Strodtbeck (1965) look at incidence and prevalence of delinquency in sixteen Chicago gangs, comparing their findings to the various theoretical expectations of Miller, Cohen, and Cloward and Ohlin (1965, 47-101). Miller sums up the literature and the problem: "Although specifically illegal activities generally constitute a relatively small proportion of a gang's activities, they are often represented as its dominant preoccupation, or even as the basis of its existence" (1976, 292).

9. We decided to edit this interview for readability. David's answers explaining how the gang formed and the impact of labeling were spread out through nearly a hundred pages of transcript. Editing seemed the best way to present David's story. In most cases we have quoted the actual answers from the transcripts and merely combined them with quotes from other answers later in the interview. All other quotes from gang respondents are word for word unless otherwise cited.

10. This quote is from notes taken after the interview with Diego. Diego pointed out homes where drugs were sold on his block.

11. Glasgow sums up our findings precisely in his important book *The Black Underclass*. He is describing the relationship of underclass males to drug sales: The drug-seller role "somewhat resembled their relation to other economic systems, principally the legitimate job world. The drug trade was reputedly able to provide 'long bread,' good money, but only for a few. The typical . . . . (black male). . . . . could not gain access to the controlling positions or to the big sums collected daily. For him, even if he became a pusher the drug system would never be a major source of income. As usual, he held options at the bottom of the pole, either as a user or one able to be manipulated by outsiders. In respect to drug use, his major concern was finding a way to ease the pain of daily living, to get a 'hum' and a little 'high,' without losing control, which would be antithetical to ghetto functioning" (Glasgow 1980, 96).

12. Klein and Maxson (1985) look at black gang involvement with sales of "rock" cocaine in South Los Angeles. Their intention seems to be to promote greater collaboration between police narcotics units and gang units. They establish, basically on law enforcement testimony, the involvement of some gang members in "rock houses." To suggest this means a trend toward all, most, or more than a few gangs getting into the "rock business" in an organized manner is not supported by any reliable evidence.

Chapter Five

1. Treatments of criminal gangs by Spergel (1964) and Cloward and Ohlin concentrated on adult criminal relationships in stable "well-integrated" communities that have little relevance for today. Juveniles in these communities "graduated" to adult criminal status. While neither call attention to the fact in their books, the "criminal opportunity structures" open to these Italian juvenile gangs studied by both Spergel and Cloward and Ohlin were traditional criminal organizations in Italian communities. While some have posited the growth of a "black mafia" through "ethnic succession" (Ianni 1975), we have little evidence to support such a notion.

2. It is important to qualify Spergel's characterization of gang violence. In Chicago, most gang-related homicides are committed by relatively older, disproportionately Hispanic, gang members. Moore also breaks down gang homicides in Los Angeles by ethnicity (1987), as do Klein and Maxson (1985). Both studies find considerably higher homicide rates for Hispanic gangs than for black or other gangs. In all instances, what is being studied is homicides, not arrests for assault or other violent crimes, fighting, or other aggressive behavior. We don't believe the findings of these studies contradict our contention that "fighting" is the central concern of younger age groups and "survival" for the older age groups.

3. In 1958, this "lower class culture," according to Miller, influenced between 40% and 60% of all Americans, with perhaps 15% of the forming up the "hard core" lower class (1958, 334). Kornhauser (1978, 204-14) sharply rejects Mill-

er's thesis. She concludes, largely on theoretical grounds, "The subculture of the lower class, as portrayed by Walter Miller, exists only in his imagination" (208). Kornhauser also points out a curious consequence of Miller's approach: since Chinese and Italians do not exhibit Miller's cultural patterns, for him they cannot be "lower class" (205). It is from another angle that Valentine (1968, 135-38) attacks Miller's attribution of certain "focal concerns" to the lower class. To Valentine, traits such as toughness and autonomy could just as well be attributed to the middle class. Among other gang theorists, only Horowitz (1983) has adopted the Miller culture of poverty paradigm, claiming to find a culture of "honor" among Chicago Chicano gangs.

4. As Bordua puts it: "Cloward and Ohlin's delinquents seem suddenly to appear on the scene sometime in adolescence and to look at the world, and to discover, 'Man, there's no opportunity in my structure' "(Bordua 1961, 134). Cloward's and Ohlin's gangs are much like Merton's conscious rebels to the existing order, ready to march in step with liberal social engineers once given the "opportunity."

5. Those interviewed, to reemphasize the point, can not be seen as representative of the gang population as a whole in a statistical sense. These were leaders and influentials from the "main group" of the founding group of Milwaukee's nineteen gangs. Eleven of the nineteen acknowledged "leaders" of the gangs were among the respondents. No "Wanna bes" were interviewed. While not randomly chosen, forty-five out of a reported two hundred and sixty founders of Milwaukee's gangs is a comparatively large sample.

6. Over half (25) of our respondents reported their families had moved to Milwaukee between 1970 and 1981. Six families had moved between 1950 and 1969. The others (14) were born in Milwaukee or did not know when their families moved here. Only eight families had moved to Milwaukee since 1978 and none since 1981. Black families came either from Chicago (19) or from the south (15). Of the Hispanics, three, all Mexican-American, moved from Texas and six from Puerto Rico. Six of the ten Hispanic families arrived in Milwaukee between 1971 and 1979. One moved here in 1953 and two did not know when their families moved to Milwaukee.

7. Of the 34 families, one third (10) had some history of gang involvement by their family in another city. Two reported slight involvement and eight reported that family members were heavily involved with gangs in another city. Of ten Hispanic families, four families were not involved with gangs in the previous city they lived in, three were heavily involved, and four reported slight family involvement with gangs prior to moving to Milwaukee. A little over 10% (6) of the families of those we interviewed said they moved to Milwaukee to escape Chicago or other big city gang problems. While the percentage of prior gang involvement seems high, the sample for the interviews was made up of key leaders and founders, not those who were followers and "Wanna bes." Our interviews concentrated heavily on gangs accused of being "branches" of Chicago gangs in order to examine the relationship between the two cities. Their families were reported by 70% (32) of those interviewed to be economically "about the same" as their neighbors while growing up. Less than a quarter (10) said their families were "better off" and less than 5% (2) said they came from families who were poorer than their neighbors.

8. Spergel's questions were aimed at validating the "strain" thesis of Merton and Cloward and Ohlin. Kornhauser cites the relevant studies testing this hypothesis and disputes Spergel's conclusions (174-80). Our study was not interested in testing "strain theory," but only in determining what the gang founders would like to do for a living compared to what they thought about their actual employment potential. Spergel's small sample of delinquents within each community (8) should warn us, however, against making generalizations from his data.

9. The following tables were not subjected to multivariate analysis for interaction effects for two reasons. First, the amount of variance is quite small and would not yield much new information. Second, this is reported data, second-hand information which is for this reason unreliable in a statistical sense. While some gang members may want to exaggerate the number of those still in the gang, others may have wanted to deemphasize gang involvement, and these two groups may have canceled each other out. Since several gang members were interviewed from the same gang, we found their respective lists of founding members and their current status to be similar, but not identical. We chose what we considered the most reliable list.

10. Milwaukee's gang founders who did not enter college fared worse in employment than the the national average. According to the *Monthly Labor Review,* 34% of black graduates and 42% of Hispanic graduates nationally who did not enter college were employed. Of the 612,000 U.S. students who dropped out of high school in 1984-85, 44% have jobs, compared to only 30% of the black dropouts and 38% of Hispanic dropouts. *Milwaukee Journal,* November 9, 1986.

11. Hispanic males in our study do show a higher dropout percentage than black males. Eighty-eight percent of Hispanic males (35 of 40) did not receive any kind of a degree, compared to 51% of black males. The percentages in all categories for the ten originals tracked from Punk Alley, the white gang, are similar to overall percentages. The one exception is the percentage of those who have spent time in jail. Less than one third (3) of white originals spent time in jail, compared to two thirds of black and Hispanic males. The small numbers, however, prohibit us from drawing any conclusions.

Chapter Six

1. As we noted in Chapter Two, the end of the bus ride did not mean a better education. The average grade for black students was no higher than a "D" in all but the two college bound high schools. In one high school in an all-white neighborhood, the average grade in 1984 for all black high school students was "F." Just as Milwaukee was embarking on its desegregation plan of scattering black children, the nature of its black youth population was also undergoing a major change. As we indicated earlier, the number of black youth living in poverty increased by 45% in the 1970s, and the 1980s have seen a more dramatic rise in poverty rates. General Assistance recipients have more than tripled since 1979,

and AFDC families have risen by more than a third. Today, most black children live in a poverty-level home. Sixty-five percent of all Milwaukee public school students come from low-income families. Just as specially designed educational strategies were needed for low-income minority students, Milwaukee began busing them all over the city. Concern was focussed on "racial balance," not on the quality of education. Not surprisingly, the resulting loss of neighborhood controls, combined with a significant increase in the number of poorer black children, contributed to unprecedented discipline problems in the schools. Black suspension rates remain among the highest in the country and have increased in relation to the white rate since desegregation. Expulsions and the confiscation of weapons in the schools have significantly increased. The Milwaukee public school dropout rate is around 40%. While a spirited battle over interpretation of various statistics has been waged in Milwaukee, it is indisputable that black and Hispanic youth do poorly in school, do worse compared to whites as they advance in school, are suspended and drop out more than whites, and go on to higher education in far smaller numbers than white students. Our source for all educational statistics is the Study Commission on the Quality of Education in the Metropolitan Milwaukee Schools, a commission appointed by then Governor Earl to investigate the performance of the Milwaukee Public Schools.

2. It should not be surprising that desegregation has had an impact on the formation and development of gangs. The recent reemergence of gang activity in some smaller cities has coincided with the implementation of local desegregation plans. What may be surprising is that there has been very little comment or analysis on the relationship between minority gangs and school desegregation. Walter Miller included a question on desegregation in his 1970s survey of twelve big cities. Respondents from two cities, Detroit and San Francisco, predicted that impending court ordered desegregation would increase interracial gang violence. A San Francisco respondent ominously noted, "But if they move ahead with plans to integrate the high schools, the gang conflict will make what is happening now look like a picnic!" (Miller 1975, 46). Miller sanguinely notes that this and other statements concerning busing may "contain elements of exaggeration." He goes on to comment that the Boston busing situation which prompted serious racial violence did not seem to increase gang conflict, casting doubt on the conclusion that "increased racial mixing in the schools inevitably leads to increased gang problems." In fact, Miller speculates that "busing might serve to lessen the danger of gang problems in that it would weaken the territorial basis of gang formation and conflict" (51). But he makes no further analysis, concluding that "additional information is needed." There are few other references to desegregation and contemporary gangs. In Columbus, Ohio, Councilman John Maloney was quoted by the Columbus Monthly in March of 1986, complaining, "Youngsters don't have a point of identity anymore. The neighborhoods are gone. The neighborhood schools are gone." Columbus crosstown busing has transported gang members to different schools and reportedly led to increased conflict.

3. Alfredo Mirande's (1987) analysis of gangs as "barrio warriors" tries to see gang members today in a political or even romantic light. Erlanger (1979) finds that gang violence receded during periods of intense political activity in Los Angeles barrios, but offers no data to verify gang participation in "movimiento"

activities. Moore, in her Presidential Address to the Society for the Study of Social Problems, points to Chicano middle-class mimicking of gang dress in the 1960s, but is skeptical of the amount of actual gang participation in the revolutionary movements of those times (1985). Perkins suggests that black Chicago gangs began to become more disruptive to the black community only in the 1960s due to the influence of drugs, prison, and the failure of community-based institutions (1987, 40-42).

4. While gang founders interviewed did not have a strong sense of community, they seemed to have a realistic sense of the status and power of black leaders in city politics. Less than one in seven black male gang founders interviewed thought black people had substantial power in Milwaukee. Half thought black people had little or no power at all. Their perceptions are remarkably similar to the surveys of the black community and elites taken over the past twenty years in Milwaukee noted in Chapter Two.

5. Most gang members would agree with Glasgow that the black drug seller was at the bottom of the drug selling heap and mainly sells to survive and get high (Glasgow 1981, 96; see our note 11, Chapter Four). Less than one in ten of those founders interviewed said they thought "major dealers" were gang members. Most explained that gang drug connections were well-known dealers not tied to any gang. Only about a third, however, thought drug use was a gang-related problem. More than four of five said they thought drug use among the gangs was "increasing."

6. Miller's 1950s and 1960s Boston gangs bear little resemblance in levels of violence to their contemporary counterparts. In Miller's sample of violent crimes, there were no gang homicides or manslaughters. Fully 30% of the gang assaults were interracial, reflecting an earlier time of gang "warfare" between ethnic groups of adjoining territory, prior to today's predominantly black on black and Hispanic on Hispanic violence (Miller1969). Also see Moore (1987) and Spergel (1984).

7. For the best reviews of the general issue of homicide causes and the "culture of violence," see Curtis (1985), Rose (1979), Silberman (1978) and Currie (1985, especially Chapter Five, 143-80).

8. Again, Miller (1969) touches on the problem in his carefully researched study of city gang violence, noting a small percentage of intra-gang violence. But he does not pursue the subject in any way. We have no way of knowing whether the intra-gang homicides in Milwaukee's Puerto Rican gangs are merely a local phenomenon, or occur in any frequency in other cities.

9. Differing definitions of what is a "gang related" homicide may account for as much as a 50% difference in the number of homicides reported. Most large cities have, since the early 1970s, changed their definition of what is a "gang related homicide" in order to demonstrate police effectiveness in decreasing gang killings (Miller 1975). Los Angeles, on the other hand, has used a much broader definition of gang homicide for equally political purposes. Regular stories about a gang murder wave have been used in Los Angeles to increase and strengthen the Gang Activities Unit of the LAPD. What is defined as a "gang homicide" differs between jurisdictions and even within police departments. It is not uncommon for police departments to keep two sets of "gang homicide" or "gang

crime" books: one set for official sources, representing generally accepted definitions, and one set by the police gang squads and given to the media to legitimate police anti-gang activities and argue for additional funding. See Miller's definitive discussion of definitions of "gang-related" homicides, (1975, 29-31). Silberman (1978, 80) points out that production of handguns drastically increased in the United States in the 1960s, corresponding to the increase in urban homicides.

10. See Short and Strodtbeck, "Aleatory Risks Versus Short Run Hedonism in Explanation of Gang Action," for the best account of the importance of situational variables in interpreting gang violence. Our interviews generally support the approach of Short and Strodtbeck (1968, 273-91).

Chapter Seven

1. The questionnaire used by the Milwaukee Gang Research Project is included as Appendix I.

2. The response to the release of our study by the Milwaukee Gang Research Project was interesting. While the evening newspaper gave it headline play and TV led their evening news shows with the story, there was very little public response after that. The "Youth Commission," a group of heads of major institutions, eventually discussed the report, but the discussion degenerated as each institution defended its own track record. One Public School official, to the embarrassment of others, actually shouted out that there were pages of jobs in the Want Ads: it was the fault of these kids that they didn't apply. In the only interesting exchange of the meeting, a social agency official wryly commented that if the public schools would have taught the kids to read, maybe they would have been able to read the want ads. On the whole, the response of Milwaukee to the Gang Study has been a disturbed quietness.

3. *Ft. Wayne Journal-Gazette,* "Opinion," August 2, 1983. "City police clearly prefer that there be no publicity about them."

4. *Milwaukee Journal,* May 5, 1983, through May 13, 1983.

5. Alderman Nabors' letter appeared in the October 8, 1983, *Milwaukee Sentinel.* Reaction came immediately in the media and in a public meeting reported on in the September 13 *Milwaukee Journal.* Letters to the editor regularly appeared in fall of 1983 alleging either that gang activity had become uncontrollable, or that undue attention had been given to minority youth gangs.

6. Interestingly, the most visible response to gangs was from black youth themselves. In 1983 the Guardian Angels formed as a group of mainly black youth organized to patrol their community to prevent crime. The Guardian Angels, as well as a similar group, the Nighthawks, enjoyed a brief popularity among minority youth as a positive, but gang-like, alternative. Both groups disbanded due to problems with the character of their leadership.

7. See the remarkable interview initiated by Breier in the *Milwaukee Journal,* February 11, 1984. The *Journal* headline read "Hagedorn a Revolutionary, Breier says." It seems the Chief took exception to Hagedorn's insistence on the existence of a gang problem and criticism of police tactics. For Breier, who was chief for life under state law, any opposition to him or his policies was almost by definition "communist" or "revolutionary."

8. *Milwaukee Journal,* April 8, 1985.

9. *Milwaukee Journal,* October 27, 1983.

10. *Milwaukee Journal,* November 15, 1983.

11. *Milwaukee Journal,* February 9, 1984.

12. J. J. Pansini, "The Gang Problem in Milwaukee: Another View." Undated, unpublished 1984 report to the United Way.

13. Chief Harold Breier had blamed busing for spreading black crime to white neighborhoods, a statement that spurred calls for his resignation. Admission of a minority gang problem was denounced as the equivalent of Breier's racist statements. See *The Milwaukee Journal,* February 9 and 11, 1984, for Breier's comments and the response.

14. Zatz looked only at public reaction to gangs. Her only observation of gangs themselves is in a comparatively narrow sample of juvenile referrals for serious crimes. While her analysis convinces us that a "gang crime wave" attributable to youth gangs was not occurring, we learn little from her article about gangs themselves. She contrasts perceptions of police and social agencies about gangs, but our study has strongly questioned the validity of the perceptions of both. While Phoenix gangs probably did not increase from 5 to 120 gangs within a year, we do not know from her article what in fact happened. In Milwaukee, the emergence of a gang fad did balloon the number of youth involved with gangs and the number of short-term gangs over a few short months in 1983. Aside from these concerns, Zatz's article is the best treatment of social reaction to gangs in the current period (see also Gonzales 1981).

15. While the City of Milwaukee was well-represented on the Task Force, the County boycotted its meetings and the Mayor refused to invite the State of Wisconsin. Warring between various levels of government crippled the Task Force and ruled out any serious attempt at "coordinated" solutions.

16. "Youth Initiatives Task Force Final Report," February 1985.

17. *Milwaukee Journal,* September 12, 1985.

18. For most interviewed, the main incarceration experience was Ethan Allen School, a juvenile institution for boys. Aside from Ethan Allen, many interviewed had personal experience with the House of Correction, a county facility for men and women sentenced to less than a four-year term. When tracking the consequences of incarceration on gang involvement for the entire founding age group, juvenile and adult incarceration are lumped together. While there seems to be little difference in attitude of those interviewed about Ethan Allen School

and the House of Correction, state prison is looked at with more fear. Gangs are now well entrenched in Wisconsin's prison system. The consequences of this development on Milwaukee's gangs has not yet been apparent.

19. Gang members resented the common tactic of police giving Municipal Court citations or "tickets" for loitering and other minor matters. Police admitted these citations were meant to discourage gang activity. The gang founders may have sound constitutional grounds for their objections. Similar use of a Disorderly Conduct charge as a means of harassment was ruled unconstitutional in Chicago in 1984 and 800,000 arrests were voided. *Chicago Tribune*, March 31, 1984.

Chapter Eight

1. NIDA grants DA 07128-01 and DA 07128-02.

2. Now that last sentence could be taken in an elitist and patronizing way. Was our study truly collaborative, or was the field staff "the workers" and the academics "the bourgeoisie"? There's no doubt *I* benefited professionally from publishing the results of our work, but what about the staff? In today's America, on the mean streets as well as on Wall Street, money is the measure of all things. So one way to judge the worth of former gang members to our study would be to see if we put our money where our mouth was. You decide. We spent about a third of the direct costs of the $1.5 million dollars grants on staff, non-professional community interviewers, interview fees, staff training, and other related community-based expenses. If costs for minority academics are included, it appears that about half of all direct costs from the $1.5 million NIDA grant went to support minority professionals and community researchers.

We paid our "community researchers" in various ways. For some on staff, we developed civil service jobs, with full benefits at the University of Wisconsin-Milwaukee. Others worked as temporary employees, and still others were paid "finder's fees" for procuring interviews and other interview-related tasks. This gave us a stable work force of upwardly mobile former gang members, while also giving us the benefit of input from gang members who were still on the streets. We included college tuition in our budget and spent as much as we could to assist those former gang members on our staff, like Jerome Wonders, Rita Lewis, and Lavell Cox, who continued on to college. Base pay was about $10 per hour. "Collaborative," to me, means that the benefits of the study must accrue to both academics and field staff, as well as to our respondents and their communities. Other academic gang research studies need to report to the public "who benefits" from all those research dollars.

3. Our interviews were all drawn from the founding group of gang members in Milwaukee. We have no way of knowing whether these young men and women may be quite different from gang members in succeeding age-groups (see Hagedorn 1996).

4. The contours of this debate are remarkably consistent with Kornhauser's (1978) discussion of the different assumptions of cultural deviance and social disorganization theory.

5. From Shaw and McKay on, social disorganization theorists have been uncertain and often contradictory in how they explain the issue of values and deviant subcultures. Cloward and Ohlin (1960) first added on Shaw and McKay and Sutherland's concept of deviant subcultures to Merton's anomie theory. Wilson and Sampson (1995, 50) apparently call subcultures "cognitive landscapes" where mainstream values "may" no longer apply. At a later date, Wilson (1996, 69–70) argued that the ghetto poor have not internalized new values at all, but are merely "adapting to difficult circumstances." Elijah Anderson (1994) seems to be the most inclined to argue that new values exist among central city gangs in his formulation of a "code of the streets." What all these social disorganization scholars share, however, is a focus on the cultural effects of social isolation on gang members, rather than on the effects of mainstream culture.

6. Violence, as will be shown below, is indicative of many different kinds of phenomena, not just social disorganization. Homicides, for example, may represent the regulation of the drug business, and this kind of homicide may vary by the opportunities to make a profit in a neighborhood, rather than by the status of local social institutions (Rose and McClain 1990). Most homicides have traditionally been between people who know one another well, often men killing men over their women, men killing women, or, more rarely, women killing men, typically in self-defense. Stanko (1994) points out that these male homicides are not "expressive" in the usual sense (Parsons 1951), but are more explicitly instrumental, in that they are acts aimed at controlling women, normally in their own homes. Thus, the number of such acts of "intimate" violence do not directly measure social disorganization, but rather measure the state of male/female relationships under economic and social stress, combined with the prevalence of a violent conception of masculinity by men (Gelles and Straus 1988). The degree to which stressed families and the prevalence of violent conceptions of masculinity indirectly measure community disorganization is an uninvestigated empirical question. Community disorganization, regardless of how it is operationalized, impacts men and women quite differently, and cannot be analyzed separately from an analysis of gender (see Hagedorn 1997).

7. What about violence? Surely wall street stockbrokers would not resort to heavily armed violence in their disputes like drug dealers do. Or given sufficient provocation and the right conditions, might even upper class financial whiz kids descend to the grubby world of violence? Steward (421–423) describes one such scene where investor John Mulheren reacts to having been ruined by Ivan Boesky:

> In the bag, Mulheren had placed a loaded, .233-caliber Israeli Galil assault rifle, purchased two weeks before, and a set of army fatigues. Already in the car were a 9 millimeter semiautomatic pistol, a .357 magnum pistol, and a 12-gauge pistol grip shotgun—a veritable arsenal.... His mission: to kill the one man behind all his torment [Boesky—ed.].... Soon Mulheren began carrying a loaded weapon everywhere. The police, he had now concluded, were in league with the government prosecutors trying to ensnare him in the Boesky scandal. Mulheren thought he should be armed in case a policemen tried to kill him.

Stewart concludes this remarkable story: "Perhaps it was inevitable, even within the confines of a white collar scandal, that violence should erupt. The money and power at stake were enormous; many have killed, or been killed, for less."

8. Three whites were excluded from the analysis. One white founder never sold and the other two made less than $2,000 monthly. Percentages may not equal 100% due to rounding. Equivalent hourly wages are based on a 40-hour week. Gang members may not have sold drugs full-time, so they may have made more per hour than indicated. Most gang members, when they sold, worked "24/7," or full time.

9. Elsewhere (Hagedorn 1997) I've categorized male gang violence as men "doing gender, doing business, and doing anomie."

10. The manufacturing sector in Milwaukee employed a total of 14,000 black males and females of all ages in 1990. In Milwaukee in 1990, the census counted a total of 10,000 black males aged 20–24, or about 15% of the male black work force, or all black males aged 20 to 59. If young black males made up 15% of a high estimate of 10,000 males in manufacturing, that means that about 1,500 black males aged 20–24 were employed at some time in manufacturing in Milwaukee in 1990, or about the same number as those employed selling drugs in Milwaukee in the 10 to 12 high drug sales neighborhoods we identified.

11. In our study, like others, the majority of the customers of gang drug sales were women, not men.

12. Larry Hoover, incarcerated leader of Chicago's Black Gangster Disciples, put it well when he said that Chicago's political machine "can't control the apathetic vote, and that's what I was advocating that we wake up—street gang members, people who live in the projects, homeless.... Mayor Daley is afraid of me because he understands the potential of the type of movement I'm trying to push" (Tyson 1996).

REFERENCES

Adler, Freda.
    1975. *Sisters in Crime.* New York: McGraw-Hill.

Agnew, Robert, Frances Ta. Cullen, Velmer S. Burton Jr., T. David
    Evans and R. Gregory Dunaway.
    1996. "A New Test of Classic Strain Theory." *Justice Quarterly*
    13:681–704.

Allen, Robert L.
    1975. *Reluctant Reformers: Racism and Social Reform Movements
    in the United States.* New York: Anchor Books.

Anderson, Elijah.
    1994. "The code of The Streets." *The Atlantic Monthly.* May.

Arnold, William R.
    1965. "The Concept of Gang." *The Sociological Quarterly* 7:1,
    59–75.

Asbury, Herbert.
    1939. *The Gangs of New York.* New York: Alfred A. Knopf.

Auletta, Ken.
    1983. *The Underclass.* New York: Vintage.

Bell, Derrick, ed.
    1980. *Shades of Brown: New Perspectives on School Desegregation.*
    New York and London: Teachers College Press.

Biernacki, Patrick and Dan Waldorf.
    1981. "Snowball Sampling: Problems and Techniques of Chain
    Referral Sampling." *Sociological Methods and Research* 10:141–63.

Bjerregaard, Beth and Carolyn Smith.
1995. "Gender Differences in Gang Participation, Delinquency, and Substance Use." Pp. 93–105 in *The Modern Gang Reader.* Edited by Malcolm W. Klein, Cheryl L. Maxson and Jody Miller. Los Angeles: Roxbury.

Black, Donald.
1983. "Crime as Social Control." *American Sociological Review* 48:34–45.

Blauner, Robert and David Wellman.
1973. "Toward the Decolonization of Social Research." Pp. 310–30 in *The Death of White Sociology.* Edited by Joyce A. Ladner. New York: Vintage.

Block, Carolyn Rebecca and Richard Block.
1995. "Street Gang Crime in Chicago." Pp. 202–10 in *The Modern Gang Reader.* Edited by Malcolm Klein, Cheryl Maxson and Jody Miller. Los Angeles: Roxbury.

Block, Carolyn Rebecca, Antigone Christakos, Ayad Jacob and Roger Przybylski.
1996. "Street Gangs and Crime." *Research Bulletin: Illinois Criminal Justice Information Authority.*

Blumstein, Alfred.
1993. "Making Rationality Relevant." *Criminology* 31:1–16.

Bloch, H. A., and Arthur Niederhoffer.
1958. *The Gang: A Study in Adolescent Behavior.* New York: Philosophical Library.

Bordua, David J.
1961. "Delinquent Subcultures: Sociological Interpretations of Gang Delinquency." *Annals of the American Academy of Social Science* 338:119–36.

Bourgois, Philippe.
1995. *In Search of Respect: Selling Crack in El Barrio.* Cambridge: Cambridge University Press.

Bowker, Lee H. and Malcolm W. Klein.
1983. "The Etiology of Female Juvenile Delinquency and Gang Membership: A Test of Psychological and Social Structural Explanations." *Adolescence* 18:738–51.

Braithwaite, John.
1989. *Crime, shame and reintegration.* New York: Cambridge University Press.

Brown, Waln K.
1978. "Black Gangs as Family Extensions." *International Journal of Offender Therapy and Comparative Criminology* 22:1, 39–48.

Bullock, Paul.
1973. *Aspiration vs. Opportunity: "Careers" in the Inner City.* Ann Arbor: Institute of Labor and Industrial Relations, University of Michigan-Wayne State.

Bursik Jr., Robert J. and Harold G. Grasmick.
1993. *Neighborhoods and Crime: The Dimensions of Effective Community Control.* New York: Lexington Books.

Camp, George and Camille Graham Camp.
1985. *Prison Gangs: Their Extent, Nature, and Impact on Prisons.* Washington: U.S. Dept. of Justice.

Campbell, Ann.
1984. *The Girls in the Gang.* Oxford: Basil Blackwell.

1990. "Female Participation in Gangs." Pp. 163–82 in *Gangs In America.* 2nd ed. Edited by C. Ronald Huff. Newbury Park, Calif.: Sage.

1993. *Men, Women, and Aggression.* New York: Basic Books.

Cazenave, Noel A.
1981. "Black Men in America: A Quest for Manhood." Pp. 176–85 in *Black Families.* Edited by Hariette Pipes McAdoo. Beverly Hills: Sage.

Chambliss, William J.
1973. "The Saints and the Roughnecks." *Society* Nov/Dec., 11:1, 24–31.

Chesney-Lind, Meda.
1993. "Girls, Gangs and Violence: Anatomy of a Backlash." *Humanity & Society* 17:321–44.

Chesney-Lind, Meda, Randall G. Shelden and Karen A. Joe
1996. "Girls, Delinquency, and Gang Membership." Pp. 185–204

in *Gangs In America*. 2nd ed. Edited by C. Ronald Huff. Newbury Park, Calif.: Sage.

Chesney-Lind, Meda and Randall G. Sheldon.
1992. *Girls, Delinquency, and Juvenile Justice*. Pacific Grove, CA: Brooks/Cole Publishing Co.

Chodorow, Nancy.
1978. *The Reproduction of Mothering: Psychoanalysis and the Sociology of Gender*. Berkeley: University of California.

Cloward, Richard, and Lloyd Ohlin.
1960. *Delinquency and Opportunity*. Free Press, Glencoe, Ill.

Cloward, Richard A. and Frances Fox Piven.
1979. "Hidden Protest: The Channeling of Female Innovation and Resistance." *Signs* 4:651–69.

Cohen, Albert.
1955. *Delinquent Boys*. Glencoe, Ill.: The Free Press.

Cohen, Michael D., James G. March and Johan P. Olsen.
1972. "A Garbage Can Model of Organizational Choice." *Administrative Science Quarterly* 17:1–25.

Community Relations-Social Development Commission.
1970. "Black Powerlessness in Milwaukee Institutions and Decision-making Structure." Milwaukee County. Undated.

Conley, John.
1982. "The Police in Milwaukee: Problems of Openness and Accountability." Future Milwaukee.

Connell, R.W.
1987. *Gender and Power*. Stanford: Stanford University Press.

1995. *Masculinities*. Berkeley: University of California.

Cook, Philip J. and John H. Laub.
In press. "The Unprecedented Epidemic in Youth Violence." In *Youth Violence*. Edited by Michael Tonry and Mark H. Moore. Chicago: University of Chicago.

Cortes, Carlos.
1972. "The Chicano social bandit as romantic hero." Unpublished paper.

Cottingham, Clement, Ed.
    1982. *Race, Poverty, and the Urban Underclass*. Lexington, Mass.:
    Lexington Books.

Currie, Elliot.
    1985. *Confronting Crime, An American Challenge*. New York:
    Pantheon.

Curry, G. David.
    1995. "Responding to Female Gang Involvement." Paper
    presented at American Society of Criminology. Boston.

Curtis, Lynn A.
    1985. *American Violence and Public Policy*. New Haven: Yale
    University Press.

Daly, Kathleen and Meda Chesney-Lind.
    1988. "Feminism and Criminology." *Justice Quarterly* 5:497–538.

Davis, Robert C. and Arthur J. Lurigio.
    1996. *Fighting Back: Neighborhood Anti-Drug Strategies*.
    Thousand Oaks, Calif.: Sage.

Decker, Scott and Barrik Van Winkle.
    1996. *Life in The Gang: Family, Friends, and Violence*. New York:
    Cambridge.

Dichiaria, Albert.
    1997. "We Ain't No Gang: We a Family." From *Gangs to Street
    Organizations to Social Movements*. Paper to be delivered at the
    annual meeting of the American Society of Criminology. San Diego.

Donziger, Stephen A.
    1996. *The Real War on Crime: The Report of the National
    Criminal Justice Commission*. New York: Harper Perennial.

Douglas, Susan J.
    1994. *Where the Girls Are: Growing Up Female with the Mass
    Media*. New York: Times Books.

Drake, St. Clair and Horace R Cayton.
    1970. *Black Metropolis*. New York: Harcourt, Brace, & World.

Drucker, Peter F.
    1985. *Innovation and Entrepreneurship: Practice and Principles*.
    New York: Harper & Row.

Durkheim, Emile.
    1951. *Suicide: A Study in Sociology.* New York: The Free Press.

Edari, Ronald.
    1977. "The Structure of Racial Inequality in the Milwaukee Area."
    UWM Urban Research Center.

Edwards, Richard.
    1979. *Contested Terrain.* New York: Basic Books.

Ehrenhalt, Samuel.
    1986. "Insight and Outlook: The New York Experience as a
    Service Economy." Paper presented before the Nineteenth
    Annual Institute on Challenges of the Changing Economy of New
    York City, May 14, 1986.

Empey, LaMar T.
    1978. *American Delinquency: Its Meaning and Construction.*
    Homewood, Ill.: The Dorsey Press.

Erlanger, Howard S.
    1979. "Estrangement, Machismo and Gang Violence." *Social
    Science Quarterly* 60:2, 235–49.

Fagan, Jeffrey.
    1996. "Gangs, Drugs, and Neighborhood Change." Pp. 39–74 in
    Gangs in America. 2nd ed. Edited by Ronald C. Huff. Thousand
    Oaks, Calif.: Sage.

Feagin, Joe.
    1984. "Sunbelt metropolis and development capital: Houston in
    the era of late capitalism." Pp. 99–127 in *Sunbelt/Snowbelt.* Edited
    by Larry Sawer and William Tabb. New York: Oxford University
    Press.

Frias, Gus.
    1982. *Barrio Warriors: Homeboys of Peace.* Los Angeles: Diaz
    Publications.

Fulbright, Karen.
    1996. *The Unintended Consequences of Incarceration.* New York:
    Vera Institute of Justice.

Gans, Herbert J.
    1962. *The Urban Villagers.* Glencoe: The Free Press of Glencoe.

Geis, Gilbert.
  1965. "Juvenile Gangs." Washington, D.C.: President's Committee on Juvenile Delinquency and Youth Crime.

Gelles, Richard J. and Murray A. Straus.
  1988. *Intimate Violence: The Causes and Consequences of Abuse in the American Family.* New York: Simon and Schuster.

Georges-Abeyie, Daniel.
  1984. "The Criminal Justice System and Minorities: A Review of the Literature." Pp. 125–42 in *The Criminal Justice System and Blacks.* Edited by Daniel Georges-Abeyuie. New York: Clark Boardman.

Gerson, Kathleen.
  1985. *Hard Choices: How Women Decide about Work, Career, and Motherhood.* Berkeley: University of California.

Gilligan, Carol.
  1982. *In A Different Voice: Psychological Theory and Women's Development.* Cambridge, Mass.: Harvard University Press.

Giordano, Peggy C.
  1978. "Girls, Guys and Gangs: The Changing Social Context of Female Delinquency." *The Journal of Criminal Law & Criminology* 69:126–32.

Glasgow, Douglas G.
  1981. *The Black Underclass.* New York: Vintage.

Goffman, Erving.
  1959. *The Presentation of Self in Everyday Life.* New York: Anchor Books.

Goldstein, Paul J.
  1985. "The Drugs/Violence Nexus: A Tripartite Conceptual Framework." *The Journal of Drug Issues* Fall: 493–506.

Gonzalez, Alfredo.
  1981. "Mexican/Chicano Gangs in Los Angeles." Unpublished Ph.D. manuscript.

Gordon, David M., Richard Edwards, and Michael Reich.
  1982. *Segmented Work, Divided Workers.* Cambridge: Cambridge University Press.

Greer, Colin.
    1972. *The Great School Legend.* New York: Basic Books.

Hagedorn, John M.
    1985. "Strategy and Tactics in Gang Intervention." Paper delivered at Juvenile Violence-Juvenile Justice conference, Milwaukee.

    1985. "Gang Youth Perceptions of Drug Treatment Programs." Report to the Wadari Foundation, Milwaukee.

    1987. "The Salience of Neighborhood for Black Gangs in an Epoch of Desegregation." Paper delivered at the Midwest Sociological Society, Chicago.

    1990. "Back in the Field Again: Gang Research in the Nineties." Pp. 240–59 in *Gangs in America.* 2nd ed. Edited by C. Ronald Huff. Beverly Hills, Calif.: Sage.

    1991. "Gangs, Neighborhoods, and Public Policy." *Social Problems* 38:529–42.

    1994a. "Neighborhoods, Markets, and Gang Drug Organization." *Journal of Research in Crime & Delinquency* 32:197–219.

    1994b. "Homeboys, Dope Fiends, Legits, and New Jacks: Adult Gang Members, Drugs, and Work." *Criminology* 32:197–219.

    1995. *Forsaking Our Children: Bureaucracy and Reform in the Child Welfare System.* Chicago: Lake View Press.

    1996. "The Emperor's New Clothes: Theory and Method in Gang Research." *New Inquiry for a Creative Sociology* 24 (2): 111–22.

    1997. "Doing Gender, Doing Business, and Doing Anomie: A Typology of Male Gang Violence." Paper presented at the annual meeting of the Association for Law and Society, St. Louis. May.

    In press-a. "Homeboys, New Jacks, and Anomie." *Journal of African American Men.*

    In press-b. "Frat Boys, Bossmen, Studs, and Gentlemen: A Typology of Gang Masculinities." In *Masculinities and Violence.* Edited by Lee Bowker. Beverly Hills, Calif.: Sage.

    In press-c. "Post-Industrial Gang Violence." In "Youth Violence." Edited by Micheal Tonry and Michael H. Moore. *Crime & Justice* 24.

In press-d. "As American as Apple Pie: A Case Study of Post-Industrial Gang Violence," in *Cross-Cultural Perspectives on Youth, Radicalism, and Violence*. Edited by Meredith W. Watts. Hartford: JAI Press.

Hagedorn, John M., Joan Moore, and Perry Macon.
1987. "Milwaukee Gang Research Project: Final Report." UWM Urban Research Center.

Hagedorn, John M. and Joan Moore.
1987. "Milwaukee and Los Angeles Gangs Compared." Paper delivered at American Anthropological Association, Oaxaca, Mexico.

Hagedorn, John M. and Mary L. Devitt.
1996. "Fighting Female: Variation, Violence, and Gender Roles in Female Gangs." Paper presented at American Sociological Association.

Hamid, Ansley.
1990. "The Political Economy of Crack-related Violence." *Contemporary Drug Problems* 17:31–78.

Hamid, Ansley and Richard Curtis.
1996. "State-Sponsored Violence in New York City and Indigeneous Attempts to Contain It: The Mediating Role of the Third Crown (Sgt. at Arms) of the Latin Kings." Paper presented at American Sociological Association.

Hannerz, Ulf.
1969. *Soulside: Inquiries into Ghetto Culture and Community*. New York: Columbia University Press.

Hardman, Dale G.
1969. "Small Town Gangs," *Journal of Criminal Law, Criminology and Police Studies* 60 (2): 173–81.

1967. "Historical Perspectives on Gang Research." *Journal of Research in Crime and Delinquency* 4 (1): 5–27.

Harring, Sidney L.
1982. "The Police Institution as a Class Question: Milwaukee Socialists and the Police, 1900–1915." *Science and Society* 46 (2): 197–221.

Heer, David.
    1986. "Undocumented Mexican: America's New Underclass?" Unpublished paper.

Helmreich, William B.
    1973. "Black Crusaders: The Rise and Fall of Political Gangs." *Society* 11 (1): 44–50.

Hobsbawm, E. J.
    1959. *Primitive Rebels: Studies in Archaic Forms of Social Movements in the 19th and 20th Centuries.* New York: Norton.

hooks, bell.
    1981. *Ain't I a Woman? Black Women and Feminism.* Boston: South End Press.

Horowitz, Ruth.
    1983. *Honor and the American Dream.* New Brunswick: Rutgers University Press.

    1983. "The End of the Youth Gang." *Criminology* 21 (4): 585–600.

Howell, James C.
    1996. "Youth Gangs, Homicides, Drugs and Guns." Tallahassee: National Youth Gang Center.

Hunter, Albert.
    1985. "Private, Parochial, and Public Social Orders: The Problem of Crime and Incivility in Urban Communities." Pp. 230–42 in *The Challenge of Social Control.* Edited by Gerald Suttles and Mayer Zald. Norwood, New Jersey: Ablex Publishing Corporation.

Ianni, Francis.
    1975. *Black Mafia.* New York: Simon & Schuster.

Irwin, John.
    1980. *Prisons in Turmoil.* Boston: Little, Brown and Company.

Jacobs, James.
    1974. "Street Gangs Behind Bars." *Social Problems* 21 (3): 395–408.

    1977. *Stateville.* Chicago: University of Chicago Press.

Joe, Karen.
    1993. "Issues in Accessing and Studying Ethnic Youth Gangs." *The Gang Journal* 1:9–23.

Joe, Karen and Meda Chesney-Lind.
    1995. "Just Every Mother's Angel." *Gender and Society* 9:408–31.

Johnson, Miriam M.
    1988. *Strong Mothers, Weak Wives.* Berkeley: University of
    California.

Johnstone, John W. C.
    1981. "Youth Gangs and Black Suburbs." *Pacific Sociological
    Review* 24 (3): 355–73.

Katz, Jack.
    1988. *Seductions of Crime.* New York: Basic Books.

Katznelson, Ira.
    1981. *City Trenches.* Chicago: University of Chicago.

Katznelson, Ira and Margaret Weir.
    1985. *Schooling for All: Class, Race, and the Decline of the
    Democratic Ideal.* Berkeley: University of California.

Keiser, R. Lincoln.
    1969. *The Vice Lords: Warriors of the Streets.* New York: Holt,
    Rinehart, and Winston.

Kirk, Jerome and Marc L. Miller.
    1986. *Reliability and Validity in Qualitative Research.* Beverly
    Hills, Calif.: Sage.

Klein, Malcolm.
    1971. *Street Gangs and Street Workers.* Engelwood Cliffs, New
    Jersey: Prentice Hall.

    1995. *The American Street Gang: Its Nature, Prevalence, and
    Control.* New York: Oxford University Press.

Klein, Malcolm, and Cheryl Maxson.
    1985. "'Rock Sales' in South Los Angeles." *Sociology and Social
    Research* 69 (4): 561–65.

Klein, Malcolm, and Cheryl Maxson and Margaret A Gordon.
    1985. "Differences Between Gang and Non-Gang Homicides."
    Criminology 23 (2): 209–20.

Kleiner, Robert J, Holger R Stub, and Jane Lanahan.
    1975. "A Study of Black Youth Groups: Implications for Research,

Action, and the Role of the Investigator." *Human Organization* 34 (4): 391–93.

Kobrin, Solomon, Joseph Puntil, and Emil Peluso.
1967. "Criteria of Status among Street Groups." *Journal of Research in Crime and Delinquency* 4 (1): 98–118.

Kornblum, William.
1987. "Ganging Together: Helping Gangs Go Straight." *Social Issues and Health Review* 2: 99–104.

Kornhauser, Ruth Rosner.
1978. *Social Sources of Delinquency: An Appraisal of Analytic Models.* Chicago: University of Chicago.

Lauderback, David, Joy Hansen and Dan Waldorf.
1992. "'Sisters are doin' it for themselves': A Black Female Gang in San Francisco." *The Gang Journal* 1:57–70.

Leach, William.
1993. *Land of Desire: Merchants, Power, and the Rise of a New American Culture.* New York: Random House.

Lemann, Nicholas.
1986. "The Origins of the Underclass." *Atlantic Monthly* (June 1986) 31–54, (July 1986) 54–68.

Leonard, Eileen.
1983. *Women, Crime, and Society.* New York: Longman.

Liebow, Elliot.
1967. *Tally's Corner.* Boston: Little, Brown, & Company.

Lipset, Seymour Martin.
1996. *American Exceptionalism: A Double Edged Sword.* New York: W.W. Norton.

Lorber, Judith.
1994. *Paradoxes of Gender.* New Haven: Yale University Press.

Maher, Lisa and Kathleen Daly.
1996. "Women in the Street-Level Drug Economy: Continuity or Change?" *Criminology* 34:465–92.

Majors, Richard and Janet Mancini Billson.
1992. *Cool Pose: The Dilemmas of Black Manhood in America.* New York: Simon & Schuster.

Martin, Susan Ehrlich and Nancy C. Jurik.
1996. *Doing Justice, Doing Gender.* Thousand Oaks, Calif.: Sage.

Maxson, Cheryl L. and Malcolm W. Klein.
1996. "Defining Gang Homicide: An Updated Look at Member and Motive Approaches." Pp. 3–20 in *Gangs in America.* 2nd ed. Edited by Ronald C. Huff. Thousand Oaks, Calif.: Sage.

McCarthy, Kevin and Burciaga Valdez.
1986. "Current and Future Effects of Mexican Immigration in California." Santa Monica, Calif.: Rand Corporation.

McCall, George J, and J. L. Simmons.
1969. *Issues in Participant Observation.* Reading, Mass.: Addison-Wesley.

McMahon, William J.,Gregory Moots F., and Sammis B. White.
1992. "Restructuring the Milwaukee Economy: 1979–1989." Milwaukee, Wis.: Urban Research Center, University of Wisconsin-Milwaukee.

Merton, Robert K.
1938. "Social Structure and Anomie." *American Sociological Review* 3:672–82.

1968, 1957. *Social Theory and Social Structure.* New York: The Free Press.

Messerschimdt, James W.
1993. *Masculinities and Crime: Critique and Reconceptualization of Theory.* Totowa, NJ: Rowman & Littlefield.

1995. "From Patriarchy to Gender: Femininst Theory, Criminology, and the Challenge of Diversity." In *International Feminist Perspectives in Criminology.* Edited by Nicole Hahn Rafter and and Frances Heidensohn. Philadelphia: Open University Press.

Messner, Steven F. and Richard Rosenfeld.
1994. *Crime and the American Dream.* Belmont, Calif.: Wadsworth Publishing Company.

Miller, Eleanor M.
1986. *Street Woman.* Philadelphia: Temple University Press.

Miller, Jerome G.

1996. *Search and Destroy: African American Males in the Criminal Justice System.* New York: Cambridge University Press.

Miller, Walter.

1969. "Lower Class Culture as a Generating Milieu of Gang Delinquency." Pp. 332–48 in *Delinquency, Crime, and Social Progress.* Edited by Donald R. Cressey and David A. Ward. New York: Harper & Row.

1969. "Violent Crime in City Gangs." Pp. 688–708 in *Delinquency, Crime, and Social Process.* Edited by Donald R. Cressey and David A. Ward. New York: Harper & Row.

1970. "White Gangs." Pp. 45–84 in *Law & Order: Modern Criminals.* Edited by James F. Short. New Brunswick, NJ: Transaction Publishers.

1974. "American Youth Gangs: Past and Present." Pp. 291–320 in *Current Perspectives on Criminal Behavior.* Edited by Abraham Blumberg. New York: Alfred A. Knopf.

1975. "Violence by Youth Gangs and Youth Groups as a Crime Problem in Major American Cities." Washington, D.C.: U.S. Department of Justice.

1976. "Youth Gangs in the Urban Crisis Era." Pp. 91–122 in *Delinquency, Crime, and Society.* Edited by James F. Short. Chicago: University of Chicago.

1990. "Why the United States has Failed to Solve Its Youth Gang Problem." Pp. 263–87 in *Gangs in America.* 2nd ed. Edited by C. Ronald Huff. Newbury Park, Calif.: Sage.

Milwaukee Department of City Development.

1977. "Population Projection." Milwaukee.

1987. "Toward Preservation Partnerships." Milwaukee.

Mirande, Alfredo.

1987. *Gringo Justice.* South Bend: Notre Dame Press.

Moore, Joan W.

1973. "Social Constraints on Sociological Knowledge: Academics and Research Concerning Minorities." *Social Problems* 21:1, 65–76.

1977. "A Case Study of Collaboration: The Chicano Pinto Research Project." *Journal of Social Issues* 33 (4), 144–58.

1983. "Residence and Territoriality in Chicano Gangs." *Social Problems* 31:2, 182–94.

1985. "Isolation and Stigmatization in the Development of an Underclass: The Case of Chicano Gangs in East Los Angeles." *Social Problems* 33 (1), 1–10.

1987. "Variations in Violence Among Hispanic Gangs." Paper delivered at the research conference on violence and homicide in Hispanic communities, Los Angeles.

1991. *Going Down to the Barrio: Homeboys and Homegirls in Change.* Philadelphia: Temple University Press.

In press. "Gangs in a Cross-cultural Perspective." In *Cross-Cultural Perspectives on Youth, Radicalism, and Violence.* Edited by Meredith W. Watts. Hartford: JAI Press.

Moore, Joan W., Ramon Salcido and Robert Garcia.
1979. "In the Barrios: Survival and Success." Presented at the Conference of the Vice President's Task Force on Youth Unemployment in the Inner City. Oakland, Calif.

Moore, Joan W. and Lionel Maldonado (editors).
1985. *Urban Ethnicity in the United States.* Beverly Hills, Calif.: Sage.

Moore, Joan W., and John M. Hagedorn.
1995. "Gangs, Neighbors, and Drug Dealing." Paper presented at Clifford Shaw Centennial Celebration. Chicago.

1996. "What Happens to Girls in the Gang?" Pp. 205–18 in *Gangs in America.* 2nd ed. Beverly Hills, Calif.: Sage.

Moore, Joan W., and James Diego Vigil.
1983. "Chicano Gangs: Group Norms and Individual Factors to Adult Criminality." Paper presented at the American Society of Criminology.

Muller, Thomas and T. J. Espenshade.
1985. *The Fourth Wave: California's Newest Immigrants.* Washington, D.C.: Urban Institute Press.

Murray, Charles.
    1984. *Losing Ground.* New York: Basic Books.

Naffine, Ngaire.
    1996. *Feminism and Criminology.* Philadelphia: Temple.

National Research Council.
    1982. *Critical Issues for Urban Policy.* Cambridge, Md.: National
    Academy Press.

Nightengale, Carl Husemoller.
    1993. *On the Edge: A History of Poor Black Children and Their
    American Dreams.* New York: Basic Books.

Needle, Jerome A. and William Vaughan Stapleton.
    1983. *Police Handling of Youth Gangs.* Washington, D.C.:
    American Justice Institute.

Oliver, William.
    1994. *The Violent Social World of Black Men.* New York:
    Lexington Books.

Parsons, Talcott.
    1951. *The Social System.* Glencoe, Ill.: Free Press.

Patrick, James.
    1973. *A Glasgow Gang Observed.* London: Eyre Methuen.

Perkins, Useni Eugene.
    1987. *Explosion of Chicago's Black Street Gangs.* Chicago: Third
    World Press.

Phoenix, Arizona, Police Department.
    1981. "Latin Gang Member Recognition Guide." Phoenix.

Piliavin, Irving and Carl Werthman.
    1967. "Gang Members and the Police." Pp. 56–98 in *The Police:
    Six Sociological Essays.* Edited by David J. Bordua. New York:
    John Wiley & Sons.

Platt, Anthony M.
    1969. *The Child Savers.* Chicago: University of Chicago.

Piven, Frances Fox and Richard A. Cloward.
    1980. *Poor People's Movements: Why they Succeed, How they Fail.*
    New York: Vintage.

Polk, Kenneth.
　　1984. "The New Marginal Youth." *Crime & Delinquency* 30 (3): 462–79.

Prothrow-Stith, Deborah, with Michaele Weisman.
　　1991. *Deadly Consequences: How Violence is Destroying Our Teenage Population and A Plan to Begin Solving the Problem.* New York: HarperCollins.

Racine Gang Project.
　　1985. "Summary of Findings." July.

Rainwater, Lee, and William L. Yancey.
　　1967. *The Moynihan Report and the Politics of Controversy.* Cambridge, Mass.: MIT Press.

Redfield, Robert.
　　1941. *Folk Culture of Yucatan.* Chicago: University of Chicago Press.

Ro, Ronin.
　　1996. *gangsta: merchandising the rhymes of violence.* New York: St. Martin's Press.

Rose, Harold M., ed.
　　1979. *Lethal Aspects of Urban Violence.* Lexington, Mass.: D.C. Heath & Company.

Rose, Harold M., Ronald S. Edari, Lois M. Quinn and John Pawasrat.
　　1992. "The Labor Market Experience of Young African American Men from Low-Income Families in Wisconsin." University of Wisconsin-Milwaukee Employment and Training Institute. Milwaukee.

Rose, Harold M. and Paula D. McClain.
　　1990. *Race, Place, and Risk: Black Homicide in Urban America.* Albany: State University of New York.

Rosenbaum, Dennis P. and Jane A. Grant.
　　1983. "Gang and Youth Problems in Evanston: Research Findings and Policy Options." Evanston, Ill.: Center for Urban Affairs and Policy Research, Northwestern University.

Rossi, Peter H., Richard A Berk, and Bettye K. Eidson.
　　1974. *The Roots of Urban Unrest: Public Policy, Municipal Institutions, and the Ghetto.* New York: John Wiley & Sons.

Royko, Mike.
  1971. *Boss.* New York: Signet.

de Santiago, Anne Akulicz.
  1980. "The Puerto Rican Community of Milwaukee: A Study of Geographic Mobility." Milwaukee: Spanish Speaking Outreach Institute, University of Wisconsin-Milwaukee.

Sampson, Robert J.
  1987. "Urban Black Violence: The Effect of Male Joblessness and Family Disruption." *American Journal of Sociology* 93:348–82.

Sampson, Robert J. and John H. Laub.
  1993. *Crime in the Making: Pathways and Turning Points Through Life.* Cambridge, Mass.: Harvard University Press.

Sanchez-Jankowski, Martin.
  1991. *Islands in the Street: Gangs and American Urban Society.* Berkeley: University of California.

Sanders, William B.
  1994. *Gangbangs and Drivebys.* New York: Aldine de Gruyter.

Sawyer, Ethel.
  1973. "Methodological Problems in Studying So-Called 'Deviant' Communities." Pp. 361–79 in *The Death of White Sociology.* Edited by Joyce Ladner. New York: Vintage.

Schwendiger, Herman and Julia.
  1985. *Adolescent Subcultures and Delinquency.* New York: Praeger.

Schlossman, Steven L.
  1977. *Love and the American Delinquent.* Chicago: University of Chicago.

Schlossman, Steven L.
  1984, Gail Zellman, and Richard Schavelson. *Delinquency Prevention in South Chicago.* Santa Monica, Calif.: Rand Corporation.

Shaw, Clifford R. and Henry D. McKay.
  1942. *Juvenile Delinquency and Urban Areas.* Chicago: University of Chicago.

Short, James F.
1964. "Adult-Adolescent Relations and Gang Delinquency." *The Pacific Sociological Review* 7:2, 59–65.

1968, Editor. *Gang Delinquency and Delinquent Subcultures.* New York: Harper & Row.

1976. *Delinquency, Crime, and Society.* Chicago: University of Chicago.

1997. *Poverty, Ethnicity and Violent Crime.* Boulder, Colo.: Westview.

Short, James F., and Fred L. Strodtbeck.
1965. *Group Process and Gang Delinquency.* Chicago: University of Chicago.

Skolnick, Jerome H.
1990. "The Social Structure of Street Drug Dealing." *American Journal of Police* 9:1–41.

Silberman, Charles E.
1978. *Criminal Violence, Criminal Justice.* New York: Vintage.

Spear, Allan H.
1967. *Black Chicago: The Making of a Negro Ghetto 1890–1920.* Chicago: University of Chicago.

Spergel, Irving A.
1964. *Racketville Slumtown Haulberg.* Chicago: University of Chicago.

1984. "Violent Gangs in Chicago: In Search of Social Policy." *Social Service Review* 58:2, 199–225.

1995. *The Youth Gang Problem: A Community Approach.* New York: Oxford University Press.

Stanback, Howard and Creigs C. Beverly.
1986. "The Black Underclass: Theory and Reality." *The Black Scholar* September/October, 24–31.

Stanko, Elizabeth A.
1994. "Challenging the Problem of Men's Individual Violence." Pp. 32–45 in *Just Boys Doing Business: Men, Maculinities, and Crime.* Edited by Tim Newburn and Elizabeth A. Stanko. London: Routledge.

Staples, Robert.
   1982. *Black Masculinity: The Black Man's Role in American Society.* San Fransisco: Black Scholar Press.

Steffensmeier, D.J. and R. H. Steffensmeier.
   1980. "Trends in Female Delinquency: An Examination of Arrest, Juvenile Court, Self-Report, and Field Data." *Criminology* 30:136–62.

Steinberg, Stephen. *The Ethnic Myth.* Boston: Beacon Press.

Stewart, James B.
   1991. *Den of Thieves.* New York: Touchstone.

Stinchcombe, Arthur L.
   1965. "Social Structure and Organizations." In *Handbook of Organizations.* Edited by James G. March. Chicago: Rand McNally & Company.

The Study Commission on the Quality of Education in the Metropolitan Milwaukee Schools.
   1985. "Better Public Schools." October.

Sullivan, Mercer L.
   1989. *Getting Paid: Youth Crime and Work in the Inner City.* Ithaca: Cornell University Press.

Sutherland, Edwin H.
   1934. *Principles of Criminology.* Chicago: J.B. Lippincott Co.

Suttles, Gerald D.
   1959. "Territoriality, Identity, and Conduct: A Study of an Inner-City Slum with Special Reference to Street Corner Groups." Unpublished Ph.D. dissertation. Champaign, Ill.: Univ. Of Illinois.

   1968. *The Social Order of the Slum.* Chicago: University of Chicago.

Takagi, Paul.
   1981. "Race, Crime, and Social Policy: A Minority Perspective." *Crime & Delinquency* 27:48–63.

Takata, Susan, and Richard Zevitz.
   1987. "Youth Gangs in Racine: An Examination of Community Perceptions." *Wisconsin Sociologist* 24:4, 132–39.

Taylor, Carl.
  1989. *Dangerous Society.* East Lansing, Mich.: Michigan State
  University Press.

  1993. *Girls, Gangs, Women, and Drugs.* East Lansing: Michigan
  State University Press.

Thrasher, Frederick.
  1963. *The Gang.* Chicago: University of Chicago Press.

Tice, Lawrence Clinton.
  1967. "The National Avenue 'Rebels': Study of a Puerto Rican
  Gang in Milwaukee." Unpublished Masters Thesis in Social
  Welfare. Milwaukee: University of Wisconsin-Milwaukee.

Toffler, Alvin.
  1980. *The Third Wave.* New York: William Morrow & Co.

  1990. *Powershift: Knowledge, Wealth, and Violence at the Edge of
  teh 21st Century.* New York: Bantam Books.

Torres, Jose, John M. Hagedorn and Greg Giglio.
  1996. "Drug Use of Milwaukee Gangs." Paper presented at the
  American Society of Criminology. Chicago.

Trotter, Joe William.
  1985. *Black Milwaukee.* Chicago: University of Illinois.

Tyson, Ann Scott.
  1996. "Feds say Larry Hoover runs a drug empire from his
  prison cell. He sees gangs as a force for good." *Christian Science
  Monitor,* 31 December.

University of Wisconsin-Milwaukee.
  1986. *UWM Report* 6 (16): 6 May.

U.S. Bureau of the Census.
  1960, 1970, 1980. "Characteristics of the Population."

Valdez, Avelardo.
  1979. "The Social and Occupational Integration Among Mexican
  and Puerto Rican Ethnics in Urban Industrial Society."
  Unpublished Ph.D. dissertation. University of California-Los
  Angeles.

Valentine, Betty Lou.
1978. *Hustling and Other Hard Work.* Glencoe: Free Press.

Valentine, Charles A.
1968. *Culture and Poverty.* Chicago: University of Chicago.

Venkatesh, Sudhir Alladi.
1996. "The Gang in the Community." Pp. 241–56 in *Gangs in America.* 2nd ed. Edited by Ronald C. Huff. Thousand Oaks, Calif.: Sage.

Vigil, Diego.
1974. *Early Chicano Guerilla Fighters.* Upland, Calif.: JDV Publications.

1983. "Chicano Gangs: One Response to Mexican Urban Adaption." *Urban Anthropology* 12 (1): 45–68.

1988 Barrio Gangs. Austin: University of Texas.

Vigil, James Diego and John M. Long.
1990. "Emic and Etic Perspectives on Gang Culture: The Chicano Case." Pp. 71–102 in *Gangs In America.* 2nd ed. Edited by C. Ronald Huff. Beverly Hills, Calif.: Sage.

Walker, Judith.
1986. "Chicago Works Together." Summary Report for the Chicago Intervention Network. Chicago.

West, Candace and Don H. Zimmerman.
1987. "Doing Gender." *Gender & Society* 1:125–51.

White, Sammis.
1986. "Research and Opinion." Milwaukee: University of Wisconsin-Milwaukee Urban Research Center.

Whyte, William Foote.
1943. *Street Corner Society.* Chicago: University of Chicago.

Wilson, William Julius.
1978. *The Declining Significance of Race.* Chicago: University of Chicago.

1984. "The Black Underclass." *The Wilson Quarterly* 8 (2): 88–99.

1985. "Cycles of Deprivation and the Underclass Debate." *Social Service Review* 59 (4): 541–59.

1987. *The Truly Disadvantaged.* Chicago: University of Chicago.

1996. *When Work Disappears: The World of the New Urban Poor.* New York: Alfred A. Knopf.

Wilson, William Julius and Robert J. Sampson.
1995. "Toward a Theory of Race, Crime, and Urban Inequality." In *Crime and Inequality.* Edited by John Hagan and Ruth D. Peterson. Stanford, Calif.: Stanford University Press.

Wisconsin Department of Industry, Labor and Human Relations.
1982. "Wisconsin Industry Projections to 1990." Madison: DILHR Labor Market Information.

Working Group on Youth Problems.
1985. "Strategies for Reducing Youth Violence." Columbus: Ohio.

Yablonsky, Lewis.
1966. *The Violent Gang.* New York: Macmillan Publishing Company.

1997. *Gangsters: Fifty Years of Madness, Drugs, and Death on the Streets of America.* New York: New York University Press.

Youth Initiatives Task Force.
1985. "Investing in Youth: Final Report." Milwaukee: Wisconsin.

Zatz, Marjorie S.
1987. "Chicano Youth Gangs and Crime: The Creation of a Moral Panic." *Contemporary Crises* 11: 129–58.

INDEX

John Hagedorn is Assistant Professor in the Department of Criminal Justice at the University of Illinois-Chicago. He was Principal Investigator of the Milwaukee Drug Posse and Homegirl Studies at the UMW Center for Urban Initiatives and Research.

Perry Macon, who collaborated in the research for this book, was the leader of one of Milwaukee's largest youth gangs. He is now studying accounting at the Milwaukee Area Technical College.